D0088146

Medical Sociology

Medical Sociology

An Introduction

Hannah Bradby

Los Angeles • London • New Delhi • Singapore • Washington DC

© Hannah Bradby 2009

First published 2009

Apart from any fair dealing for the purposes of research or private study, or criticism or review, as permitted under the Copyright, Designs and Patents Act, 1988, this publication may be reproduced, stored or transmitted in any form, or by any means, only with the prior permission in writing of the publishers, or in the case of reprographic reproduction, in accordance with the terms of licences issued by the Copyright Licensing Agency. Enquiries concerning reproduction outside those terms should be sent to the publishers.

SAGE Publications Ltd
1 Oliver's Yard
55 City Road
London EC1Y 1SP

SAGE Publications Inc.
2455 Teller Road
Thousand Oaks, California 91320

SAGE Publications India Pvt Ltd
B 1/I 1 Mohan Cooperative Industrial Area
Mathura Road
New Delhi 110 044

SAGE Publications Asia-Pacific Pte Ltd
33 Pekin Street #02-01
Far East Square
Singapore 048763

Library of Congress Control Number: 2008925525

British Library Cataloguing in Publication data

A catalogue record for this book is available from the British Library

ISBN 978-1-4129-0218-2
ISBN 978-1-4129-0219-9 (pbk)

Typeset by C&M Digitals (P) Ltd, Chennai, India
Printed in Great Britain by The Cromwell Press Ltd, Trowbridge, Wiltshire
Printed on paper from sustainable resources

CONTENTS

Acknowledgements		x
Preface		xi
Introduction		1

Part 1   The social context of health and illness — **19**

1   A very brief history of medicine and society — **21**
Chapter summary — 21
Introduction — 21
1900 – the dawn of the twentieth century — 23
First World War: 1914–1918 — 26
1918–1939 — 27
Second World War: 1939–1945 — 27
1945 to the twenty-first century — 28
Costs and benefits of twentieth century medical innovation — 30
Health inequalities — 33
Medical transformations — 34
    Further reading — 35
    Revision questions — 36
    Extension questions — 36

2   Defining the doctor's remit — **37**
Chapter summary — 37
Introduction — 38
Diagnosis: legitimate and illegitimate illness — 38
Treating diagnosed disease — 41
Defining death — 43
Doing death — 44
Defining doctors as special healers — 45
Overlap with other professionals' work — 46
Specialization to the point of incoherence? — 47
Medicine's place in society — 48
    Further reading — 49
    Revision questions — 50
    Extension questions — 50

3   Defining health, defining disease   **51**

Chapter summary   51
Introduction   52
Biomedical disease model   52
Limitations of the biomedical model   53
Defining health   57
Lay understandings of health   58
Dimensions of lay models of health   59
The context of health   60
Biomedical disease and the value of health   61
     Further reading   62
     Revision questions   63
     Extension questions   63

Part 2   Getting ill, being ill   **65**

4   The social causes of disease   **67**

Chapter summary   67
Introduction   68
Class, ill health and industrial revolution   68
Social class and inequality   71
     Public policy approaches to inequality   71
     Mechanisms causing health inequalities by class   76
Ethnicity and inequality   81
Age and gender   83
Tackling health inequalities   83
Future prospects   84
International health inequalities   84
     Further reading   85
     Revision questions   86
     Extension questions   86

5   Risk, choice and lifestyle   **89**

Chapter summary   89
Introduction   90
Individuals and their behaviours   91
Risk taking and thrill-seeking   98
Risky sex and gay men   98
Prejudice and blame   99
Cousin marriage and congenital problems   100
Risk and preventative medicine   101
New risks, new diseases – we're all patients now?   102
Risk, lifestyle medicine – what next?   104

Further reading   105
Revision questions   106
Extension questions   106

6   Experiencing illness   **108**
Chapter summary   108
Introduction   108
The sick role   110
Sickness as deviance   111
Stigma and illness   112
Illness as failure   113
Biographical disruption and illness narratives   114
Autopathography   115
Remaking lives?   116
    Further reading   116
    Revision questions   117
    Extension questions   117

7   Ill bodies in society   **119**
Chapter summary   119
Introduction   120
Bodies in society   120
Embodied illness   121
Dualist thinking   122
Bodies as machines   124
Suffering bodies   126
Impaired bodies and disability   126
    Further reading   128
    Revision questions   128
    Extension questions   128

8   The process of disability   **131**
Chapter summary   131
Introduction   132
Disability and the life course   133
Chronic illness, impairment and disability   135
The social model of disability   137
The cultural model of disability   139
Special or universal needs   142
    Further reading   143
    Revision questions   143
    Extension questions   143

Part 3 Getting healthcare   145

9   **Doctor–patient relationships**   **147**
    Chapter summary   147
    Introduction   148
    Self-care   148
    Appropriate consultation   149
    Compliance, co-operation, conflict   150
    Inverse care law   152
    Evidence on medical consultations   153
    Communicating across the divide   155
    Co-operation and challenge   157
        Further reading   158
        Revision questions   159
        Extension questions   159

10 **Healthcare organization**   **161**
    Chapter summary   161
    Introduction   161
    What's so special about the NHS?   162
        Socialized medicine   162
        Insurance system   163
        Pluralist socialized system   163
    Evaluating the NHS   164
    Reforming the NHS   165
    Clinical governance   166
    Medical dominance   168
    The role of the hospital   168
    Commercial and industrial interests in the NHS   170
    The context of care   173
        Further reading   174
        Revision questions   174
        Extension questions   175

11 **Challenges to medicine**   **176**
    Chapter summary   176
    Introduction   176
    Changing medical practice   177
    Disappearing doctors, disappearing patients   179
    Doctors' difficulties   183
    Regulating medicine   184
    Reform from within   186

Non-human threats   187
Prospects   189
   Further reading   189
   Revision questions   190
   Extension questions   190

12   Conclusion   **192**
Chapter summary   192
Introduction   192
Change and continuity   193
Effective care: competing priorities   193
The politics of communication   194
Uncertainty   197
Context   197

References   **199**

Index   207

ACKNOWLEDGEMENTS

Thank you to both the British Medical Association (BMA) and the General Medical Council (GMC) for their kind permission to reproduce material from their websites.

The Crown copyright elements of the publication 'Inequalities in Health' a.k.a 'The Black Report', 1980, produced by the DHSS, are reproduced under the terms of the Public Sector Information (PSI) Licence. The figure was supplied courtesy of Martin Rathfelder, Director of Socialist Health Association, www.sochealth.co.uk. The National Statistics Socio-economic Classification (www.statistics.gov.uk) is also reproduced under the terms of the PSI Licence.

Material from 'Poverty Inequality and Health in Britain' © George Davey Smith, Daniel Dorling and Mary Shaw is reproduced with permission from The Policy Press.

All of the photographs in this book were taken by Phil Mizen, to whom the author is indebted. The fee for the photographs has been donated to 'Médecins Sans Frontières'.

PREFACE

Teachers collaborating on a medical curriculum tend to argue that their own specialist subject requires a significant amount of time to be devoted to it and fierce debates over the relative merits of histopathology, biochemistry and anthropology as part of a doctor's education can ensue. Medical sociology has proved no exception to this rule and it has had a powerful ally, in the form of the General Medical Council and its publication *Tomorrow's Doctors* (first published in 1999 with a second edition in 2001, available from www.gmc-uk.org/education/undergraduate/tomdoc.pdf), in arguing that an understanding of the social nature of illness and healthcare is essential for a medical education. Of course, the contribution of sociology (or any other discipline) to medical education should, ideally, be judged on what difference it makes to practice. In this regard sociology has been extremely successful in that many sociological ideas about healthcare have become mainstream, for instance, the various debates about institutionalization, care in the community, excess medical intervention in childbirth, racism in the mental health services and class inequalities in mortality.

This book distils a selection of the insights offered by a critical social science perspective for a medical audience. The range of material on health, illness and the medical profession seeks to engage practitioners of medicine and to encourage ongoing critical thinking of the type that can be worn down by the exigencies of getting through a medical education. The pressures of passing the assessment hurdles *en route* to becoming medically qualified are felt especially strongly by those following a four year accelerated course, and it was teaching these students in the medical school at the University of Warwick that made me want to write this book. These students have been challenging, engaged, lively, combative, dismissive, emotional, enthusiastic, naive and cynical – sometimes all in the space of a single lesson. However, their shared sense of purpose in wishing to provide medical care for people in need is impressive.

Many thanks must go to the seminar tutors and lecturers with whom I have shared the work of teaching medical students and who have contributed greatly to my understanding of how sociological ideas can be applied to medicine. Further thanks must also go to: the anonymous referees, for their constructive comments; Hayley Davies, who worked on an early version of the manuscript; Stuart Robertson, who produced a master document; Mila Steele and Jai Seaman of SAGE; and Phil Mizen who took the photographs.

INTRODUCTION

Chapter summary

This chapter describes:

» some indicators of medicine's power as an institution;

» the relationship of trust between an individual doctor and a patient as central to medicine's influential role;

» how critics have suggested that medicine's influence is overbearing and that trust in the beneficence of medicine has been eroded by recent scandals;

» how medicine's obligations to promoting equitable levels of health between social groups and the need to promote equity in its own ranks are linked to similar prejudices;

» how inequalities within medicine reflect those in the wider world.

Useful terms for this chapter

iatrogenesis: an illness or injury introduced as a result of medical intervention that was intended to be therapeutic

medical sociology: the study of the structural and cultural features of medicine as an institution, a profession and a discipline: scholarship in this area is also termed the 'sociology of health and illness' to underline that understandings of health and illness in society are not confined to medicine, but encompass a broader field of enquiry

medicalization: a process whereby conditions formerly seen as non-medical come to be defined and treated as medical problems

paternalistic: acting on behalf of other people and claiming to promote their best interests, without seeking their views or asking their permission

racism: discriminatory attitudes or practice based on prejudices about ethnic or cultural groups *sexism*: discriminatory attitudes or practice based on prejudices about men and women

sociology: the study of human society and social relations, initially associated with the social problems of industrializing nations

MEDICINE'S POWER, INFLUENCE AND REPUTATION

This book is about how society understands and responds to those who get ill and, in particular, the role that medicine plays in this relationship. Maintaining health, preventing illness, treating disease and coping with death all occur in daily life, in people's homes, with their friends, neighbours, work-mates, partners and families. While the main source of support for the sick is usually networks of kith and kin, societies of all types have healers who specialize in attending and assisting the sick. Healers use their experience of the expected course of an illness to advise an invalid's supporters on caring for him or her.

A striking feature of contemporary wealthy nations is that healing as an occupation has developed from a small-scale enterprise to become an enormous industry that provides health services through public and private funding. The organization of modern health services is complex, as is the pattern of interaction with other statutory services, such as education and welfare and non-statutory services including religious organizations (churches, missions, temples, and mosques), charities (Scope, The Terence Higgins Trust) and voluntary organizations such as self-help groups and hospital visitors. Multi-national commercial interests form part of the healthcare industry, by manufacturing and supplying products and services to the National Health Service (NHS) and other health and social care organizations, including medical machines, software, pharmaceuticals, orthotic and prosthetic devices, private health insurance, institutional care for the elderly, and alternative therapies. At the heart of this network of interconnections is medicine which plays a central role in managing not only medical services, but also nursing, midwifery, physiotherapy, audiology and other allied professions, in regulating the limits of alternative or complementary therapies, in shaping the direction of research and policy and exercising influence in neighbouring disciplines such as psychology, genetics and public health.

Medicine's role as key player in the broad business of healthcare means it is regularly in negotiation, in contention and sometimes in conflict with other interest groups. Groups with whom medicine negotiates over whose interests are being best served include those citizens whose taxes fund healthcare, patients who use the service, politicians who formulate health policy, healthcare professionals, including management and other clinicians, and regulatory and advisory bodies such as the Human Fertilization and Embryo Authority.

Medicine's official bodies – the British Medical Association (BMA) and the General Medical Council (GMC) – relate to other public bodies including national and local government health officials and associations of other health professionals, such as nursing and dentistry, through representation on committees and the membership of official working parties.

BOX 0.1

The General Medical Council

The purpose of the General Medical Council is to protect, promote and maintain the health and safety of the public by ensuring proper standards in the practice of medicine. The law gives us four main functions under the Medical Act:

- keeping up-to-date registers of qualified doctors;
- fostering good medical practice;
- promoting high standards of medical education;
- dealing firmly and fairly with doctors whose fitness to practise is in doubt. (Available at: http://www.gmc-uk.org/)

Collectively, doctors' views are represented to the general public through reports and press releases on a range of matters, from drugs licensing to immunization uptake and are also discussed through journals of research and practice (*The British Medical Journal, The Lancet*) and other professional journals (*Hospital Doctor, Doctor, Pulse, Health Services Journal*). Medical issues are not confined to formal policy, service provision and academic circles, since their salience and human interest are covered in television, radio programming and in fictionalized form in medical soap operas and dramas as well as in newspaper, magazine and internet health pages.

BOX 0.2

The British Medical Association

The British Medical Association is the doctors' professional organisation established to look after the professional and personal needs of our members. The BMA represents doctors in all branches of medicine all over the UK ... We are a voluntary association with over two-thirds of practising UK doctors in membership and an independent trade union dedicated to protecting individual members and the collective interests of doctors ... We are the voice for

(Cont'd)

---

doctors and medical students – in constant contact with ministers, government departments, members of the UK, Scottish, Welsh and Northern Ireland administrations and many other influential bodies. We are committed to keeping members in touch with the profession's collective views and policies and to being at the forefront of healthcare development … We promote the medical and allied sciences, seek to maintain the honour and interests of the medical profession and promote the achievement of high quality healthcare. (Available at: http:// www.bma.org.uk/)

Medicine uses all available communication channels and lobbying opportunities and as a professional group is influential, well connected and vociferous. But despite the large scale, wide range and great complexity of medicine's interests, its view of its own worth is based on the nature of the relationship between doctor and patient. The idea that doctors are regarded as professionals who, when consulted, can be trusted to act in the best interests of their patients is crucial to underpinning the influential role that medicine enjoys. The power that medicine has wielded in determining the development of publicly funded health services has been offset by the sense that altruism and a desire to help others are doctors' prime motivations. The vocational nature of medicine is well established in the public's view so that seeking medical training and employment is seen as a good thing for society at large, as well as for the individual who will be employed as a doctor. The material reward that individual doctors receive has generally been viewed as a side issue and not as a measure of medicine's worth to society. Relative to other professions with a similar length of training, medicine is a well-remunerated occupation, with good conditions of employment, which have been achieved through skilful negotiation. The state has been prepared to underwrite the costs of employing doctors because medicine has been seen as an essential service, important to national wellbeing, and doctors are seen as trustworthy professionals.

TRUST IN MEDICINE

In terms of understanding the dilemmas that face medicine today, the paradox of a profession that justifies its international political and commercial influence on the basis of the trustworthiness of its one-to-one interactions with clients is important. Medicine's claim that doctors are professionals with a vocational calling whose extensive training and distinctive knowledge are harnessed to serving the public good is challenged by evidence of less noble motivations in some quarters. Medicine's emphasis on the beneficent relationship with clients has been subject to criticism, not least from research that has demonstrated the ways that the interests of the institution of medicine often outweigh those of patients in the organization of healthcare (see Chapter 8). For example, the independent inquiry into paediatric cardiologists' practice in Bristol found that professional rather than patient interests had been paramount. Such evidence that professional ethics do not, in fact, guarantee disinterested, impartial behaviour has received media attention in Britain and it has become abundantly clear that doctors, like any group in society, demonstrate all of our inherent human failings, including, sadly, the ability to murder. The withdrawal of respect for and trust in professionals is not confined to doctors, however, with politicians, social workers and the clergy suffering a similar fate. Yet this is particularly worrisome for medicine which depends on intimate access to people's bodies, and to details of their daily lives, in order to diagnose and practise. Medical scandals are assessed by the medical press in terms of the impact on the trust between doctor and patient. An editorial in the *British Medical Journal* after Harold Shipman's conviction for murdering fifteen of his patients stated

> Serial killers in healthcare like Shipman ... are particularly shocking because they damage the trust that exists between clinicians and their patients. (O'Neill, 2000)

The maintenance of trust between doctor and patient is of prime concern to today's medical profession, but it is not a new preoccupation for medicine. Only one hundred years ago physicians were part of a small-scale trade, lacking any potent means of altering the course of disease and competing with other types of healers for clients (see Chapter 1). Relying on the fees paid by patients meant that a doctor's sympathetic and authoritative bedside manner was crucial to attracting and retaining clients. Medicine has since developed to be part of a vast 'medical-industrial complex' (Illich, 1976) which has confidence in its ability to defeat disease. During the period when faith in the scientific approach accompanied a massive expansion in research activity, the issue of patient respect may have been less pressing than scientifically informed advances.

However, even without such evidence of malpractice attracting news headlines, medicine's authority and social standing would inevitably be subject to criticism. One consistent criticism has been that medicine's success and power have led it to ignore the interests of other players involved in the delivery of healthcare. Patients' groups complain that the disease rather than the sick person is the focus of medical interest and that the patient's occupational, financial and caring roles are ignored when they should be taken into consideration when planning treatment for optimal recovery. Nurses protest about their relegation to the role of handmaiden to the medical project, when they should be respected as clinicians with specific skills and responsibilities.

Alternative therapists dispute their exclusion from the legally sanctioned, state-funded monopoly on healing that medicine enjoys and midwives point to their eviction as the expert occupational group dealing with birth. Critics describe how medicine's methods can damage individual and collective health in the name of effecting a cure (referred to as iatrogenesis). Others from within and beyond the medical profession also suggest that medicine's influence is too pervasive and its perspectives have been overbearing in matters of mental illness, assisted reproduction and genetic research, and need to be tempered.

CHANGING EXPECTATIONS AND PRIORITIES

Justifying a medicalized view of disease by asserting the altruistic vocational nature of the medical calling has been increasingly challenged. The paternalistic model of medicine, where the expert doctor manages the compliant patient and their disease with minimal negotiation, has been cast as an oppressive abuse of power. The call to understand the doctor–patient encounter from the point of view of the patient, the patient's carers and non-medical professionals has become difficult to ignore. Concomitant demographic and economic changes have made the need to incorporate patients' views more urgent. Chronic conditions have taken over from infectious disease as the main burden of disease for the population and therefore the main work of healthcare providers, and as life expectancy has increased so too have people's expectations of quality of life and of health services. People expect to live longer than their grandparents did and to receive good services from the NHS if and when their health fails.

Medicine's difficulties in responding to an apparently unending increase in the demand for health services have been compounded by the anticipation that scientific medicine would be able to mend all ills. Astonishing innovations in some branches of medicine have occurred while other problems remain untouched by new medical techniques. Medical expertise, technology and research effort have tended to focus on health problems which are fixable, so organ transplantation and cardiac bypass are now routine operations. By contrast, conditions that are less amenable to medical intervention have received less attention and fewer funds. For instance, strokes are the biggest cause of disability in Britain yet do not attract the levels of funding associated with other diseases that affect smaller numbers of people. Defining the medical profession's priorities for curing or containing the sick and maintaining the healthy is not a simple task and remains one in which different branches of medicine may not agree with one another. In addition, the voice of the service user is increasingly expected to be represented in defining priorities on management boards of healthcare trusts and steering committees for research work.

To understand the relationship between medicine and society a first step is to appreciate both the complexity of medicine as an institution – its clinical, research and teaching functions – and the difference between the institutional interests of medicine and the motivations and aspirations of individual doctors working within the profession. Stories of individual, heroic doctors seeking to improve people's quality of life, and the cases of rogue, criminal doctors are together important in understanding the public's expectations of medicine. Nonetheless, it is the institutional questions that preoccupy this book as the legitimate and appropriate limits of medicine's remit now and in the future are considered. Should medicine concern itself with issues beyond the boundaries of what is currently the formal healthcare system? A compelling reason why medicine should look beyond the clinical is that the vast majority of ill health is treated beyond organized clinical care: people can maintain their health, develop symptoms, treat them and recover from illness without ever consulting a medical professional.

Lack of contact with a doctor does not mean that people have not drawn on medical knowledge: part of the power of modern medicine lies in its penetration of the whole population's understanding of illness. In our highly literate and knowledge-based society, where most people have access to radio and television and a growing proportion to the internet, e-mail and mobile telephones, medical knowledge is widely accessible. Not only can ordinary people use medical handbooks and patient information systems, we can consult pharmacists, internet sites and NHS Direct. Information about health matters is provided not only for that crisis moment at the onset of an illness, but also as entertainment in dedicated newspaper and magazines pages and as part of regular broadcast scheduling. The means of accessing medical know-how may be diffuse, and largely independent of face-time with a doctor, but it is nonetheless a medical understanding to which most of us turn when illness strikes. Critics have described how medicine has accrued responsibility for an ever widening range of social problems, with the medicalization of childbirth, madness, criminal activity and addiction seen as a sometimes inappropriate assumption of responsibilities, or more sinisterly as medical colonization. In this view medicine's interest in preventing disease, whether through genetic or public health intervention, cannot be welcomed wholeheartedly given the inevitable extension of medicine's influence to cover 'pre-patients' who are not (yet) ill.

Medicine is the central and most authoritative institution that deals with health and illness, as is shown by the widespread influence of medical ideas about the process, treatment and prevention of disease. Understanding how this professional authority has built up over recent history and its links with falling mortality rates and the evolution of other economic and social systems is the subject of Chapter 1. Despite various challenges to medicine, its power has persisted, as has been demonstrated by the perpetuation of a system of professional self-regulation despite high profile cases of serious

Figure 0.1 A large proportion of regular healthcare takes place outside the NHS and without recourse to the profession of medicine whereby people diagnose and treat their own symptoms, with informal help from friends or family as well as paid help from people without medical qualifications

misconduct. The GMC regulates professional conduct and it is doctors themselves who oversee and govern this process. While efforts to increase non-medical, lay representation on the GMC's governing body have been successful, it is nonetheless numerically dominated by doctors and has remained remarkably free of outside interference in its decisions about the fitness to practise medicine. Self-regulation has been the key to medicine's most important coup in assuring its own prestige and power: the idea that only doctors can stand in judgement on their fellow doctors rests on the peculiar reverence with which medical knowledge is treated. The idea that non-medics cannot gauge, understand or intervene in the clinical relationship has, at least until recently, served to shelter medicine from the increasingly invasive system of outside inspection that accompanies other public sector professional practice. Medical regulation is currently undergoing significant reform (as discussed in the government White Paper, *Trust, Assurance and Safety – The Regulation of Health Professionals in the 21st Century*, February 2007) and, while self-regulation is set to be modified, it has been important in understanding medicine's place in society today.

MEDICINE'S STANDING

While medicine has successfully limited the degree to which other professionals can judge its quality of practice, it regularly stands in judgement over others. Society relies on medical judgement for the regulation of various dilemmas and the extent of this reliance is an index of medicine's power. Medicine's jurisdiction extends well beyond medical matters since doctors testify during the regulation of aspects of public and private life, including judgements about criminal responsibility, fitness to parent and eligibility to receive state benefits. These decisions have significant effects in terms of the level of intervention that is justified by public agencies into people's private life and the financial and material support which they are entitled to claim and medicine has been seen as being sufficiently trustworthy to wield this responsibility.

Belonging to a profession that enjoys high levels of power and prestige does not, of course, mean that individual practitioners necessarily enjoy happiness and contentment. Regret is often expressed for a recently passed golden age of medicine when the great autonomy of, and respect for, doctors made the job more satisfying. Doctors' individual autonomy has been eroded, with the upsurge of quality audits and non-medical management structures and the increasing access that ordinary people have to medical knowledge through old and new media. At the same time the range of things that doctors can do for patients has increased while expectations have been raised, all of which may have contributed to expressions of discontent by doctors. The debates about terms and conditions of employment for doctors is part of a wider debate about medicine's place in society: what can doctors expect of their patients and of the general population whose taxes pay their salaries? What can individual patients expect in return and how is the contract between society and the medical profession to be regulated? Should the special nature of medical work, the unsocial hours, the painful emotions and the proximity to death and disease, attract high financial reward? Or should the work be its own reward? Can patients' viewpoints be meaningfully included in healthcare decision making? Given the emphasis on preventative work and consumer choice, is it still appropriate to refer to 'patients', or should the term 'clients' be used?

CRITICAL APPROACHES TO HEALTH AND MEDICINE

In order to begin to answer these questions we will start by defining the scope of the work that doctors undertake. Describing what doctors do is no mean feat in itself, given the breadth and variety of tasks undertaken by medicine: from laboratory-based histopathology to public health education campaigns; from opthalmology to forensic psychiatry. At our disposal we have a tradition of sociological research that offers various approaches to analysing what happens at the individual level between doctors and patients and at the collective level between the profession and society. Sociology examines how social situations are structured by social class, ethnic group and gender which may, for instance, influence how a patient is treated in the health services. Sexism and racism are two of the ways that prejudice and discrimination systematically disadvantage particular groups. Common-sense explanations have often justified the poor conditions of women or minority ethnic groups in terms of those groups deserving their own misfortune, whereas a sociological approach looks at how those in power benefit from such inequality. Research into the meanings that influence our daily lives shows that illness is redolent with meaning and interpretation that do not rely on scientific models of causation. For instance, seizures have been associated with supernatural possession, which in some cultures has implied special visionary powers but in others has been seen as a bad omen leading to the shunning of the affected individual. To be diagnosed with epilepsy is still to be faced with the prospect of stigma, despite the condition being understood as a neurological condition that is treatable. Negative assumptions have not disappeared in the face of neurological explanations of the patterns of brain activity that cause seizures, because prejudice is not simply or straightforwardly a result of ignorance. Stigmatizing views, as with other cultural evaluations, are often assumed and implicit and may only become obvious when they are disrupted. The implicit nature of culture's influence on our beliefs is part of its power.

Many of us would be reluctant to admit to adhering to superstition or 'old wives' tales' but would nonetheless be reluctant to walk under a ladder or put an umbrella up indoors for fear of bad luck, and would be similarly disinclined to 'speak ill of the dead'. The misfortune of illness is often explained in terms of luck rather than social inequalities and, especially in seeking to explain the onset of illness, non-scientific answers around destiny, fate, morality and spirituality are often invoked. Sociology is concerned with the structural distribution of resources that determine our material wellbeing and the shared interpretations that give meaning to our lives. This attention to the shared, social aspects of life can appear to be somewhat at odds with medicine's focus on a treatable bodily pathology that is located in the individual.

How useful is this sociological view of the power and meanings around health and illness to doctors when actually faced with patients? This book considers medicine's deficits and shows how many of them derive from having excised the spiritual, personal and contextual aspects of illness and suffering from the clinical encounter. A patient who consults a doctor wants symptoms attended to and the underlying condition treated, while the doctor's duty of care is to that individual person. If the doctor–patient relationship is contracted on a one-to-one basis, how useful is it to consider the wider context in which the consultation is situated? The patient may be identified with a particular ethnic group, gender and socio-economic class and this identification could place the patient in a statistically high-risk group for a specific condition. Is it useful to a clinician to know about inequalities in the incidence and outcome of disease in sub-sections of the population? Is it relevant to the quality of one-to-one care?

It might be argued that providing the doctor does his or her best for each individual patient, it matters not one iota whether that patient is, for instance, black, nor that black minorities tend to receive poorer treatment compared to other ethnic groups. The social dimensions of illness – the influence of socio-economic class, religion, ethnicity, gender, or sexuality – have been regarded as being of little concern to the practise of medicine, being more properly the business of social workers, politicians, policy specialists, activists and academics. But such a view is disingenuous, since, despite the individual focus of much clinical care, preventative interventions such as immunization and screening, which are at the heart of the modern medical mission, are aimed at the wellbeing of the population rather than the individual. State-funded health services ensure the supply of employable workers and reduce the burden of disease and disability on the public purse. Medicine addresses population health problems both in terms of individual clinicians administering public health policies and by acting as gatekeepers for benefits aimed at alleviating the suffering of disability, chronic conditions and ensuring healthy pregnancy. What then is the doctor's obligation towards the population rather than the individual? Is there any responsibility or even requirement to practise in a way that addresses the social inequities in health? Should doctors' practice be aimed at society's overall health by aiming to reduce differentials?

Medicine has a long tradition of campaigning reformers working for the betterment of others by reducing the effect of inequalities through political as well as medical means. The Quaker physician John Coakley Lettsom (1744–1815) used some of the fortune made from his London medical practice on philanthropic activities and, more recently, the General Practitioner Julian Tudor Hart (1927–) worked in a mining village in South Wales to improve living conditions as well as to treat illness. Tudor Hart's description of the inverse care law, whereby those most in need of healthcare receive the poorest service, has been important in directing efforts to tackle inequalities in mortality (see Chapter 4). Using the influence and prestige of their discipline, some doctors have seen their job as addressing, if not redressing, the consequences of the unequal distribution of power and money. Doctors have played a significant role in describing how being born into poverty is associated with premature death and disease when compared to being born into wealth (see Chapter 4). One of the ways that social class influences the risk of premature death is through its association with the available avenues of education and employment open to a person.

INEQUALITY WITHIN MEDICINE

Professionals, including doctors, make up the social classes associated with the lowest mortality rates. Despite the NHS and the Welfare State having been established for more than 50 years, class-based inequalities in health still persist. Despite medical education being state-funded and open to anyone, the medical profession remains structured by class, gender and ethnicity. Although women now make up more than half of the annual intake of medical students, they are significantly under-represented at senior levels and in competitive specialities (for instance, after a concerted, nation-wide, effort to increase their representation, women still only occupy 6 per cent of consultant surgeon posts in England). People of minority ethnicity are also at a disadvantage, given that non-Anglo-Saxon names have been routinely de-selected as interview candidates for training places and employment. Thus the medical profession is still overwhelmingly white and middle class, with nearly a third of medical students having parents who are or were doctors. Middle-class white men, who as a group were the pioneers and beneficiaries of medicine's establishment as a scientific, rational enterprise, continue to be its most powerful constituent. These inequalities evident within its own ranks in turn raise further questions about medicine's obligations to promoting an equitable society.

Does it matter that one group is over-represented in sought-after medical employment? Does it matter that the lower social classes are over-represented in experiencing premature mortality? These are parallel questions about how opportunity and material wealth are distributed in society. Those with power and privilege have sought to justify their own position as having been earned on the basis of merit alone, and by blaming the less fortunate for their own plight. Medicine has indeed, at times, been complicit in the justification of its own privilege and it has participated in confirming the marginalized status of some groups of patients: for instance, the moral failings of unmarried mothers had been defined as a form of madness in the twentieth century and their incarceration in asylums was thereby justified; the low pain threshold of black patients was used as a reason to limit analgesia for people with sickle cell crises; newborns with Down syndrome were refused treatment and even feeding in the 1960s on the grounds that these were lives not worth preserving. More recently, people with HIV have been denied treatment altogether or have been given treatment in a punitive fashion. In this respect medicine is not especially wicked, but it certainly reflects the prejudices of wider society.

Evidence of discrimination and the failure to challenge prejudice does not set medicine apart from other contemporary professions. Medicine's tendency to reproduce prejudice against stigmatized groups must be set against the philanthropic and radical reforming traditions of providing healthcare for society's powerless in opposition to the mores of 'respectable' society. Contemporary defenders of medicine point to the value of the scientific method in moving medicine away from moralising medical judgements. Medicine's focus on the pathogen should mean that an intra-venous drug user's HIV-related symptoms will be treated with the same dispassionate care and expertise as a haemophiliac who contracted the virus via the blood transfusion service. Science's claim to value neutrality has certainly helped to remove religious morality from clinical decision making, but prejudice can nonetheless be found in the delivery of care. The cost of scientific neutrality and the focus on objective diagnostic criteria has been to deny that the subjective suffering of the patient has a place in the medical setting, as will be explored in Chapters 6 and 7.

The paradoxes of modern medicine are fascinating. Medicine is a noble profession, which, in Britain, works in a nationalised service to ameliorate the conditions of the marginalized and also accommodates private consultations which command high fees sometimes for procedures which are cosmetic rather than therapeutic. Some of medicine's techniques have remained largely unaltered for centuries (bone-setting for example) and these exist alongside techniques that rely on highly developed technology. Medicine insists upon the special individual nature of the relationship with the patient, yet pursues interventions to improve population-level health, which, in the case of screening and immunization, carry a level of risk for the individual. An important feature of medicine's rise, described in Chapter 1, is the demonstration of the efficacy of its methods: antibiotics can arrest the progress of previously fatal infections and immunization programmes will prevent the infections even arising. The decrease in mortality rates and the increase in longevity that have characterized the twentieth century have together been seen as triumphs of scientific medicine's methods.

PARADOXICAL MEDICINE

However, the extent to which medicine's ability to intervene in disease processes has been responsible for the increased longevity of the population as a whole continues to be debated. While improvements to nutrition and housing in the first half of the twentieth century were crucial to improvements in the population's health, the medical administration of antibiotics and other newly developed drugs also played a role. Certainly the overall effect helped to establish medicine's increasingly scientific approach as effective and reliable. The public's trust in the great potential of medicine to improve quality of life was a necessary condition for the post-Second World War expansion of health and social care services. Throughout the twentieth and into the twenty-first century these developments have continued to accrue and technology that was unknown in medicine only a century ago is now routinely deployed: ultrasound scans, magnetic resonance imaging (MRI) scans for diagnosis and battery-powered brain implants to stimulate or suppress specific bodily functions. The process of disease at the genetic and molecular level has become a standard element of medical training and information about disease at the cellular level is regularly communicated to patients: the effects of chemotherapy on lymphocytes; testing for T-cell levels in people with HIV; the examination of individual gametes in assisted reproduction. The sub-cellular level of analysis, as in genetic testing where specific sequences of DNA are sought, is becoming more usual. The range of diagnoses that can be made continues to expand, as does the variety of therapies and treatments available. And yet, alongside technological and therapeutic innovation, other aspects of medicine have remained fairly constant: the UK continues to have a community-based network of General Practitioners (GPs) or family doctors who deal with bodies rather than cells and where examination and intervention are fairly low-tech. The common cold, flu and backache which account for the majority of days off work continue to make up much of a GP's caseload, where diagnoses remain largely based on the history that the patient offers.

And this brings us to a problem: medicine is a rapidly developing discipline that nonetheless retains much of the longstanding character of its practice. The breadth of the activities that medicine encompasses can make it difficult to discuss 'medicine' in the singular. Medicine is a dynamic and heterogeneous profession with such diverse clinical, research and academic practices that we might ask whether it is legitimate to discuss medicine as a single enterprise. It is difficult to prescribe what it is to be a doctor or, indeed, what might be the common features of doctors' work (see Chapter 2), so is it legitimate to analyse medicine as a single profession? Medicine considers itself and is considered by others to be a unified whole, and to a remarkable extent it behaves with a unity of purpose. That is to say, we all recognize what a doctor is even if we find it hard to offer a convincing definition or an adequate and succinct description that covers everything that a doctor might do. The doctor exists in our shared culture as a figure recognizable by his or her stethoscope, bleeper or scrubs, and is expected to be a useful, caring person who deals with illness. One of the markers of medicine's phenomenal success is that a caring, competent doctor is internationally recognized as a social good, cutting across language barriers and cultural divides.

OVERVIEW OF THIS BOOK

The paradoxes raised in this introduction together represent the subject of this book. Chapter 1 relates the current context of medicine and its role in society to recent historical developments. The challenge of defining what doctors do, and how this relates to patients' expectations of medicine, is considered in Chapter 2 and further developed in Chapter 3 as the medical definition of disease is compared with how lay people understand illness and health. The second part of the book explores the processes and experience of getting ill. Chapter 4 covers the body of evidence suggesting that the onset of illness is not a purely random matter, with people who live in disadvantaged conditions in terms of income, housing, employment and education consistently having the least favourable patterns of morbidity and mortality. Rates of ill health and of death are structured by socio-economic inequalities and yet there is a persistent emphasis on lifestyle and risk whereby an individual's behaviour is held responsible for the maintenance or breakdown of that person's health. The correlation between specific behaviours and the risk of disease has become a central tenet of health promotion and public health. The ubiquity of risk as an idea that informs health and its status in modern life more generally is the focus of Chapter 5.

Illness involves not simply individuals who may feel the stigma and failure of being ill, but also the families, friends and supporters who undertake their care. The effects on social networks of illness in terms of the physical and emotional labour of caring work is the subject of Chapter 6, which also deals with the sense of impending mortality that illness carries and about which medicine has little to say. This line of enquiry is extended in Chapter 7, which looks at the challenge which ill and dying bodies present, especially bodies which seem to be uncontrolled and uncontrollable by medical or other means. Chapter 8 focuses on disability, to ask how we can develop ways of understanding disability that more closely reflect how people experience it and how we may also avoid negative assumptions about people's inabilities.

Part 3 considers how organized healthcare provision responds to the challenges described in parts 1 and 2. The doctor is an important resource for ill people but the general crisis of faith in science and the professions, and a specific series of medical failures and abuses, have led to concern over a diminution of trust in doctors. Evidence of this damage to the doctor–patient relationship and the consequences of a reduced respect for and trust in medicine are discussed in Chapter 9. In terms of society's relationship with medicine, the organization and funding of the NHS, as successive governments attempt to improve general health and quality of care without losing control of spending levels, are dealt with in Chapter 10. Chapter 11 makes an assessment of the various challenges to medicine's autonomy as a profession, its role in defining and diagnosing disease and its dominance in the field of healthcare, and weighs up likely future changes. The concluding chapter offers a few practical steps that doctors in their clinical practice can take to respond to some of these challenges. The development of medicine's professional profile as an institution able to respond to the ever-changing demands of society has depended on an ability to reflect upon the mutual responsibilities of the providers and recipients of healthcare. No simple formula exists for deriving this contract but a reflective, mature medical profession needs to be involved in an active and constant search for the best available consensus in order to avoid being outdated.

Using this book

Each chapter in this book has summary points at the beginning to give the reader an overview of what is about to be covered. Revision questions at the end of each chapter prompt the reader to recap the key points of the preceding chapter. Extension questions use the ideas in the chapter together with new material to ask about novel situations. There is also further reading indicated at the end of each chapter, where the interested reader can get a fuller and more detailed picture of the issues described in the chapter.

Further reading

Armstrong, D. (2003) *An Outline of Sociology as Applied to Medicine* (5th edn). London: Arnold.

An influential and authoritative account of the significance of sociology's insights for medicine.

Lantos, J.D. (1997) *Do We Still Need Doctors?* New York: Routledge.

A provocative and readable book which introduces many of the dilemmas that face medicine in its relationship with the public; most of the evidence presented is from north America.

REVISION QUESTIONS

1 Are medicine's institutional obligations to the individual patient, or to the population that it serves?

2 Are individual doctors' obligations to the individual patient, or to the population that he or she serves?

3 Which groups need to be involved in setting priorities for research and service provision in healthcare?

EXTENSION QUESTIONS

1 Hierarchies within medicine

- Working with others, list all the specialities in medicine you can think of, in no particular order.
- Can the various specialities be divided by status? How is a high status specialism distinguished from a low status specialism? Are hospital doctors higher or lower status
than community doctors? Is salary level more or less important than the specialist
techniques that a doctor must learn to employ? Does the potential that a doctor has to
improve someone's quality of life make a difference to the status of a specialism?
- Thinking about the esteem in which specialisms are held by other doctors, rank the
specialisms that you've thought of in a single hierarchy.
- Rank the specialties in terms of the relative salary that each attracts.
- Are the rankings of esteem and of salary the same?

Compare your rankings with information given on renumeration and working conditions in the
following book: Ward, C. and Eccles, S. (2001) *So You Want To Be A Brain Surgeon?* (2nd edn).
Oxford: Oxford University Press.

Are there any discrepancies between your rankings and the information in the book? Is it
appropriate that different forms of medical practice attract differential financial reward? Is it
appropriate that specialists in public health, palliative care, histopathology and thoracic
surgery are all regulated by the same structures and legislation?

2 Feminised medicine?

At least 50 per cent of the intake for medical schools in the UK is now female. However, while
the numbers of women consultants have risen, the numbers in some surgical specialities have
dropped. There have been very few women presidents of Royal Colleges.

- What is preventing women from progressing up the ranks of all the specialisms of
medicine?
- Should gender equality in all sections of the profession be a goal of twenty-first
century medicine?
- Paid maternity leave and the provision of pre-school childcare (largely private sector)
have not resulted in gender equality in the medical profession (or in many other professions). What further structural changes need to occur to permit women to succeed
and reach the top of the medical profession?

PART 1

THE SOCIAL CONTEXT OF HEALTH AND ILLNESS

1

A VERY BRIEF HISTORY OF MEDICINE AND SOCIETY

Chapter summary

This chapter describes:

» the social, economic and political changes affecting health and healthcare;

» developments in the practice of medicine;

» the initial documentation of health inequalities;

» the establishment of the NHS;

» and introduces ideas about priority setting in the NHS.

Useful terms for this chapter

germ theory: the idea that many diseases are caused by micro-organisms, invisible to the naked eye, which was controversial when first proposed, but which now underpins micro-biology and basic hygiene practice (see Box 1.3, p. 25)

knowledge explosion: expansion of knowledge initially associated with mass printing technology and now with digital technology, which means that no single person can keep up with all of advances in understanding, even in a limited specialist field

INTRODUCTION

What is the value to today's medical students of learning about the history of medicine? Apart from the inherent interest of exploring the past, the dilemmas and anxieties as well as the success and confidence of our times can be understood to have developed from what has gone before. Developing an understanding of the conditions that have led up to the present can promote reflection on the likely direction of change for the future of the profession and can also engender a sense of the range of possible alternatives. Appreciating the tensions inherent when treating illnesses that have faced previous generations may encourage the type of reflective practice that is the goal of today's professionals.

This chapter gives some of the historical context that is necessary for understanding contemporary British medical practice by surveying developments and continuities over the last century in health outcomes, health policy and medicine's role in managing illness. Over the last hundred years remarkable changes have taken place in the practice of medicine while the effects of social and economic changes and of scientific discoveries have become apparent in the nation's health and its expectations of medicine. From the time of the ancient Greeks up until the First World War (1914–1918) medicine's tasks had remained relatively stable and fairly simple, namely 'to grapple with lethal disease and gross disabilities, to ensure live births and manage pain' (Porter, 1997: 718), and medicine's success in this enterprise has, with some justification, been described as 'meagre'.

In the eighteenth century medicine had been practised by a range of different occupational groups that included bonesetters, dentists, apothecaries, surgeons, midwives, herbalists and druggists. Hospitals were mainly voluntary and were funded by local subscribers who had the right to control access to services. Throughout the nineteenth century a set of reforms saw the physicians and surgeons wrest control over hospital admissions from these subscribers. After 16 unsuccessful attempts, the 1858 parliamentary bill brought about the Medical Registration Act that conferred considerable advantage on the medical profession by restricting certain appointments to those practitioners who were registered with the General Medical Council (which was established as a result of the bill).

Public expectations at the time of medicine's ability to combat disease were low and although medicine had attained the status of a profession (rather than a mere occupation), it carried relatively little prestige or power. The retreat of infectious disease and the rise of chronic conditions occurred in parallel with the evolution of the doctor from small-scale, self-employed service-provider to high status professional at the heart of the machinery of modern medicine. The twentieth century saw health indicators for the British population improve and medicine claimed some notable victories against disease while growing in prestige, power and influence. Critics have interrogated how much of the improvement in health and wellbeing can be attributed to the effects of the growing apparatus of medicine and have pointed to the positive effects of improved social and economic conditions over the same time span. Assessing the contribution of medicine to human health and happiness is crucial given the large proportion of public spending that is devoted to medical services, although the attribution of benefit to different causes is difficult to gauge with certainty.

1900 – THE DAWN OF THE TWENTIETH CENTURY

As the nineteenth century turned into the twentieth, medicine had become a profession regarded as more-or-less fit for a gentleman's son. The hospital was still in the process of becoming an important concentration of expertise and technology and medicine was practised largely in patrons' homes or in consulting rooms.

A precursor to the NHS was established through the National Insurance Act of 1911 that founded an insurance scheme against sickness for every working person in the country. The bill was passed despite some strong objections raised by the BMA (British Medical Association – see Box 0.2, pp. 3–4) that were primarily concerned with the lack of medical representation in the administration of the scheme. The Medical Registration Act of 1858 had created the conditions for a unified and autonomous profession to develop, since it would eventually permit only legally qualified medical practitioners to practise, although in 1900 it was not yet illegal for someone to practise medicine if they were not registered. The General Medical Council (see Box 0.1, p. 3) had responsibility for the register and replaced the 22 licensing bodies that had previously accredited doctors. It drew on the membership of pre-existing associations of surgeons, apothecaries and physicians and acted as an effective pressure group in representing the interests of the profession to the authorities of the state. Hospitals were beginning to be recognized as places where medical expertise and innovative treatment could be found and their role as providers of services to the poor who could not afford fee-for-service consultation at home or in surgeries was fading. A few women had also won the right to qualify in medicine and the London School of Medicine for Women had been established.

The generalist physician still held sway as the most influential voice within medicine, but the tendency to specialize, which characterizes medicine nowadays, was emerging. Family doctors' practice at the start of the twentieth century was largely continuous with that of the nineteenth century, with their role consisting mainly of observation, interpretation and reassurance at the patient's bedside. This general practice took place in small-scale consulting rooms, often in doctors' own homes, and relied on a limited range of equipment and pills and potions of dubious efficacy. The division was growing between generalists and consultants who were beginning to make the most of the new equipment and auxiliary staff available in hospital settings. Surgery in alliance with anaesthesia and professional nursing had established itself in city hospitals as a skilled speciality, with other areas such as obstetrics, paediatrics and orthopaedics emerging as distinct areas of knowledge and practice.

The transformation of Britain from a mainly agricultural to an industrial economy was well under way, with the proportion of the population living in cities standing at 80 per cent in 1880, compared with only 15 per cent in 1750 (and compared with about 88 per cent at the start of the twenty-first century). The number of men employed in agriculture continued its nineteenth century decline and would continue to fall steadily until the end of the twentieth century. The numbers employed in mining were still increasing, as they had done since the mid-1800s, and these would peak around 1920 before dropping down to minimal levels by the end of the twentieth century. Residential areas had grown up near to industrial centres and were often squalid, over-crowded and impoverished, with their ill effects on residents apparent in the levels of disease, despite ongoing public health reforms. The authorities were shocked by the effects of deprived living on the population's health when recruitment for the Boer war (1899–1902) found that 35 per cent of conscripts were unfit for service. The right to vote had been extended during the nineteenth century to an increasing proportion of lower-class men (women remained disenfranchised until well into the twentieth century), thereby concentrating politicians' attention on the needs of the growing proportion of working-class voters. The state's relationship with the nation's health was in flux: the Depression and the Industrial Revolution had taken their toll on workers' bodies and the difficulties in raising a fit army paved the way for subsequent public health measures.

Parliamentary acts legislated for a series of reforms to protect the poor, including school meals for children, the prohibition of the sale of alcohol and tobacco to children, minimum wages in certain trades and a national insurance unemployment benefit in the event of job loss. Local authorities began to improve the systems of sewage and rubbish removal and the supply of uncontaminated drinking water. The statutory regulation of working conditions in factories and workshops and of the adulteration of foodstuffs slowly improved conditions and marked the beginning of official intervention in the health of the working population. These reforms may have contributed to the ongoing decline in the death rate, which stood at 18 per thousand at the turn of the century. The rate, which had been dropping since records began in the first half of the nineteenth century, would continue to fall until the First World War, but historians agree that the work of personal physicians had little to do with improving survival rates. Nonetheless, increased longevity combined with scientific advances in understanding the disease process supported medicine's growing confidence as a profession. Evidence of the benefits of Listerian surgery (see Box 1.4, p. 25) in reducing infection and the elegant experiments of Pasteurian bacteriology (see Box 1.3, p. 25) made a clinical practice whose efficacy against disease was informed by scientific findings a distinct possibility.

Technological inventions were also becoming available and adding to the reputation of hospital medicine: the thermometer and stethoscope were used in hospital training and were soon to become routinely used; the X-ray (invented in 1895) and electrocardiograph (invented in 1901) were yet to find their place as standard diagnostic tools. Clinical medicine had a system of diagnosis based on the interpretation of physical signs, increasingly aided by technology, with the search for physical causes of disease justified by scientific reasoning. Despite these signs of the rise of medicine as a scientific discipline, the early part of the twentieth century was a time when the doctor had the ability to diagnose disease scientifically while remaining therapeutically powerless.

BOX 1.3

Louis Pasteur

Louis Pasteur (1822–1895) was born in the Jura region of France and educated in Paris as a biologist and a chemist. In 1854 he became a professor of chemistry at the University of Lille where he studied fermentation in wine and beer. His series of elegant experiments confirmed the 'germ theory of disease' to his contemporaries and showed that microorganisms could be killed by heating liquid to 55 degrees Celsius for a short period of time (a process known as pasteurization that is applied to milk and other comestible liquids to this day). His work became the foundation for the science of microbiology and a cornerstone of modern medicine, with immunology growing directly from his work on developing a rabies vaccination.

BOX 1.4

Joseph Lister

Joseph Lister (1827–1912) discovered the antiseptic technique which has been crucial to the development of modern surgery. Born in Essex, the son of a wealthy wine merchant, Lister graduated from University College, London in 1852 and began his surgical career in Edinburgh, becoming professor of surgery at the Royal Infirmary in Glasgow by 1860. Working on Pasteur's 'beautiful researches' demonstrating his theory that bacteria cause infection, Lister proved the effectiveness of antisepsis by using lint-soaked carbolic acid to dress a boy's compound fracture in 1865. During operations Lister had carbolic acid constantly sprayed, which saturated all those present and was a practice ridiculed by some colleagues, but, together with the heat sterilization of instruments, this resulted in a dramatic decrease in postoperative fatalities. He became professor of clinical surgery at Edinburgh University in 1869 before returning to London for an appointment at King's College in 1877.

Hospitals, which were central to the rise of medicine, were largely located in the cities, and the urban poor were catered for by charitable institutions and by specialist foundations funded through donations. Rural general practitioners offered some services at cottage hospitals in return for a fee, but compared to their urban counterparts rural populations were under-served. The insurance principle, administered through friendly societies or co-operatives, put hospital treatment within the reach of an increasing proportion of the population and the demand for hospital services grew consistently with their availability.

Anatomy, bacteriology and physiology were taught in medical schools using textbooks and written examinations, a new feature of medical education. The standardized assessment of the transfer of professional knowledge was a key feature of medicine's emergent professionalism. The recognition of an ever-expanding range of human diseases was under way and doctors' key role in classifying the cause of death (see Chapter 2) was well established.

FIRST WORLD WAR: 1914–1918

In the run up to the 1914–1918 conflict, also called the Great War, the gains in longevity among the affluent classes benefiting from improved standards of living had yet to filter down to the poorer classes. Mortality for women and children, including those in the poorer classes, continued to drop during the war years, probably due to a more equitable distribution of the food supply which had come under state-control. The increased provision of health surveillance and services for mothers, together with maternity benefit, reflected the state's concern with producing future healthy generations, particularly young men who could serve in the war. Better survival rates for babies led to a falling birth rate and the effect of smaller families together with an increase in women's employment was a rise in the average standard of living. The improvement may also have been supported by state restrictions on the availability of alcohol (a staple foodstuff and safe drinking source only a few generations earlier), justified to keep war-time factory workforces to regular hours. In addition to the provision of obstetric services, medicine's war effort involved the maintenance of the fighting machine by tending to the armed forces.

In many ways war has been good for the development of medical expertise, not least because people and governments have a heightened tolerance for medicine's more brutal methods to repair the damage wrought by warfare's violence. The shift in medicine from the nineteenth century's observational bedside craft to a scientific interventionist calling had begun before the onset of the First World War, but the conflict offered continuing opportunities for this development. Techniques to repair firearm wounds and innovations in the treatment of the psychological effects of sustained fighting were notable medical legacies of the Great War. But more important than these technical advances was the centrality accorded to health in the post-war re-making of society. There was a willingness to improve environmental health and social conditions for the whole population, which included a concerted effort to build 'homes fit for heroes' through raising public funds. Having played an important role in the war effort, medicine was seen as a central profession in building society back up. Changes to the national insurance scheme made it more accessible and widened the availability of medical services.

1918–1939

The period between the world wars saw infectious disease continue to retreat, with effects on longevity as the proportion of people over 65 years in the population increased from 6 per cent in 1920 to 9 per cent in 1940. The long-term effects of better nutrition, living standards and environment contributed to the retreat of tuberculosis, meningitis, polio, rheumatic fever and pneumonia as routine infections. The arrival of sulpha drugs – chemical compounds with a bacteriostatic effect – from the mid-1930s meant that doctors finally had an effective chemotherapy for fever and bacterial infection. The early sulpha drugs slashed the mortality rates of puerperal fever, responsible for much postpartum maternal mortality, and were seen as miraculous. Pharmaceutical regulations were minimal and these sulpha drugs were prescribed in vast quantities. They may also have supported ongoing gains in longevity, which had the concomitant effect of the rise of chronic and degenerative diseases in later life. Lung cancer, coronary artery disease, diabetes, stroke and chronic degenerative disease emerged as major diseases as the era of acute infection slowly gave way to that of chronic disease.

While long-term health outcomes were improving steadily, the Great Depression, whose onset was marked by the New York stock market crash of 1929, made daily life difficult for much of the population, particularly the working classes. National debts incurred in order to fund the Great War contributed to economic instability on a global scale and economic recovery was slow. While Britain was not hit as hard as some other European countries, unemployment in the industrial areas was devastating. A government-funded unemployment scheme was introduced in 1934, which paid out according to need as determined by a means test rather than according to the level of contributions that had been made. A widespread unwillingness to revisit the hardship of the 1930s contributed to the national enthusiasm for further reform to the Welfare State and the establishment of the NHS following the Second World War.

SECOND WORLD WAR: 1939–1945

The initial shock of the Second World War was not so much combat casualties as the poor condition of the city children evacuated to rural settings. The dirtiness, scabies, head lice and incontinence of some evacuees became public knowledge and showed up the inadequacy of the public health measures and health surveillance that had been established since the First World War. When fighting started in earnest after the so-called phoney war, the proportion of casualties and fatalities among the civilian population was far higher than in previous conflicts. Hospitals had not previously had to cope with the aftermath of bombing and inadequacies in the system were exposed. Innovations in healthcare organization resulting from these experiences included the establishment of the public health laboratory system, mobile paramedical teams and the blood transfusion system. Specialist areas of medical interest continued to develop within the generalist hospital, with psychiatry being particularly important in getting soldiers back to a fit state of mind to fight once their bodily wounds had healed.

In addition to the move away from generalist clinical practice, the lasting change to the medical care of the Second World War was the use of penicillin – a biological agent that destroyed pathological bacteria more effectively than chemical sulpha drugs. Penicillin cured wound infections and sexually transmitted diseases among the armed forces and was greeted as another miracle drug, boosting morale and dramatically increasing doctors' power to influence the course of disease.

1945 TO THE TWENTY-FIRST CENTURY

Since the end of the Second World War in 1945, Britain has not had to cope with mass civilian or armed forces casualties and medicine's development has been focused on civilian healthcare. The national mood in 1945, following years of rationing, fighting and fear, was doubtless worn down, but it was also determined to build a better future, with science being seen as the rational and progressive means to this end. Scientific medicine was viewed as playing a key role in relieving society of its burden of disease, disability, premature death and depression through the appliance of innovative technology and pharmaceuticals. The introduction of penicillin to treat civilian illness after the war established its reputation as a wonder drug and cemented the public's faith in scientific medicine. However, the unwanted side-effects of scientific intervention were already apparent: by 1948 nearly 60 per cent of staphylococci isolated at the Hammersmith Hospital in London were already penicillin resistant.

The establishment of the NHS was key to the commitment to a happier, healthier future and was accompanied by the introduction of family allowances and the education act that made schooling available to all 5–15 year olds. Meanwhile a revolution in manufacturing was in full swing that would bring unprecedented change to domestic life, with the arrival of cars, televisions and washing machines for the masses.

The NHS was established shortly after the Second World War in order to make medical care available to the entire British population, free at the point of delivery. The ideal was that an adequate service would be provided for all, regardless of their social position, and it was assumed that such universal care together with public health measures would result in a decrease in the population's need for healthcare. The NHS was not, in reality, newly made in 1948, since existing hospitals – both charitable and municipal – were nationalized and GPs were employed on new contracts while remaining in existing premises without additional equipment or personnel. Existing interest groups had to be accommodated in the new system and the most powerful and the most resistant of these were hospital consultants. Aneurin Bevan (1897–1960), Minister of Health in the post-war Labour government, claimed to have 'won over consultants by choking their mouths with gold' and negotiated a set of compromises to establish a system that addressed professional concerns to a considerable degree.

The NHS has been described as representing a compromise between the principles of traditional medical authority and rational public administration (Klein, 2000). Having bought out the existing system, without much in the way of re-organization or reformation, the inequities of the pre-NHS healthcare system persisted: London was very well served with hospitals, with few in the north, east and west of the country where they were confined to the cities. The distribution of GPs was uneven as were their facilities and skills and, since there was no obligatory additional training after leaving medical school, their reputation as less expert than hospital consultants might have been warranted. The establishment of the NHS did nothing to disrupt the division between hospital doctors and GPs, indeed it may have been deliberately reinforced. Unable to satisfy all the constituents of the medical profession, Aneurin Bevan deliberately encouraged rifts and then sought the support of the most influential sections of the profession to push through a deal. Hospital consultants gained various perks such as study leave and merit awards, while the BMA (representing the GPs) persisted in its opposition to the terms under which the NHS was established.

Inequities and compromises notwithstanding, figures on the uptake of national health services in the immediate aftermath of its establishment suggest it was a success. Millions of sets of teeth and pairs of spectacles had been supplied by the time charges for them were introduced in 1951 by the then Chancellor Hugh Gaitskill, seeking revenues for the Cold War arms race. Aneurin Bevan resigned from government in protest, but a year later a charge was introduced for prescription drugs. These charges did nothing to temper the ever-increasing demand for GPs' services and prescriptions.

The dramatic improvements in mortality rates apparent in the first half of the twentieth century could not be sustained at the same rate after 1945. Nonetheless, the 25 per cent of deaths attributable to infectious diseases in 1900 had fallen to less than 1 per cent by 1990, having declined throughout the century. Academics and researchers have argued about how much credit medicine can take for this change. Thomas McKeown's (1912–1988) well-known and widely cited thesis says that improvements in life expectancy can be better explained by improvements in social, economic and environmental factors than by progress in medical science (McKeown, 1979). Others have suggested that the picture is more complex, with changes instigated by medicine shaping the environment in which infectious agents failed to thrive. In particular, the public health movement and the work of medical officers contributed to creating clean water, safe sewage disposal and other innovations to clean up the urban environment, such as dustbins with lids to deter flies.

BOX 1.5

Thomas McKeown

Born in Northern Ireland in 1912 and educated in Canada, Thomas McKeown worked at Oxford University and Guy's Hospital medical school during the 1930s before qualifying in medicine in 1942. He was appointed to the Chair in Social Medicine at the University of Birmingham in 1945. While he had interests in foetal medicine and congenital malformations, it is his interest in society and medicine for which he is chiefly remembered.

He developed ideas about the contribution of medical interventions to the improvement of the human condition in analyses that were published as collaboratively written papers and later elaborated upon in books which included *The Modern Rise of Population* (1976), and *The Role of Medicine* (1979). His thesis challenged the belief, promoted by establishment medicine, that improvements to the population's health and particularly reductions in mortality had sprung from clinical practice. McKeown argued that population health ameliorated in line with social, economic, public-health engineering, and dietary improvements.

His realistic reappraisal of the origins of progress was not universally well received, competing as it did with vested professional interests and challenging hagiographic accounts of medical men. He was a founder of the social medicine movement and a proponent of the application of scientific analysis to healthcare planning to provide services on the basis of identifiable need.

COSTS AND BENEFITS OF TWENTIETH CENTURY MEDICAL INNOVATION

The development of a polio vaccine in 1953 and its use in mass immunization programmes in the 1960s were followed by vaccinations against diphtheria, tetanus and whooping cough, and later by measles, mumps and rubella vaccinations. The second half of the twentieth century was a period of economic expansion combined with rapid innovation and development for the western world and medicine has been very much part of this process. The development of effective vaccinations against so many infectious diseases, together with drugs effective against many bacterial conditions and some viral infections, not to mention metabolic disorders, is an impressive record for biomedical sciences and represents an important reduction in human suffering and premature death. The high speed of identification and the adoption of new ideas and practices seen in the post-Second World War years has been unprecedented in human history.

However, rapid progress against infectious agents has been accompanied by the catastrophic effects of other innovations, such as 'Thalidomide', marketed to pregnant women as a safe anti-emetic which also had sedative and hypnotic properties, but which actually caused serious foetal defects and was withdrawn in 1961. Other casualties of pharmacological innovation include a synthetic oestrogen, prescribed to prevent miscarriage, which was subsequently linked with a rare form of cancer, and a non-steroidal anti-inflammatory drug prescribed to over 80 million people worldwide for osteoarthritis and other acutely painful conditions before being withdrawn in 2004 because of its association with an increased risk of heart attack and stroke associated with long-term, high-dosage use. No products introduced since penicillin or vaccines have had a comparably positive impact and even that impact cannot be counted as purely beneficial. Antibiotic resistance was first noted in the 1940s soon after widespread prescription started and the search for products to evade resistance has remained an important and ongoing part of research and development in the pharmaceutical industry ever since. Half a century later, the public health implications of the widespread use of antibiotic medicine are coming to the public's attention. The routine dosing of farmed animals with antibiotics and inappropriate antibiotic prescription for viral infections in human populations have been linked with the identification of multiply-resistant lines of bacteria responsible for acute and life-threatening infections in hospital settings.

Assessing the role of medicine in the improvement of human health and happiness is difficult because, as the story of penicillin shows, each innovation changes not only the world in which the pathogens act, but also our own perceptions and expectations of disease and of health. For example, while the founders of the NHS imagined that the population's health would improve as a result of free access to services to the point where demand would drop, they were unfortunately misguided. Rather, our perceived need for healthcare has expanded in line with medicine's ambitions and capabilities and our expectations have shifted a long way from those held in 1948.

BOX 1.6

Dangerous childbirth

At the beginning of the twentieth century having a baby was a relatively risky business, with maternal death rates around 1 in 100 for live births. The number in developed countries today is about 1 in 10,000. Perinatal mortality rates have also dropped with developed countries' rates being below 10 per 1,000 live births, compared to more than 100 per 1,000 live births a century ago. Improved pre-natal care has contributed to these improvements, as have the medical management of birth with asepsis preventing postpartum infection, the use of Caesarean section and assisted delivery for obstructed or stalled birth, and the use of blood transfusion to mitigate the effects of hemorrhaging. Obstetricians' interventions undoubtedly save mothers' and babies' lives, yet the routine use of the elective Caesarean section for normal births as well as the emergency or planned Caesarean for abnormal births has changed expectations about birth. Women and babies no longer routinely die in childbirth, but critics argue that the price for increased safety through medically managed birth has been the brutalizing and dehumanizing of most births. The question of whether increased safety offsets the other costs is debated in both medical and non-medical circles.

The development of organ and joint replacement techniques in the twentieth century represents the realization of the highest expectations of high-tech, pharmaceutically sophisticated medical interventions. Thanks to the timely development of immunosuppressant drugs, together with advances in surgical techniques and the availability of cadaver organs, often as a result of road traffic accidents, it has become possible to replace a diseased heart. Given the very poor success rate of early attempts at transplantation, another factor in the eventual success of transplant surgery has been a supply of patients willing to be subjected to experimental and uncertain procedures carrying little hope of success. The mood of confidence in medicine and optimism about a scientifically shaped future that prevailed during the 1960s and 1970s, when these techniques were in development, doubtless made such willingness more likely. By the start of the twenty-first century transplant surgery had become routine for renal problems, taking place in 23 centres throughout the UK performing about 1,700 transplants per year. Transplant medicine is currently recognized as a distinct branch of surgery, with separate training routes for those doctors specializing in transplantation of the kidney and the liver.

While death from infectious disease is now a rarity, the number of deaths from cancer has continued to increase. Improvements to radiotherapy regimes and the introduction of chemotherapy, followed by screening programmes for breast and cervical cancers in the early 1960s, represent medical advances in tackling cancer. Despite notable progress in the case of some rarer cancers, the prospects for those with common adult-onset cancers continue to be moderate with early detection remaining the best chance for recovery. Where cancer has disseminated through the body, management rather than cure is the aim of medical treatment. Increasing numbers of cancer deaths represent an unwelcome continuity with the nineteenth century and one which continues to resist the progress of scientific medicine.

HEALTH INEQUALITIES

The major causes of death towards the close of the twentieth century were cardio-vascular disease, stroke and cancer. The inequitable social class distribution of rates of premature death, which had been noted by nineteenth century philanthropists such as Charles Booth and Edwin Chadwick, re-emerged as a political issue towards the end of the 1970s. Analysis of statutory data showed that, despite the NHS having been in operation for 30 years, men and women of the poorer social classes continued to experience significantly higher rates of premature death. The establishment of the NHS meant that people were no longer excluded from receiving healthcare because they could not pay for the service or for an insurance premium. Nonetheless, the NHS did not address the inequitable national distribution of healthcare facilities, nor the uneven availability of good quality services. Research continues to investigate the relative contribution of individual lifestyle behaviours (for example, smoking, excess drinking and unhealthy food) and the more diffuse and widespread effects of persistent poverty (damp housing, material deprivation, a sense of the unfairness of inequality) on mortality inequalities. A discussion of health inequalities is picked up again in Chapter 4.

The economic recession of the 1970s did not forestall the continued rise in demand for health services and meant that governments were in search of new solutions to persistent health problems. Containing health and social care bills for the long-term mentally ill and for the elderly who, throughout the twentieth century, continued to grow as a proportion of the population was much of the impetus behind 'community care' programmes for both of these groups. People who had been confined to institutions became more visible when living in community settings and, arguably, were more vulnerable to prejudiced attitudes. Further discussion of the funding of health and care services is to be found in Chapter 9.

Global health inequalities and old prejudices against marginalized groups were reinforced in 1983 with the identification of the Human Immunodeficiency Virus, or HIV, as the agent responsible for a syndrome of rare conditions associated with the breakdown of the immune system – Acquired Immunodeficiency Syndrome or AIDS. Gay men, drug users, sex workers and Africans have all been identified as having increased risk of contracting the virus for different reasons and, at times, have been held culpable for their own suffering. The spread of HIV and other rare viral diseases, together with the inability to produce a cure, suggests that confidence in the retreat of infectious diseases in the face of scientific progress has perhaps been misplaced, or is at least premature.

Medicine has over-reached its own and its patients' expectations in areas such as transplant surgery. Barriers to the development of technologically sophisticated medicine have been moral and ethical as well as practical and scientific as people have struggled to come to terms with the extraordinary treatment options that have become available with such speed. In other respects medicine has failed to fulfil the hopes of those who sponsored and implemented a national health service in Britain, in that, despite improved access, inequalities persist in the quality of service available to groups defined by locality, social class, ethnic group, age and medical diagnosis. The apparently limitless demand for healthcare and the colonization of areas not previously seen as medical (such as infertility, short stature and sexual performance) mean that, even in a nationalized, publicly funded system, the opportunities for the accumulation of profit are considerable. The profit motive in pharmaceutical and medical technology multi-national companies makes the eradication of national and global health inequalities unlikely in the foreseeable future.

MEDICAL TRANSFORMATIONS

To visualize the changes that have taken place in the medical profession since 1900, imagine the rural GP of a hundred years ago, solely responsible for the day-to-day health of his community of patients, from birth to death. He (women doctors were still rare) would have carried most of his equipment, tonics, sugar pills and perhaps morphine with him when he made house visits, and would have done so by foot, bicycle or horse. He would have expected to be able to cope with whatever condition he faced as a good diagnostician and generalist physician. He would have had to bill his patients in order to make a living, and, particularly in poor areas, would have needed to enjoy a decent reputation and an extensive patient list in order to make a good living. Doctors with a social conscience may have chosen to present smaller bills to their poorer patients, since there was no statutory health insurance system. In contrast, today's doctors are embedded in a more formally regulated, institutionalized enterprise which could not operate without equipment, services and the infrastructure of the state, industry and research communities which brings medical practitioners into constant contact with other professionals. At the start of the twentieth century when the ideal of a generalist physician was still defended, medicine was already in the process of becoming highly specialized. This process has developed throughout the twentieth century so that even most GPs in the community and physicians practising general internal medicine in hospitals have areas of particular expertise. The knowledge explosion has made it impossible for any doctor to keep abreast of all aspects of medicine and potentially threatens medicine's status as a unified discipline. What constitutes the core material of a medical education and how much of this is subsequently relevant in daily practice continue to be debated.

The daily context of patients as well as doctors has changed dramatically since 1900: our lives are almost unrecognizable compared to those of our early twentieth century forbears for whom television, supermarkets, mobile telephones, personal computers and widespread access to air travel were science fictions and a national health service was still a generation away. The limitless desire for the consumer goods that populate our daily lives has been equally influential in medicine. While ownership of ever more powerful machines is perhaps its own reward, medical consumerism may have more drastically diminishing returns. Even if money and other resources were no barrier, no amount of medical expertise can budge the bottom line that we share with our ancestors: despite the great expectations of scientific medicine, death, disease and degeneration remain our fate. The implications of this obvious assertion represent a truth with which modern society and the medicine that serves it have yet to come to terms.

Further reading

Davey Smith, G., Dorling, D. and Shaw, M. (eds) (2001) *Poverty, Inequality and Health in Britain 1800–2000: A Reader*. Bristol: Policy.

A selection of papers chosen to illustrate the continuities and changes in the ongoing investigation of poverty and health over the last two centuries, with a useful historical time line showing key moments and pieces of legislation.

Hardy, A. (2001) *Health and Medicine in Britain since 1860* (Series: Social History in Perspective). Basingstoke: Palgrave.

A succinct account of a discrete period of British social history which gives a good sense of the development of the British health services and doctors' place therein.

McKeown, T. (1979) *The Role of Medicine: Dream, Mirage or Nemesis?* Oxford: Basil Blackwell.

A book that can rightly be called a classic, given its profound influence on the criticism of the profession and discipline of medicine.

Porter, R. (1997) *The Greatest Benefit to Mankind: A Medical History of Humanity from Antiquity to the Present.* London: HarperCollins.

This is a big (800-plus pages) book which surveys the history of medical thinking and medical practice, with a focus on the development of western medicine. Described as a 'blockbuster' by a review in the Guardian *newspaper, it is an enjoyable read, offering an informed and wide ranging view of the past, interestingly connected to current concerns.*

REVISION QUESTIONS

1 What were the significant historical events that permitted the development of medicine as a powerful profession?

2 What were the significant historical events that led to the establishment of the NHS?

3 To what extent can medicine claim responsibility for the improvement in mortality rates in the second half of the twentieth century?

EXTENSION QUESTIONS

Think about the phrase 'the golden age of medicine' and decide which of the following phrases you agree with most.

– The golden age of medicine is characterized by patients respecting their family doctors with whom they enjoy a trusting, lifelong relationship.
– The golden age of medicine will occur when the potentials of stem cell research for organ regeneration and of pharmacogenetics for personalized medicine are fulfilled.
– The reduction of mortality rates to historically unprecedented low levels marks the golden age of medicine.

At which historical period were the costs of medicine smallest compared to the benefits?

If you could choose any historical period between 1900 and 2050, when would you most like to be, or to have been, a doctor?

When would you most like to be, or to have been, a patient?

Are the benefits of scientific medicine set to increase in the future?

2

DEFINING THE DOCTOR'S REMIT

Chapter summary

This chapter describes:

» how doctors' work can be distinguished from that of other health professionals;

» key features of the doctor's role which are identified as:

- determining what constitutes legitimate disease;
- defining when a person has died;
- overseeing death when it is sanctioned by the state.

However, these features do not apply exclusively to physicians and not all physicians undertake this type of work.

Useful terms for this chapter

diagnosis: the process of identifying a disease or condition through its symptoms and signs

disease: a medically recognized and diagnosable pathological condition associated with an underlying lesion, such as an infection or tumour. Disease is an organic process, usually distinguished from injury or a stable disability

illness: state of sickness, subjectively identified by the sufferer or his carers but not necessarily presented to, or recognized by, medical authority

medical pluralism: the co-existence of a number of traditions of medicine which rely on different underlying principles and may be consulted simultaneously by a single patient

signs: when a patient arrives at a consultation the doctor identifies pointers or signs which signify an underlying pathological lesion

symptoms: feelings experienced by patients suggesting that something is wrong, sometimes leading to help seeking from a health professional

INTRODUCTION

In the previous chapter society's changing expectations of medicine were outlined, suggesting that both achievements and failures in combating disease affect the evolution of the relationship between patients and their doctors. This chapter returns to the present, to ask 'What do doctors do?' Doctors diagnose and treat disease, with a view to curing or at least alleviating its symptoms. Diagnosis and treatment are crucial aspects of a doctor's work for those patients receiving healthcare and these are activities that have wider significance for the way that society works. Decisions and judgements made by doctors are crucial to the functioning of the institutions of contemporary society in which medical authority arbitrates in non-medical dilemmas. For instance, doctors can give evidence in determining who is considered sane and therefore able to stand trial to answer for the consequences of their actions, while medical evidence has also been given enormous weight in cases of suspected child sexual abuse or 'suspicious' cot death. The role of medical evidence given by individual doctors in legal arbitration is key to understanding medical power in society. The next two sections cover the functions of diagnosis and of treatment that go beyond the individual patient, to gain purchase on the wider social effects of these aspects of doctors' work.

DIAGNOSIS: LEGITIMATE AND ILLEGITIMATE ILLNESS

Before medicine offers treatment, it has to arrive at a diagnosis. Patients experience symptoms and this experience motivates them to seek medical help. Medical diagnosis uses the symptoms described by the patient, and other visible or palpable signs, to detect the lesion that underlies the disease. When the patient is conscious and communicative he can describe his symptoms, but even where this is impossible, signs of pathology can be detected by looking, feeling, smelling and listening to the patient's body without the aid of instruments as well as with simple aids to observation, such as lenses and light sources to examine the eye, ear canal, mouth and throat. Abnormalities in the expected parameters of bodily functioning are sought by counting and timing pulse rates, taking blood pressure, measuring body temperature and listening to the rhythm of the heart and lung function.

The rise of hospital medicine has made possible the use of more complex machines and techniques to collect indications of the inner workings of the body, including X-rays, barium washes, electronic monitors and ultrasound scans. Sophisticated visualizing technologies have been developed, such as CAT (computerised axial tomography), PETT (positron emission transaxial tomography) and MRI (magnetic resonance imaging) scans to give a three dimensional body image on a screen and endoscopes to look inside the body via orifices or surgical incisions. Better understandings of the metabolic and genetic nature of disease and its biochemistry have spawned tests that can detect the pathogen itself or by-products of its activity in blood, or other tissue samples or in bodily waste products. Genetic tests allow certain conditions to be associated with specific features of the genotype.

Biomedicine places particular significance on detectable lesions in order to distinguish disease-related symptoms from those which are not recognized as disease-related. A fractured bone will show up on an X-ray; swollen glands imply a pathogen which may also be causing a raised temperature; a palpable lump may be a tumour whose presence can be confirmed by histological examination; a piece of wood sticking out of a wound might be visible to the naked eye and any accompanying infection may cause a distinctive smell. Foreign bodies, pathogens and tumours are all lesions to which symptoms and signs can be attributed. The availability of diagnostic technology to identify underlying pathological processes means that disease is increasingly diagnosed with reference to numerical values. Normal ranges are defined on parameters such as weight, height, circumference, haemoglobin level, blood pressure, heart and respiratory rate, hormone and electrolyte levels, heart size and visual acuity. Values inside the defined range are normal and therefore healthy, whereas outside the range (and accompanied by associated changes to bodily organs or systems) these are defined as unhealthy or diseased. In this sense disease has come to be defined as deviation from the norm and its detection has become dissociated from the experience of symptoms (a subject which we return to in Chapter 5).

There has been a shift in emphasis from the subjectivity of the patient's descriptions of the experience of his own symptoms and the doctor's interpretation of bodily signs to the objectivity of numerical values generated by the technologically aided examination of the body. The nineteenth century family doctor with a good bedside manner compared the patient's current symptoms and signs with experience of that individual's health history and identity. With the rise of hospital medicine and diagnostic technology, it is the identity of the disease rather than the patient that comes to the fore: disease is conceptualized as a stable entity with its own 'personality' that will be consistently manifest through symptoms, signs and numerical printouts. The doctor's expertise no longer lies in recognizing the significance of symptoms for the individual patient, but in a detailed knowledge of the manifestation of the disease. This focus on objectively measurable disease, independent of the bodily or social context in which it occurs, is a distinctive feature of the way that modern medicine is practised.

Recognition of a disease through its diagnosis is central to the clinical and administrative aspects of medical treatment. Patients progress through the NHS by each individual doctor recognizing symptoms and signs that indicate a disease which they are competent to treat and, where they cannot help, by referring that patient to a suitable specialist. Despite the emphasis on multi-disciplinary team-working, the responsibility for diagnosis remains with the doctor and the patient's pathway through, and experience of, health-care services hinge on diagnosis. Diagnosis is crucial to gain access to services including referral to specialists: it opens the way for diagnostic, palliative and therapeutic procedures. People who suffer symptoms without a recognizable diagnosis will find their trajectory through the health services is hindered: an appropriate diagnosis facilitates referral between medical specialists. Diagnosis is also significant beyond clinical care, since it determines patients' access to a variety of other benefits.

In Britain the state provides benefits for those considered unable to support themselves such that, in theory, the ill effects of disease and disability on the individual and their household are mitigated. Getting access to the system of sickness and disability benefits turns on a person's incapacity and inability to engage in normal activities and this inability is legitimated by a medical diagnosis. The financial and other assistance available to those who are designated diseased or disabled can include dispensation from paying taxes, prescription and dental charges and subsidies for the cost of housing, home care, leisure facilities and transport. What is more, unlike most employers' benefit schemes, which are time-limited, state assistance is available regardless of the afflicted person's prospects of a return to economic productivity. Furthermore, statutory benefits are available regardless of the sufferer's role in the genesis of his own ill health: the effects of recreational drug-taking are, at least in theory, treated with the same standard of care as are the symptoms of any other disease. Statutory health services, and the social care services with which they work in a closely integrated fashion (as distinct from pre-welfare state charitable support), are not meant to distinguish between deserving and undeserving cases.

Sickness and disability benefits are funded through general taxation, so the burden of supporting the incapacitated is shared across the population. Doctors act as gate-keepers for people seeking to claim these statutory benefits with medical certification of a condition determining whether or not it warrants such support. Suffering that cannot be attributed to a recognized disease or disability may not attract statutory benefits, as was illustrated by the generally sceptical response to people with Chronic Fatigue Syndrome and Gulf War Syndrome during the 1990s. Medical certification is integral to the way that the Welfare State is administered and is the main way in which the public purse is protected from unscrupulous citizens who would fake symptoms to live in able-bodied idleness. The problem with relying on medical certification is two-fold: some symptoms can be faked, and yet symptoms that are severely debilitating are not necessarily recognized as stemming from a diagnosable disease. The medical model of disease overlooks the complexities of human suffering so that people with real difficulties can nonetheless be excluded from receiving benefits. Symptoms that are considered vague and therefore not related to a real biological cause may be denied a diagnosis and dismissed as psychosomatic or faked. To have a condition that is not diagnosed as disease has implications for a person's material and financial circumstances, as well as his or her clinical care; it also has more subtle implications for the person's place in his or her social network.

Beyond the administrative and financial significance of diagnosis, there is an informal validation to having one's suffering medically recognized: 'The doctor says I have Beijing influenza' validates illness. Receiving a doctor's diagnosis makes sense of symptoms and gives people permission to be ill, thus authorizing remedial actions: going to bed, neglecting daily tasks and refusing meals. While it is possible to behave like an ill person on one's own initiative, it is easier to do so with impunity when supported by medical authority. Indeed, self-certification of illness for absence from employment is now encouraged to reduce unnecessary GP-consultations, but many institutions still rely on medical definitions of legitimate illness. Education and training establishments rely on medical certification of illnesses for decisions about people's rights to claim special support in education and to re-sit examinations, while commercial organizations use medical diagnosis to judge an employee's rights to remain in employment and to gain access to private sickness benefit and pension schemes.

The categorization and confirmation of states of disease and disability are crucial parts of medicine's work for the regulation of education, employment and the distribution of statutory and non-statutory benefits for those exempt from their normal activities. Diagnosis is also the lynchpin for the aspect of the doctor's remit consequent upon diagnosis – namely, the treatment of the diagnosed condition which we consider next.

TREATING DIAGNOSED DISEASE

What is expected of the doctor treating diagnosed disease? In the age of scientific medicine, doctors are expected to draw on the best available scientific evidence, which, especially in hospital medicine, means co-ordinating the contributions of a range of specialists and various investigation and test results. Diverse evidence must be weighed up including expert opinions which may not be in agreement, test results that may be contradictory, the published evidence base, the doctor's instinct and his experience from previous cases – all of which have to be given their proper weight in deciding upon a course of treatment to recommend. The integration of health and social care means that a variety of professionals will manage a person's treatment and recovery. It is not only professional and scientific evidence that must be considered, but also the individual circumstances and preferences of each patient.

Medical educators have long instructed students to listen to patients' own stories when coming to a diagnosis, but the idea that patients should be involved in the decision making that follows diagnosis is more contentious. Wider access to post-compulsory education and to medical information means that patients' ability and willingness to comment on and contribute to decisions about treatment have increased over the last few generations. User-involvement and patient choice are politically favoured so that, where expressed, the patient's opinion should be taken seriously. Where clinicians do not share the language or culture of the patient, proactive efforts to overcome communication barriers are increasingly expected from healthcare providers. Greater longevity and the rise of chronic disease mean that diagnosis and ensuing treatment tend to be ongoing processes of constant updating, re-balancing and integrating the various forms of evidence. The long-term nature of much of medicine's case-load makes the involvement of the patient crucial, and over the course of a chronic condition the weight given to different forms of evidence will shift: biopsy results may be central in establishing a cancer diagnosis but later in the disease process the patient's priorities may shift away from seeking a cure through aggressive treatment and towards maintaining a good quality of life over a limited period of time. The priority given to different forms of evidence must shift and this can be complicated by disagreement between patient and professional and between various professionals on the balance of risk of particular courses of action. And it is the doctor who is the professional at the helm, responsible for keeping this complex process of balancing evidence and opinion in making treatment decisions on course.

The evidence-based pursuit of treatment, delivered by a multi-disciplinary, co-ordinated team of professionals who consult appropriately with the patient and/or the patient's carers is already a demanding expectation. But we also expect our doctors to steer this process with humanity and compassion. Respectful care should be extended to all patients, whether conscious or unconscious, regardless of their prognosis. Furthermore, dead bodies should be treated respectfully and this humanity and compassion must be apparent not only to the patient (when alive), but also to his or her family, friends and carers. Doctors who have good diagnostic skills, can integrate diverse evidence in decision making and offer treatment and prognoses in a way that continues to treat the patient as a unique human are, rightly, highly valued by their colleagues, not to mention their patients. Where successfully combined, the extraordinary mixture of knowledge, skills and qualities demanded of a good doctor may justify the prestigious and powerful role they enjoy beyond the immediate field of medicine. The question of whether such demanding expectations are reasonably applied to most doctors, or indeed whether they are fulfilled with any regularity, is another matter. One of the issues that this book explores is the extent to which the failures of medicine are attributable to a systemic flaw in medicine's methods and society's expectations of them.

High expectations of medicine are problematic for routine therapeutic work in the sense that anything less than a total recovery can be seen as a failure. In the last century medicine redefined death to an extent never previously dreamed of by promoting recovery from what had been fatal or debilitating diseases (polio, smallpox, measles). Antibiotics and immunization programmes mean that formerly common bacterial infections of childhood, which were feared as regularly causing death, are now rare (see Chapter 1). At the other end of the lifespan, opportunistic infections such as pneumonia and bronchitis are curable in old age, bypass operations to treat angina are now common for people over 80 years of age, and medical technology such as pace-makers, nebulizers, ventilators, dialysis machines and fibrillators manage some of the effects of chronic conditions and effectively delay death.

Death is an equivocal business for medicine; its deferral is modern medicine's goal but inevitably the most successfully treated disease eventually reaches a point where scientific methods can no longer intervene. Medicine seeks to make premature death a less and less common experience but, with society increasingly relying on scientific rather than religious or magical means of delaying death, medicine is inevitably associated with death. So while medicine has been credited with promoting our longevity it is also associated with death, to the extent that doctors have replaced priests as the professionals who oversee the end of life. At times of grave illness it is medical rather than religious or spiritual expertise that is generally sought in the first instance. Medical personnel are the first port of call if life is threatened and are expected to be able to staunch its ebbing away, or if this proves impossible, to ease the process of dying. Death may represent the failure of medicine's enhanced therapeutic interventions, but the activity around death has remained part of medicine's remit nonetheless.

DEFINING DEATH

A hospital death has become the norm, with most people in the UK dying in a medical institution and the vast majority of us dying under some type of medical management. Death usually takes place on medical territory and the practical and legal business incurred by death is dealt with by hospital employees for whom the tasks rapidly become routine. Where death takes place beyond the hospital, medicine plays a role as the arbiter of death nonetheless, since medical professionals must certify death for legal and statutory purposes. The legal oversight of death requires that every demise is certificated by a medical practitioner who must designate a cause of death. Without such a certificate a person cannot be buried, nor can his estate be divided amongst any inheritors. The certificated cause of death is collated for national mortality statistics the analysis of which forms the basis of various health policies, with the long-term aim of improving the population's health. Doctors divide illegitimate from legitimate deaths: dying from the natural processes of bodily ageing, or from disease or random accident, must be distinguished from death which may have been caused by unusual or suspicious circumstances. While coroners (or in Scotland, the procurator fiscal) must establish the cause of death in unusual circumstances, it is doctors who, most often, define death as natural or unnatural.

A professional association with death is popularly seen as sinister, with undertakers, grave-diggers and coffin-makers assumed to be morbid or creepy. But medicine's oath to 'first, do no harm' perhaps off-sets the disturbing aspect of medicine's familiarity with death. Medicine's honourable intentions around death are recognized given that the profession is entrusted with overseeing and certificating the portal between life and death.

Overseeing and defining the process of death is not a one-off responsibility but a continuously changing process, given the development of techniques to support or replace the parameters that have defined life in the past, in particular, respiration and heart-beat. With the arrival of machines that could take over heart and lung function, the definition of death has, inevitably, shifted. The enormous research interest and funding devoted to transplant medicine in the late 1960s and 1970s has had the effect of re-defining death. Before the 1950s a body with a beating heart was considered to be alive and one without a heart-beat was considered dead. The development of the novel concept of brain death was linked to the need for organs to be retrieved from bodies through which oxygenated blood was still circulating: if breathing and heart-beat stopped before organs were 'harvested' they would not be fit for a transplant recipient. Transplant surgery could not have developed to the extent that it has today without this shift in the definition of death taking place. The phrase 'non-heart-beating cadaver' which has common currency in medical settings today would not have made sense in the 1930s, since by definition a cadaver had no heart-beat. The phrase implies the possibility of the 'heart-beating cadaver' – a body whose heart is beating but is considered dead nonetheless because of a lack of brain activity.

DOING DEATH

In addition to documenting death, doctors also, to a limited extent and usually at the extremes of the life course, do death. In the exceptional (peacetime) occasions where the state sanctions the ending of another's life, it is doctors who carry it out. It is a mark either of the trust and esteem invested in doctors, or more critically, of the excess power that the profession wields – that where death is permitted, doctors do it.

In those countries where euthanasia is legal, it is overseen by medics and known as 'physician assisted suicide'. In Britain, where abortion is currently permitted under certain circumstances, it is doctors who interpret the conditions of each case and decide whether it is appropriate, with two doctors required to certify an abortion in the UK. Highly emotive debates surround the issue of abortion, where the termination of a pregnancy is defined as the murder of an unborn child by 'pro-life', anti-abortion groups. Where capital punishment by lethal injection takes place in the USA, it is undertaken only after the prisoner has been certified as in a fit state of mental and physical health to take responsibility for the crimes of which he (very few women are killed as legal punishment) is convicted. The insertion of cannulae and intravenous tubing and the remote delivery of lethal drugs by injection may be executed by trained technicians rather than a doctor, yet even where physicians are not required to administer the lethal injection, they are required to be in attendance to certify the death of the prisoner. Many doctors would argue that the deliberate taking of a life, even assuming that the legal conviction for the crimes is safe, is inappropriate for the medical profession and contravenes a doctor's duty to do no harm. However, my argument does not concern individual doctors' morality but the role of the profession which this level of responsibility implies.

Regardless of whether abortion, euthanasia or capital punishment are considered moral or justified, the medical profession not only distinguishes between the dead and the living, but also, under very specific conditions, terminates pregnancy, assists the very ill towards death and oversees the medical execution of convicted prisoners who are judicially executed in certain countries. This is an important indication of the trust invested in medicine by the institutions of the state, and in democratic states it is, by extension, a reflection of the general population's trust.

DEFINING DOCTORS AS SPECIAL HEALERS

So far then, the defining features of doctors' work have been identified as: the diagnosis of disease; treating disease with humanity and compassion in the light of the evaluation of the available evidence; and wielding the authority to oversee, certificate and administer death. How useful is this initial attempt to define what doctors do, in understanding medicine's relationship with the rest of the health service and with society? There are two main problems which mean that this definition is inadequate. The first problem is that the definition is not *specific* enough to distinguish doctors from other health professionals who diagnose and, in the case of midwives, can certify infant deaths. Second, the definition is not *detailed* enough to cover the range of doctors' work across the field of medicine; the high degree of medical specialization means that some doctors' work entails neither diagnosis, nor treatment, nor death. These two problems of specificity and detail are discussed below in setting out the parameters of this book's subject matter.

OVERLAP WITH OTHER PROFESSIONALS' WORK

Doctors are not the only professionals who diagnose and treat disease. (As mentioned above, midwives have the right to certificate infant deaths around birth but in practice it is usually a doctor.) Osteopaths, homeopaths, acupuncturists, herbalists and chiropractors diagnose and treat conditions without necessarily referring to the biomedical model. Trained practitioners of Chinese medicine can be found in many British cities and spiritual healers that call on various traditions of religious, supernatural or magical belief, from hakims to druids, regularly dispense treatment for illness. Medical pluralism, whereby a number of traditions of medicine which rely on different underlying principles are used simultaneously, is a widespread phenomenon with a growing proportion of the British population using alternative systems in tandem with biomedicine. But even within the biomedical field, there are different approaches to diagnosis and treatment: nurses diagnose and treat certain conditions without recourse to a doctor and there have been recent moves to extend the range of these conditions by developing the role of the 'nurse practitioner'. Nurses' expertise and experience have long been influential in the diagnosis and treatment decisions of hospital doctors, particularly when the doctor is a novice, but it is only recently that nurse practitioners have begun to prescribe a limited range of drugs, thereby blurring professional boundaries. Within a working hospital or clinic, members of staff are likely to know one another's status: only a very green hospital worker would mistake a senior physician for a staff nurse or an auxiliary for a cleaner. However, from the patient's point of view, and particularly a new patient, these distinctions may be hard to make. What is the difference between a clinical psychologist and a psychiatrist? In a busy hospital setting, how easy would it be to distinguish a phlebotomist from a doctor taking blood? Could you tell the difference between a maxilla-facial surgeon and a highly specialized and surgically skilled orthodontist?

Anyone who has spent time in healthcare settings knows that even when the tasks performed by an orthodontist and a surgeon are similar, the difference in professional status remains distinct. The special status of the medical practitioner, even when the tasks that he or she performs are very similar to those of other health professionals, is of interest in understanding medicine's role in society. Medicine's exceptional status and responsibility for managing other health professionals rest on claims for the superior efficacy of medical methods over other healing arts, and its extended period of education and training revealing the mysteries of medical knowledge that non-physicians cannot appreciate. The phrase 'Professions Allied with Medicine' (PAM) defines medicine as the central or index profession with which others have become associated. 'Allied Health Professionals' (which is replacing 'PAM' as the acceptable term) makes the centrality of 'medicine' as the reference profession less obvious.

What is the significance of some of the tasks associated with medicine being indistinguishable from those performed by other professionals? And can we draw any conclusions from evidence that some of medicine's methods are not especially efficacious, nor very different from the methods used by other healing traditions? These observations could be significant to medicine's claims to professional authority, since they raise the prospect that medicine's distinctive professional character derives, at least in part, from its strategic triumphs in out-manoeuvring rivals, rather than being solely determined by a coherent scientific approach to disease and healing. 'Professionals' distinguish themselves from run-of-the-mill 'occupations' with reference to their extended period of formal training, which acts as a justification for higher rewards in terms of salary and pension. Medicine is prominent, even among other professions, since it benefits from a state monopoly facilitated by The Medical Registration Act of 1858 (see Chapter 1) and its professional dominance has been maintained by the development of an individualized model of pathology and the emphasis placed on the doctor–patient relationship (see Chapter 9).

SPECIALIZATION TO THE POINT OF INCOHERENCE?

The second problem in defining the doctor's remit in general terms is the degree of specialization within medicine which means that having completed training some doctors' work will never again involve the diagnosis or treatment of patients. Doctors concerned with laboratory-based research or with preventative health policies never meet living patients. Pathology examines the disease process in dead bodies and histopathology concentrates on cell samples, with neither specialism necessarily contributing directly to the treatment of disease. Anaesthesia concerns a very specific aspect of the patient's wellbeing, which, while crucial to the success of medical intervention, is not in itself therapeutic or curative. Defining medicine by attempting to describe the work that doctors do unravels the view of medicine as a single profession with common interests: a psychiatrist's work may resemble that of a clinical psychologist in terms of working methods and expertise, and share almost nothing with that of a vascular surgeon.

Medicine's harshest critics have suggested that the greatest aid to its success was the establishment of the medical monopoly, which means only those licensed by the General Medical Council are permitted to practise as physicians. Licensing is only permitted after the successful completion of a limited number of regulated education and training routes. So even if a surgeon and an orthodontist are performing very similar dental-maxilla-facial operations, and giving the same training opportunities to junior doctors, the only way an individual with a background in dentistry can be recognized as a hospital surgeon is by re-training in a medical school. The strong professional ethos whereby doctors identify their own interests as lying with other doctors, rather than with other professionals who might share similar work, suggests that trying to define doctors by the content of their work is to miss the point. Medicine's strength as a profession relies on professional solidarity and astute lobbying at a national political level as much as on the content and methods of its work. Indeed, it is arguable that medicine has attained its social status as a profession in the face of evidence that some of its methods are inefficacious and, in some cases, positively harmful to patients.

MEDICINE'S PLACE IN SOCIETY

The question of the benign versus the detrimental effect that medicine has had on human health and happiness underpins much of the criticism surrounding medicine. Is medicine's distinctive profile as a profession in public life due to its contribution to our wellbeing or largely a result of effective professional lobbying? This question has become more pressing with the general erosion of our unquestioning faith in science, experts and professionals, as the sometime failure of medicine's methods has become recognized and discussed. In this scheme of enquiry, the definitional difficulties of describing the commonality of doctors' work, and the features that distinguish it from the work of other health professionals, are largely irrelevant: a doctor is a recognizable type which we can all identify. Like a detective, footballer or gangster, doctors enjoy a clear-cut public image; they exist as a category. While individual doctors and hospitals are known to have failed, people are nonetheless keen for curative medicine to work and for good quality health services to be available. And for the most part, doctors enjoy a good public image: recruitment to medical schools remains healthy, despite the expansion in the number of places available over the past decade and problems with the allocation of training places in 2007. Notwithstanding concerns about regulating medicine (discussed in Chapter 10), medicine remains at the heart of the great public interest in health, as shown by its profile in current affairs, in entertainment, in lifestyle choices and marketing. Medicine is rarely out of the headlines with health and the provision of health services continuing to be the topic that no political party seeking re-election can afford to ignore. The enormous interest in all matters medical is shown by the popularity of hospital-based British and American television series that achieve consistently high ratings, and the appearance of health pages, dealing with illness, cures and the organization of healthcare, in a range of newspapers and magazines.

This interest in medicine is part of an aspiration towards maintaining health and fitness and avoiding disease. This aspiration is used to promote an array of products ranging from yoghurt to enhance biotic growth in the gut, to soya milk to reduce cholesterol, to socks to prevent deep vein thrombosis, to copper anti-rheumatism bracelets. Health claims are used to sell food, clothes, toiletries and gym membership, and it is this same promise of improved health that has underwritten the public's faith in medicine's scientific project. The distinctive way that biomedicine diagnoses and treats disease, however, has led some people to question whether medicine has anything useful to say about health. Can medicine define what constitutes health or help us to recognize a healthy state in ourselves or in others? If we have a diagnosed disease does that mean that we are unhealthy? These questions are explored further in the next chapter.

Further reading

Academic texts: a number of edited collections of papers sample the main preoccupations of medical sociology that inform this book.

Annandale, E., Elston, M.A. and Prior, L. (eds) (2005) *Medical Work, Medical Knowledge and Healthcare: A Sociology of Health and Illness Reader*. London: Blackwell.

Bury, M. and Gabe, J. (eds) (2004) *The Sociology of Health and Illness: A Reader*. London: Routledge.

Nettleton, S. and Gustafsson, U. (eds) (2002) *The Sociology of Health and Illness Reader*. Cambridge: Polity.

Reading the journals Social Science and Medicine (published by Elsevier) and The Sociology of Health and Illness (published by Blackwells), both of which are available and searchable online with an appropriate subscription, will offer a fuller and more varied range of the topics covered by medical sociology.

Popular texts: the following books introduce some of the themes and dilemmas of medical sociology in an easily readable form.

Foxton, M. (2003) *Bedside Stories*. London: Guardian.

Short chapters that originally appeared as a newspaper column, describing the difficulties that one young man faced as he trained for and practised medicine in the UK.

Mercurio, J. (2002) *Bodies*. London: Jonathan Cape.

A novel based on the author's medical training, which portrays the worst aspects of being a very junior doctor in an unforgiving hospital environment and highlights how institutional practice works to cover up medical errors and uncertainty.

REVISION QUESTIONS

1 Distinguish between the profession, discipline and practice of medicine.

2 What are the important features of doctors' work?

3 In what sense has disease come to be defined as a deviation from the norm?

4 What forms of evidence must be evaluated in coming to a diagnosis?

5 Is there a common feature of all clinical doctors' work?

6 Can doctors' work be distinguished from other health professionals' work?

EXTENSION QUESTIONS

1 Medical impostors

Periodically un-qualified people are prosecuted for impersonating a doctor. The extent of the deception varies, as does the impact it has on patients: impostors may simply be pacing hospital corridors with a stolen identification badge; however they may also undertake complex surgical procedures which can wreak damage upon unsuspecting patients. Sometimes impostors can carry out medical work and go undetected for a number of years.

– Are medical impostors threatening to the medical profession?
– Is the competent impostor more or less damaging to the medical profession than the incompetent, negligent, qualified doctor?
– If an impostor successfully poses as a doctor for a number of years, is it right to prosecute him?
– Should he be offered the chance to train in medicine?

2 Death and doctoring

Where capital punishment is state sanctioned should doctors:

– administer lethal injections?
– certify criminals to be dead?

Where a patient has a progressive and severely painful condition which can no longer be treated other than palliatively, should doctors administer progressively large doses of analgesic to combat pain?

Morphine, known to be a highly effective analgesic for severe pain, also has a depressive effect on respiration which could hasten the death of a bed-bound patient. Should a contraindication, such as respiratory depression, prevent a doctor from treating a person palliatively?

What are the contrasts between the case of lethal injection and the case of a patient requiring palliative care for severe pain?

3

DEFINING HEALTH, DEFINING DISEASE

Chapter summary

This chapter describes:

> » how medical models posit lesions as the cause of symptoms of disease, but this model is problematic when a disease has no associated lesion or when the lesion causes no symptoms that prompt the sufferer to seek medical help;

> » how the biomedical focus on disease means that health is viewed as an absence of disease;

> » how lay understandings of health are multi-dimensional, including strength, vitality and ideas around functional fitness, and that these vary by class and gender;

> » how folk models of health and illness co-exist with medical ideas;

> » how people's non-medical ideas about illness and health are significant to doctor–patient understanding in the clinical encounter.

Useful terms for this chapter

autonomy: both the independence with which individual practitioners act in clinical medicine and the self-regulation that has been a mark of the profession of medicine reflect the high degree of the profession's legitimated autonomy

Cartesian: relating to the ideas of René Descartes who proposed a dualist view of mind and body where mental phenomena are thought to be non-physical. See Chapter 7 for further discussion

INTRODUCTION

The previous chapter explored some of the difficulties of defining doctors' work in a way that distinguishes it from other healthcare professionals' work and which adequately covers the doctor's remit. Definitional details notwithstanding, medicine is clearly the profession most closely allied with disease and its treatment. Furthermore, it is a profession that enjoys considerable autonomy and social standing with concomitant power and influence. Medicine's reputation and status are predicated on the efficacy and effectiveness of its campaign against the symptoms and causes of disease and the promise of technological, pharmaceutical, genetic and surgical cures for human ailments, suffering and debilities. The biomedical understanding of disease dominates thinking about the processes of health and illness in western culture. Specific aetiological agents which bring about changes to the body's structure and function are held to cause disease, and this model of causation has its roots in the eighteenth century when disease first came to be seen as being located in specific anatomical structures. Cartesian-influenced ideas of the body as separable from the mind led to so-called pathological medicine, whereby the onset of illness is located to pathology in a particular organ. The implications of this model for medicine's relationship with its patients will be considered in this chapter.

BIOMEDICAL DISEASE MODEL

The disease-centred organization of biomedicine, with its division of specialities according to the location of the disease (Cardiology; Neurology; Respiratory; Ear, Nose and Throat) or disease type (Oncology; Rheumatology), suggests that the pathogen and the pathology, rather than the person, are at the centre of medical interest. Successes in the battle with disease have been emphasized in the history of medicine: the defeat of smallpox and polio, the ability to operate on diseased hearts and to remove cancer are all emblematic of medicine's potential to improve the human condition. High-risk interventions against virulent, invasive diseases whereby brain surgeons and oncologists save young lives enjoy heroic prestige when compared with the so-called Cinderella specialisms of Rehabilitation and Geriatrics. Slow onset, chronic disorders of old age such as dementia for which no simple cure exists and which lead to complex care needs do not offer the same ability for a dramatic cure. Saving a young, previously fit person from a fatal condition has an appeal that responding to the slow degenerative effects of a condition does not.

In the effort to diagnose and treat disease medicine will locate its cause in a lesion inside the body whose presence can be detected via symptoms and signs. Having presented symptoms, the patient will allow their doctor to act as a kind of detective, inferring the existence of disease from the clues available. The patient will then defer to the doctor's expertise in interpreting the disease and will be expected to respond to questions but not to challenge medical opinion. This model is an effective description of some instances where medicine is very effective: when a patient detects an unexpected lump, an unusual headache, or a raised temperature which leads to the detection of a tumour, foreign body, or microbial infection which can then be effectively treated with surgery, chemotherapy, radiotherapy or antibiotics.

LIMITATIONS OF THE BIOMEDICAL MODEL

However, even a limited experience of clinical practice shows that this model does not account for all eventualities in the presentation of symptoms and the diagnosis of disease. The first problem is that the relationship between symptoms, pathology and disease is not always as straightforward as the model suggests. A person may experience symptoms without the detection of any underlying pathology and, in other cases, a serious pathology does not provoke symptoms. How does pathological medicine cope with the absence of a lesion to explain manifest symptoms? One response is to leave the basic model intact by assuming that while a lesion may not have been detected, it nonetheless exists; for instance, when a primary site cannot be located, despite evidence of metastasis, the primary cancer is assumed to have escaped detection. Similarly, multiple sclerosis may be diagnosed in someone who has experienced a characteristic combination of symptoms in their legs, vision and sense of balance, even when an MRI scan fails to show evidence of demyelinization of the nerves, thought to be the underlying pathological process. In the case of multiple sclerosis, there is an assumption that with the passage of enough time and with appropriate testing nerves that have shed their insulating myelin sheath will eventually come to light.

Another medical response to the absence of a lesion to explain symptomology is to assume that there is no legitimate disease in evidence. This response can be seen in the unfolding history of Gulf War Syndrome and of Chronic Fatigue Syndrome (or CFS, and also known as Myalgic Encephalitis or ME), as in both cases sufferers have struggled to have their symptoms taken seriously. Illness that is not recognized as real disease often involves symptoms that can only be assessed subjectively by the sufferer, such as aches, pains, cramps, nausea, tinnitus, dizziness, loss of libido and fatigue. Without an accompanying lesion these symptoms are often assumed to be indicative of a psychological disorder rather than organic pathology. Such symptoms can be assumed not to require therapeutic intervention other than anti-depressants or talk-therapy, and may be dismissed as of limited clinical importance.

This is difficult territory since people do sometimes invent symptoms, and, as described in the previous chapter, doctors must play a role in policing legitimate from illegitimate illness. On the other hand, the International Classification of Disease (see Box 3.1) has consistently expanded its number of diagnostic categories, with each subsequent edition including numerous new diagnoses. The ongoing expansion of diseases that are recognized is, in part, due to scientific progress as pathogens are identified; for instance, what was once known as Gay Men's Syndrome has become Acquired Immuno-Deficiency Syndrome, as the methods of transmission of the Human Immuno-Deficiency Virus have been understood. HIV or Avian Flu Virus are pathogens that can have devastating effects on carriers. But not all new diseases are so tightly linked to a pathogen. Alcoholism and anorexia nervosa, while now widely recognized as distinct diseases, cannot be linked with a single underlying lesion.

BOX 3.1

International Classification of Diseases (ICD)

The classification of diseases has its origins in the 1850s. William Farr (1807–1883), the first medical statistician of the General Register Office of England and Wales (established in 1837), and Marc d'Espine of Geneva were each asked to prepare an internationally applicable, uniform classification of causes of death for presentation to the International Statistical Congress in 1855. The two men submitted separate lists which were based on very different principles. Farr's classification was arranged under five groups: epidemic diseases; constitutional (general) diseases; local diseases arranged according to anatomical site; developmental diseases; and diseases that were the direct result of violence. D'Espine classified diseases according to their nature (gouty, herpetic, haematic, and so on). The Congress adopted a compromise list of 139 rubrics. In 1864, this classification was revised in Paris on the basis of Farr's model and was further revised subsequently in 1874, 1880 and 1886. Although this classification was never universally accepted, the general arrangement proposed by Farr, including the principle of classifying diseases by anatomical site, survived as the basis of the International List of Causes of Death. This list was adopted by the International Statistical Institute in 1893 and was, in effect, the first International Classification of Diseases.

The World Health Organization took over the responsibility for the ICD at its creation in 1948 when the Sixth Revision, which included causes of morbidity for the first time, was published. The tenth version of the International Classification of Disease, known as ICD-10, was endorsed by the 43rd World Health Assembly in May 1990, and came into use in WHO member states as from 1994. There are 12,420 codes included in ICD-10, as compared to 6,969 in ICD-9.

The ICD has become the international standard diagnostic classification for all general epidemiological and many health management purposes. These include the analysis of the general health situation of population groups and the monitoring of the incidence and prevalence of diseases and other health problems in relation to other variables such as the characteristics and circumstances of the individuals affected.

The ICD is used to classify diseases and other health problems recorded on many types of health and vital records including death certificates and hospital records. In addition to enabling the storage and retrieval of diagnostic information for clinical and epidemiological purposes, these records also provide the basis for the compilation of national mortality and morbidity statistics by WHO member states.

(Adapted from material at http://www.who.int/classifications/icd/en/)

Disease does not exist as a stable set of categories, but shifts in response to the changing micro-biological environment (we return to this in Chapter 11), progress in medical research and changing social attitudes. Medicine does not simply react to the changes going on around it, but is an active agent in altering those categories of disease that are recognized and treated. Recognizing alcohol addiction as a condition that can be treated, rather than as a moral failing to be condemned, has arisen from the combination of changes in social attitudes and the efforts of pioneering doctors. The active creation of new disease categories, often in the absence of a specific lesion, is an unavoidable aspect of medical practice. The recent history of treatment for male sexual dysfunction is a case in point. Before the arrival of the patented drug Viagra (see Box 3.2, p. 56) in the marketplace, male impotence was a side effect of disease, of treatment for disease and of the aging process for which no simple, non-invasive treatment was available. The prescription and use of Viagra have been important for the quality of life of some of those who take it, although others find the side effects of headache and nasal congestion outweigh the benefits in terms of erectile function.

Viagra's success as a drug of choice has created enormous profits for the pharmaceutical company that owns the patent and has led to the search for an equivalent drug to be marketed to women. Women who have a reduced desire for sexual intercourse unconnected with a specific disease have been referred to as suffering from 'sexual dysfunction', although no identifiable associated lesion exists. Arguably, the experience of a reduction in libido is a normal part of growing older, or when suffering from mental health problems or from fatigue. The search for a 'female Viagra', and the use of Hormone Replacement Therapy (HRT) to counter the effects of menopause, have been termed 'life-style medicine' to differentiate them from the real, organic disease which serious medicine treats.

BOX 3.2

Viagra

Sildenafil citrate is a drug developed by the commercial company Pfizer, originally in the hopes of finding an effective treatment for hypertension and angina. Clinical trials suggested that it had little effect on these diseases but did induce penile erection. The drug is available by prescription from a physician, although in the USA it was advertised direct to consumers on television and it is widely available via the internet. Viagra has sold in huge quantities (annual sales in the period 1999–2001 exceeded $1 billion). While its primary clinical use is by those with erectile dysfunction, it is also used as an aphrodisiac by people without dysfunction and is taken to counteract the side effect of impotency induced by the recreational use of Ecstasy. Viagra has been a hugely successful brand drug, known as a 'little blue diamond wonder', and the distinctive shape and colour of the pill have made it highly recognizable the world over and the direct selling of the drug via e-mail possible. The term 'Viagra' is also used to sell other products such as 'herbal Viagra' and various materials marketed as 'Viagra for the mind'.

In addition to absent lesions, the sometime absence of symptoms is another potentially troubling feature of the biomedical model of disease. When a pathology does not lead to symptoms which could prompt medical consultation, the biomedical model of disease is challenged; for instance, cancers of soft tissue do not always provoke troublesome symptoms until the disease is well established. If a pathology is not betrayed by symptoms, screening is required to prompt treatment at an earlier point in the disease process. For instance, the prostate-specific antigen (PSA) is produced by the prostate gland and when detected at elevated levels in a man's blood it may indicate prostate cancer. However, screening is not highly specific since an enlarged prostate which is not cancerous also produces similarly elevated levels of PSA.

Screening may detect signs of a pathological process in the form of abnormally high blood, cholesterol or PSA levels and yet individuals can experience no symptoms. This diagnosis of the asymptomatic as potentially diseased is anomalous to the medical model of disease, since diagnosing disease in the absence of symptoms disrupts basic assumptions about the division between health and illness. Screening relies on a deviation from the norm as an indicator of potential disease and this has led to the creation of a new category of pre-patient who is 'pre-diseased' or 'at risk'. The emphasis on risk (explored further in Chapter 5) over and above any symptoms has contributed to the 'worried well' becoming an important component of a doctor's workload. Raised cholesterol and high blood pressure may be unaccompanied by feelings of illness and so the idea that disease brings about symptoms which prompt people to visit the doctor is dislocated. In this respect we are all, in some sense, potential patients, at least until tests prove us to be free of the indicators of disease risk.

As well as asymptomatic pathology, people can experience symptoms that are painful or disruptive and potentially indicative of disease, but will not be prompted to consult a doctor. The so-called symptom iceberg describes the empirical finding that the majority of symptoms experienced in day-to-day life do not result in people seeking medical help. One survey showed that one in 200 headaches lead to a consultation and while this may not be surprising for a minor symptom, the finding that only one in 14 instances of serious pain in the chest were taken to a doctor is more worrying (Scambler et al., 1981). Since people's experience of a serious symptom (such as passing blood or intense pain) does not trigger medical consultation in a predictable or systematic fashion, there is no guarantee that disease will be seen before it is too advanced to be treatable. At the same time minor symptoms are regularly presented which do not need a doctor's detective skills to understand or treat: GPs report that between one-third and one-half of their patients present with insignificant complaints that they could treat themselves.

These various contradictions of pathological medicine – symptoms without lesions, pathology without symptoms, and the unpredictable way in which the experience of symptoms is related to help-seeking – can be explained in terms of the public being ill-informed. Periodically public education campaigns will seek to raise people's awareness of the appropriate response to signs and symptoms of disease through the timely seeking of medical advice. But no amount of re-education will overcome two inherent problems of this model. First, not all disease has an underlying lesion or pathology (or not one that can be detected currently) and second, symptoms and signs cannot be mapped onto pathology in a simple one-to-one process. Minor symptoms such as headaches may be due to a hangover, a lack of sleep, a knock to the head, constipation, a brain tumour, or all four of these. In addition to the problematic assumption that the pathology causing a disease will be indicated by symptoms and detectable through signs, there is a binary implication in the biomedical model that is troubling; either you are disease-free and healthy or diseased and therefore unhealthy. That people without serious symptoms can feel ill, and those with indications of pathology may consider themselves healthy, suggests that the relationship between health, illness and disease is more complex than the reliance on detectable lesions allows.

DEFINING HEALTH

A final problem with a disease-centred pathological medicine is that it has very little to say about health. Where medicine seeks to promote health, the focus is on disease prevention through screening and immunization. The idea of a preventative medicine that could thwart disease before it brought pain, suffering and disablement has been, and remains, a powerful ideal. But disease prevention is not the same as conceptualizing, understanding and promoting health.

In medical terms health is the absence of disease, yet this is an impoverished understanding of good health. The aspects of health missing from the biomedical model are summed up in the World Health Organization's (WHO) definition of good health as 'a state of complete physical, mental and social wellbeing'. The virtue of this definition is its great breadth, since it covers spiritual happiness, material sufficiency and social justice, but this is also a problem, since many doctors see such matters as beyond medicine's remit, being more properly the concern of religious leaders, social workers and politicians. However (as we will see in Chapter 4), the important role of social and economic disadvantage in premature death has led others to place the promotion of an equitable society at the heart of the practice of socially responsible medicine. While medicine may not have a great deal to say about it, health is nonetheless a quality that is much discussed in daily life.

LAY UNDERSTANDINGS OF HEALTH

From the 1970s onwards the discrepancy between the biomedical model of health as an absence of disease and lay conceptions of health has been the subject of sustained research. Research has explored how people think about their own and their family's health, and how their thinking contradicts medical models. The frequent comparison of 'lay health beliefs' with 'medical knowledge' has implied that doctors have neutral, objective certainties, whereas we also need to consider the evidence of uncertainty, inconsistency and variation in medical knowledge and practice in Chapter 11. While some non-medical ideas can be dismissed as 'merely beliefs', belief does play a crucial role in recovery and non-medical explanations can offer an aetiological certainty that medical ideas lack.

Dividing lay beliefs from medical knowledge implies that they are separate domains of knowledge that do not overlap. The dispersal and availability of medical knowledge and its interpretation in both old (books, magazines) and new (websites, interactive television) media means that this is not a realistic picture. Medical models exert extensive influence on how we think about health, and the way that they are interpreted by non-experts is of considerable interest. There has been a growing recognition of the influential role of class, gender and ethnicity on the subjective experience of health and healthcare and the importance of taking this into account when organizing service provision. A variety of quantitative and qualitative research methods have been employed to elicit what ordinary people think about health. Enough research has now been undertaken for patterns to emerge in people's responses, which are described in the next section.

DIMENSIONS OF LAY MODELS OF HEALTH

An absence of disease appears as part of many (but not all) conceptualizations of health, but people's expectations of good health and resistance to illness form a wider, more complex and nuanced picture than this alone. People who themselves suffer poor health or chronic illness seem more likely to emphasize the absence of illness as an indicator of health. However, people can also feel able to describe themselves as healthy, even if suffering from a chronic condition such as diabetes or arthritis. To be able to see oneself as healthy in the face of disease involves conceptualizing health as a reserve to be called upon in times of need. People say that having a good reserve of health is shown by being able to recover quickly from illness or accident. Lay accounts often conceptualize health as functional fitness and as a reserve of strength which represents the biological capacity to resist or cope with illness which could fluctuate over time. The idea of balance and equilibrium frequently crops up in ideas of 'normal' health, although this desirable state may rarely be actually attained. Good health as energy and vitality is also a frequent finding, often described as the ability to get up and get on with paid employment and household tasks, even the least attractive ones.

Survey work with a sample representative of the British population (Blaxter, 1990) found that definitions of health varied by gender and life course, with younger men emphasizing physical strength and fitness whereas younger women cited energy, vitality and the ability to cope as important. In middle-age people's concepts of health became more complex, with mental wellbeing and contentment becoming more significant. Older people, and particularly men, defined health in terms of function, although ideas around contentment, happiness and a good state of mind, even in the face of disability or disease, were also prominent. Women were consistently more expansive in their descriptions of health and more likely to emphasize social relationships than men. In sum, these ideas about health challenge the biomedical model that health is simply an absence of disease, by suggesting that an absence of disease is not necessarily valued for its own sake. Instead, health is more characteristically valued for what it makes possible in terms of social relationships, leisure-time pursuits and productive activity. Different dimensions of health change in significance through the life course and vary by gender, and this change and variation in health are missing from medical models of health.

THE CONTEXT OF HEALTH

The social context in which people are asked to define good health has an influence on the dimension that is emphasized. Compared with middle-class women, the working-class women in one study assessed their own circumstances as too constrained to afford the 'luxury' of being ill: they felt they had to get their work done, no matter what.

> I haven't got time to worry about anything being wrong. Not only that, I think with a family you can't afford to be ill, you know what I mean? You think, well you'll be ill after you've cooked tea. (Pill and Stott, 1982)

The influence of gender on ideas about health has also been noted in a number of studies. Working-class women in London felt that women's domestic responsibilities and their lack of support meant that they were unable to be ill, whereas men had more freedom to indulge their symptoms.

> I'd say women have more aches and pains than men, but ... when you've got a family you will find a woman will work till she's dropping. But she'll do what she's got to do and then she'll say, 'right, I'm off to bed'. (Cornwell, 1984)

This idea that illness is a luxury that women with family responsibilities cannot afford is an idea that crosses cultures, as is shown by the following quote by a Pushto-speaking Pathan woman now living in England.

> We do not have time to be ill. I have not been ill at all ... whether we are well or ill, happy or unhappy, we do our work. (Currer, 1986)

Changes to the social context in which health is experienced feature in the ways that people define and re-define health. Middle-aged French women interviewed during the 1980s reflected on the changes to health and healthcare in their lifetimes, and had a 'memory of the terrors of the past' described by researchers as 'astonishingly vivid' (Herzlich and Pierret, 1984, 1987). For British women, the NHS and raised standards of living have meant that the terrors of the past are receding: epidemics of childhood infections, maternal mortality and famine are no longer day-to-day fears. Yet historical fears may nonetheless influence behaviours that are relevant to health. People who lived through food shortages in the 1940s who are now grandparents or great-grandparents will often value those rich, calorific foods that were once rationed and will include them preferentially in children's diets. However, the present generation of children is somewhat unlikely to suffer from a calorific or micronutrient shortfall that requires their diet to be supplemented with full-cream milk, butter, chocolate and meat; indeed, they are more at risk from obesity and diabetes. Migrants who learnt their health behaviour in another culture and climate will also bring their ideas about health and health maintenance and will adapt them for the new British context. For example, women who had grown up in India or Pakistan had learned about the heating and cooling nature of foods, weather and bodily states before migrating to Glasgow on the west coast of Scotland (Bradby, 1997). They regarded the Glaswegian climate as excessively wet and cold and therefore likely to exacerbate 'cool' conditions such as colds and flu. These women described their daily efforts to protect themselves and their children from the effects of the climate; for instance, children would never be given milk to drink without first heating it to counter-act its cooling properties. In winter-time some of the women suggested that drinking milk, even when it was heated, might be foolhardy. Eating foods with a warming effect (such as ginger) and avoiding cooling foods (such as yoghurt) were seen as sensible precautions against infection. However, ideas around the cooling or heating nature of foods, climates and physical conditions did not replace or compete with germ theory and a doctor's advice which was valued and taken seriously.

Regulation of the wet, dry, hot or cold nature of food, climates and conditions to maintain health and fend off infection is not confined to minority ethnic groups in Britain. Older patients born during the Second World War have described causes and treatments for illnesses seen in general practice that employ a folk classification of the wet, dry, hot or cold symptoms underlying the once familiar advice to 'feed a cold, starve a fever' (Helman, 1978). These folk beliefs pre-date medical ideas about the transmission of microbial pathogens, but have also adapted and gained new elements, notably germ theory. Helman's study concluded that in certain respects GPs resembled their patients in adhering to folk models: the indiscriminate prescription of antibiotics suggests that doctors have not been good at distinguishing between viral and bacterial infections, while the prescription of cough mixtures of dubious efficacy suggests that doctors have not been over-reliant on scientific evidence.

BIOMEDICAL DISEASE AND THE VALUE OF HEALTH

The search for disease-causing lesions has had some notable triumphs against pathogens and has thus contributed to improving human health. One of the ironies of pathological medicine's widespread influence is that the deficits of medical ideas have become clear. For instance, germ theory tells us that an infection follows exposure to an infective agent, but since we are all continuously exposed to pathological micro-organisms, this is not a sufficient explanation. Genetic markers for conditions have been identified, and the functional genes associated with many conditions have also been discovered. But having a genetic trait does not necessarily result in a disease, since even dominant genes with high penetrance do not always express themselves.

Lay understandings can make up the deficits of medical thinking: the onset of an infection can be explained in terms of features that are not acknowledged by medicine, such as properties of heating and cooling or fate. These are not necessarily alternatives to medical thought, but are in addition. Health is understood to be multi-dimensional and the balance of the dimensions varies through the life course and with gender and class. While lay ideas value the absence of disease as an aspect of health, it is also conceived as a social and interactive quality that can exist at the same time as illness. Health is valued as strength, vitality and the ability to fend off disease, and the activity and interaction that good health makes possible seem to be more important than health as an isolated phenomenon. The process by which pre-scientific beliefs are accommodated within a scientific model and the ways that migrants use their health beliefs to make sense of a new environment illustrate the dynamic and flexible ways whereby people use ideas to understand their situation. This pragmatism means that lay ideas may not be internally consistent, for instance, a chronic condition does not preclude a person from describing himself as healthy. This apparent contradiction is not illogical, providing health and illness are not seen as binary opposites or mutually exclusive categories.

The range and variety of ideas about health that lay people deploy, and the complex evaluation of what health is good for, have not always been appreciated by the providers of health services. The medical model has tended to dominate despite patient advocacy groups working to keep medical services in touch with patients' priorities. Groups campaigning around specific diseases or conditions have promoted the priorities of particular health-service users, and increasingly the 'user-perspective' is required to be represented at all levels of planning, commissioning, providing and evaluating services as well as in the training and educating of healthcare professionals. Whether the trend towards the inclusion of user-perspectives will significantly alter the evaluation of health which clinicians work towards remains to be seen.

Further reading

Lupton, D. (2003) *Medicine as Culture: Illness, Disease and the Body in Western Societies* (2nd edn). London: SAGE.

Offers a readable overview of the way medicine is experienced, perceived and socially constructed in western societies.

REVISION QUESTIONS

1 How does the medical model of disease evaluate symptoms without lesions?

2 How does the medical model interpret a pathology which does not provoke symptoms?

3 Contrast different models of health.

4 How do lay ideas about health vary with gender?

5 Are folk models additional or alternative to medical models for most people?

EXTENSION QUESTIONS

1 Defining health

How do you define good health for yourself?

– If you have a chronic illness such as asthma or colitis does this influence the definition?
– If you come from a family with a history of a particular illness, such as diabetes or high blood pressure, does this make a difference to the definition?

How might a person in his or her seventies who has diabetes mellitus and a hip replacement define good health?

– What constitutes good health in the context of chronic illness?
– Can good health be defined, regardless of chronic conditions and old age?

Imagine what might constitute good health for the following three cases:

– a middle-aged man, employed as a road-mender, who has occasional outbreaks of psoriasis;
– a woman in her late twenties, in the ninth month of pregnancy, who is keeping well;
– a child refugee, recently arrived from a country where she witnessed violent conflict.

Are there any dimensions of health that are common for all three of these cases?

2 Discussing disease

Diseases aren't entities and the names they go under are no more than handy generalizations: 'It is vulgar medical error to speak, write and ultimately to think as if these diseases we name, these general references we symbolise, were single things with external existences ... the next time you go to the doctor you don't want to know which entity, in a word, you've got but what, in rather more words, may be the matter

(Cont'd)

with you. '(Sturrock, J. (2004) 'Short cuts', *London Review of Books*, 7 October, page 22, quoting F.G. Crookshank's appendix to a book entitled *The Meaning of Meaning*, by C.K. Ogden and I.A. Richard from the 1920s)

Does the way in which we think of the relationship between symptoms and disease influence the relationship between doctor and patient?

– What are the advantages for the doctor of discussing disease as a stable entity?
– What are the advantages for the patient of discussing disease as a stable entity?

3   Premature babies

Babies born prematurely at only 24 (out of the more normal 38–42) weeks of gestation can now be kept alive in special care baby units. Such treatment may carry a price in terms of a lifetime of eye, lung and other developmental problems.

– Can individuals born this prematurely ever be considered healthy?

Critics of modern medicine have argued that one of its paradoxical effects is to produce a population that may survive longer, but at the cost of carrying a heavy burden of symptoms. In Denmark, as a result of a public consultation, premature babies are observed for the first few hours and not given interventionist treatment in the first instance (ventilation or CPR).

– To what extent should medicine be responsible for ensuring that its practice is applied in order to decrease the overall burden of ill health in society?

In the developing world, full-term babies and children continue to die as a result of diarrhoeal infections and poor sanitation.

– To what extent should medicine be responsible for ensuring that its practice is applied in order to decrease the overall global burden of ill health?

PART 2

GETTING ILL, BEING ILL

THE SOCIAL CAUSES OF DISEASE

Chapter summary

This chapter describes:

» how the chances of premature mortality are not randomly distributed throughout the population;

» how the positive association between poor living conditions and poor health has been documented since the nineteenth century;

» how reports in the twentieth century confirmed that more favourable rates of morbidity and mortality continue to be associated with higher socio-economic class;

» how explanations for the causes of health inequalities, supported by research findings, include behavioural and cultural influences and materialist or structural effects, as well as relative poverty having an effect via psycho-social pathways;

» how health inequalities by ethnic group and gender are partially explicable in terms of material deprivation, but effects on health across the life course also need to be considered;

» how the extent to which national and international health inequalities are seen as a problem to be tackled depends on political views.

Useful terms for this chapter

life tables: a means of tabulating the probability that a cohort of people will survive to their next birthday and hence the probability of that group surviving to any particular year of age, assuming that they continue to experience the same mortality rates

socio-economic class: a means of defining the hierarchical strata in society using social as well as economic indicators of status

standardized mortality ratio (SMR): number of deaths usually expressed per 1,000 of the population standardized for age

INTRODUCTION

Microbiology has contributed enormously to understandings of the proximate causes of infectious disease, but what do we know about the overall patterns of illness in society? Medicine has been criticized for emphasizing the role of the pathogen in the diagnostic process but failing to explain why a pathogen produces illness in one individual but not in another. Exposure to an infectious agent – viral or bacterial – is part of the explanation for the onset of illness, but it is not a sufficient answer since not all episodes of exposure lead to infection. What of injuries and non-infectious diseases – is the misfortune of being struck down equally likely to befall any one of us, or are some people more at risk than others? How should we interpret an unequal distribution of poor health and accidental injury throughout society? When particular social groups are found to be at a higher risk of death, disease or disability, what responsibility does an equitable society have to mitigate such risk?

As described in Chapter 1, the transition from infectious to chronic disease has occurred over the last two centuries and a general increase in longevity has been a result of the falling risk of premature mortality. In addition to be able to trace changes in mortality rates over time, we can measure and contrast standardized mortality rates between socio-demographic groups and across localities. The development of increasingly sophisticated means to measure the distribution of disease in populations has coincided with the retreat of infectious disease and the appearance of chronic illness as significant features of human existence.

CLASS, ILL HEALTH AND INDUSTRIAL REVOLUTION

A person's position in society will influence his or her chances of experiencing disease and premature death. Being born into deprivation and continuing to live in deprivation increases the chances of disease and early death. The observation that poverty and mortality are associated has been documented since the early nineteenth century, when poor living and working conditions in urban settings were associated with elevated rates of disease and death. The industrial expansion of the nineteenth century was known to expose workers to specific environmental risks that would lead to associated conditions: for example, scrotal cancers with chimney sweeping, silicosis and pneumoconiosis with mining. Other occupations, such as corn-milling, millinery and snuff-making, had their own particular disabilities and diseases. But over and above occupation-specific disease, as cities were surveyed and death rates were calculated the positive association between over-crowded poverty and mortality could not be ignored. Tuberculosis was known to be a disease of the urban poor in the first half of the nineteenth century and the over-crowded, squalid conditions of the tightly packed industrial cities allowed newer diseases such as cholera to flourish among the working classes.

In France, an ex-army surgeon named Louis René Villermé (1782–1863) published evidence in 1832 that the poorest neighbourhoods in Paris consistently had the highest mortality rates. Meanwhile, across the Channel in London, William Farr (1807–1883) working at the government's General Register Office developed a registry of diseases and linked birth and death registrations with decennial censuses of population. His medical training and practice, together with a passion for statistics, gave rise to work which established what we now call epidemiology. His innovative methods, still used today, included the use of life tables as a means of measuring society's health, with infant mortality as a key indicator. Farr's work was also important for other investigators of the social context of disease. Among these was Friedrich Engels (1820–1895), a Manchester factory owner (who later collaborated with Karl Marx), who described the ill effects of capitalist industrialization and urbanization on the health of the poor in his 1845 publication *The Condition of the Working Class in England*. Around the same time Edwin Chadwick (1800–1890) was commissioned by the government to survey sanitation in response to the influenza and typhoid epidemics of 1837 and 1838. The resulting report on the 'Sanitary Conditions of the Labouring Population' was published in 1842, and was part of the mounting evidence that disease was directly related to living conditions.

Chadwick, like Engels and other researchers and reformers of the era, felt that the association between environment and disease implied an urgent need for public health reform to improve the conditions in which the poor lived. Better sanitation and ventilation were seen as especially critical for disease prevention. Like other champions of reform Engels and Chadwick benefited from family fortunes that had been accumulated via the Industrial Revolution, so they were not disinterested parties in the development of capitalism. Arguments for reform stressed the interests of the middle and upper classes that would be better served by improving the health of the poorest: when malnourished and ill the working classes were less able to work productively than when they enjoyed better health. The insanitary conditions of the poor encouraged disease and disability and kept a proportion of people unable to support themselves. Public health reform was presented as a good, long-term investment of public money which would eventually improve the stock of productive workers available for employment and would cut the cost of supporting the infirm.

This type of argument together with the increasing value placed on individual lives was, in the long term, effective in reforming welfare provision, but in the mid-1800s there was still considerable opposition. Entrenched argument against reform included the idea that mortality was nature's brutal corrective for populations that had become too big. Thomas Malthus (1766–1834) published an essay in 1798 that described how populations grow faster than the means of subsistence and that poverty and famine are the natural corrective outcomes. While Malthus later came to acknowledge that poverty and famine could be avoided by individual or group efforts, others viewed poverty and sickness as resulting from the degeneracy of the lower classes. Any reforms that reduced disease and death and so preserved sickly, unfit individuals were viewed as storing up trouble for the future, since these people and their inadequate offspring would simply burden society at a later date. This complexity of the association between poverty, disease and premature death was such that those who resisted reform could cite the considerable expense and the uncertainty of success as reasons for inaction. An ethic of individual responsibility and the logic of free trade unfettered by state regulation had together allowed traders and industrialists to amass enormous riches while relying on charity to rectify the hardships that befell the working classes.

Despite some marked divisions of wealth and ownership, in the pre-penicillin era when infectious disease thrived among the impoverished classes, the upper classes were not immune either, despite their superior living conditions. Fears about their own risk of contracting disease which was rampant in slums, and upper-class anxiety about potential widespread social insurrection along the lines of the French Revolution, were both reasons why the balance of opinion shifted away from the prevailing *laissez-faire* attitude and towards concerted action to relieve the suffering of the poor. The nineteenth century saw much debate about ensuring a clean, healthy population who were fit for work which, together with better understandings of the mechanisms of disease transmission, led to the institution of public health as the concern of a professional civil service.

The horrific conditions of Britain's industrial cities of the nineteenth century have been compared to the shanty towns and refugee camps of contemporary developing countries in their propensity as breeding grounds for sickness. The overflowing cesspools, gross over-crowding and pollution of air and water were all characteristic of British urban life. The alleviation of the abject misery of the poor through regulation of the food supply, working conditions and housing was part of the move towards improved health amongst the population, as was indicated by a rapid population rise and increased longevity after 1900.

Before this process (outlined in Chapter 1) got under way, at the start of the nineteenth century the crude death rate was 18 per 1,000 people, which included deaths from disease and injury among other causes. The average age at death of a working-class man was 25 years, whereas that of a gentleman was almost double at 46 years. These crude averages show that a large proportion of the whole population died prematurely by today's standards, and that the risk of an early death was closely tied to occupation and social position.

Table 4.1 Death rates by sex and social (occupational) class (15–64 years). Rates per 1,000 population England and Wales 1971

Social (occupational) class	Males (all)	Females (married, by husband's occupation)	Ratio M/F
I (Professional)	3.98	2.15	1.85
II (Intermediate)	5.54	2.85	1.94
IIIn (Skilled non-manual)	5.80	2.76	1.96
IIIm (Skilled manual)	6.08	3.41	1.78
IV (Partly skilled)	7.96	4.27	1.87
V (Unskilled)	9.88	5.31	1.86
Ratio V/I	2.5	2.5	

SOCIAL CLASS AND INEQUALITY

At the start of the twenty-first century the overall crude death rate was about 10 per 1,000 people (10.5 per 1,000 women and 10.1 per 1,000 men in 2001 (ONS, 2003)) and life expectancy had improved dramatically when compared with two centuries earlier. In 2004–2006 the life expectancy of girls at birth was 81.3 years as compared with 76.9 years for boys, and this continues to rise (see http://www.statistics.gov.uk/ for recent figures). This increase in life expectancy at birth is to be celebrated as a singular achievement, with most people born in the UK now enjoying the reasonable expectation of a long life. However, within the improvement in life expectancy, the gap between the rich and the poor within Britain remains. Being born into a professional-class family means enjoying about 10 more years of life, on average, when compared to those born into unskilled workers' families. In the face of impressive progress in the prevention of premature mortality, the persistence of this gap between social groups has been deplored by some and ignored by others.

The upheavals of the two World Wars in the twentieth century were important in eroding the hierarchical nature of British society: barriers to consorting between social classes, occupational, religious and ethnic groups were reduced during these conflicts. The impediments to social mixing were indeed re-established after peace was declared, but they could not be restored to their previous impermeability. The Second World War took the lives of all classes, disrupted social hierarchies, promoted the ideals of class and gender equality and advanced the sense that every individual in society should be valued. The idea that everyone should benefit equally in the effort to re-build a just and equitable society after the war was manifest in the establishment of the NHS in 1948.

Public policy approaches to inequality

At the end of the 1970s the Labour government commissioned a working group chaired by Sir Douglas Black, a former president of the Royal College of Physicians, to review the available evidence on inequalities in health. The group published its findings (Townsend et al., 1988 (DHSS, 1980)) which have come to be known as the Black Report, and its primary discovery was the existence of large differentials in mortality and in morbidity that favoured the higher social classes. The death rate for adult men in social class V (unskilled workers) was twice that of adult men in social class I (professional workers).

BOX 4.1

Social and economic class in Britain

The British are accused by other nations of being class obsessed, with an almost irresistible urge to categorize people according to their class origins. The question for those researching inequalities in health is whether a person's position within the social hierarchy can be reliably located and whether its measurement can be repeated. In the effort to map social class, an individual's occupation, income, education, home ownership and area of residence have all been used to pin-point a person's position. In a rapidly changing society, the measurement of social position has to change also; for instance, 30 years ago car and television ownership was an indicator of wealth, whereas in the early twenty-first century a television is now seen as an essential piece of equipment, necessary for social participation, with its ownership almost universal, and in many areas of Britain car-ownership has become the norm. Similarly, whereas owning one's own home and being educated to degree level used to be fairly reliable indicators of an upper middle-class background, widening access to higher education and the selling of public housing stock mean that this is no longer the case.

The nineteenth century studies that demonstrated the human costs of the Industrial Revolution used occupation and neighbourhood to divide up the population into different status groups. Occupation-based classifications, like the version shown below, are routinely used in national data sets and, since they have been used for such a long time, they facilitate the description of trends over time. However, they are based on an assumption that a person's job is a good indicator of his or her social status and that most households are headed by a man who is the main earner plus his dependants who earn less than him.

Table 4.2 Occupations within social class groupings

Social	Occupation
I Professional	Accountants, engineers, doctors
II Managerial and technical	Marketing and sales managers, teachers, nurses, journalists
IIIN Non-manual skilled	Clerks, shop assistants, cashiers
IIIM Manual skilled	Carpenters, goods van drivers, joiners, cooks
IV Partly skilled	Security guards, machine tool operators, farm workers
V Unskilled	Building and civil engineering labourers, cleaners

Table 4.3 The National Statistics Socio-economic Classification Analytic Classes

1		Higher managerial and professional occupations
	1.1	Large employers and higher managerial occupations
	1.2	Higher professional occupations
2		Lower managerial and professional occupations
3		Intermediate occupations
4		Small employers and own account workers
5		Lower supervisory and technical occupations
6		Semi-routine occupations
7		Routine occupations
8		Never worked and long-term unemployed

Source: from http://www.statistics.gov.uk/methods_quality/ns_sec/

Leaving aside the debate over whether this has ever been a good working assumption, it has meant that women, the self-employed and the unemployed have been difficult to classify in this hierarchy.

In acknowledging some of the problems of a purely occupational-based classification, in 2001 the National Statistics Socio-economic Classification (NS-SEC) was adopted (shown above in Table 4.3) for use in all official statistics and surveys.

For many who study inequality, social class is more than simply a means of pinpointing social position. A Marxist analysis classifies people according to their position within a capitalist system, where the poor are forced to sell their labour to survive. Those who own nothing else sell their labour to others who own the 'means of production' which, during the Industrial Revolution, meant mills and factories. Nowadays the owners of the means of production are often global corporations and, as well as factories, they own call centres, hotels, leisure facilities, internet servers, oil refineries, pharmaceutical laboratories and hospitals. Furthermore, those who are forced to sell their labour for very low wages are a global rather than a national class, with, for instance, low paid manufacturing work now largely carried out in the developing world and, increasingly, the service industry recruiting low-wage populations as call centres relocate to India.

The durability and power of a Marxist explanation of the inequalities inherent in a capitalist system, nationally and internationally, ensure its influence as a means of understanding and criticizing the development of society. However, the focus on class relations to the exclusion of other social divisions means that inequalities by gender and ethnicity have not always been adequately explained. Women and minority ethnic workers are routinely subject to discrimination and marginalization which are not directly related to their class position.

The Black Report asserted that inequalities in health were unacceptable and that they were not being adequately addressed by the health or social services. Confirmation that the position in the social hierarchy into which a person is born had an important effect on their life chances was, to some people, a shocking demonstration that the modern democratic nation was failing to offer its citizens equal life chances. After commissioning the report, the then Labour government was defeated in the general election of 1979; the incoming Conservative administration was not interested in the report's findings or in the implications they might have for designing policy. Their policy was to increase inequality as a motor for economic prosperity, by deregulating marketplaces and undermining the welfare provision for those who had failed to accumulate wealth. The so-called 'nanny state' was seen as a disincentive for individuals to strive for the means to look after themselves and their own family. This can be seen as a reiteration of the ethic of individual responsibility that informed resistance to public health reforms during the nineteenth century.

BOX 4.2

Prime Minister Thatcher and individualism

While she was Prime Minister, Mrs (later Lady and then Baroness) Thatcher gave an interview to a popular women's magazine, in which she described her view of the relationship between the individual and the collective:

> I think we've been through a period where too many people have been given to understand that if they have a problem, it's the government's job to cope with it. 'I have a problem, I'll get a grant.' 'I'm homeless, the government must house me.' They're casting their problem on society. And, you know, there is no such thing as society. There are individual men and women, and there are families. And no government can do anything except through people, and people must look to themselves first. It's our duty to look after ourselves and then, also to look after our neighbour. People have got the entitlements too much in mind, without the obligations. There's no such thing as entitlement, unless someone has first met an obligation. (Prime Minister Margaret Thatcher, talking to *Women's Own* magazine, 3 October 1987, pp. 8–10)

The phrase 'There is no such thing as society' came to sum up the individualism of the Conservative administrations which justified the systematic dismantling and under-funding of health and social care services.

Perhaps unsurprisingly, the Conservative government led by Mrs Thatcher printed only 260 copies of the Black Report and very little official publicity or credence was given to its findings. The report was clear on concluding that 'recent data show marked differences in mortality rates between the occupational classes, for both sexes and at all ages' with 'available data on chronic sickness tend[ing] to parallel those on mortality' (summary point 1) (Townsend et al., 1988: 198). The report stated that 'much of the evidence on social inequalities in health can be adequately understood in terms of specific features of the socio-economic environment ... (work accidents, overcrowding, cigarette smoking) which are strongly class-related in Britain and have clear causal significance' for health inequalities (summary point 5) (Townsend et al., 1988: 199). Evidence of inequalities of health service-use that favoured the most privileged classes was also presented. The report's recommendations centred on giving children a better start in life, using preventative measures and educational action to encourage good health in a larger proportion of the population and improving the quality of life of people with disabilities. The report outlined policy suggestions together with a budget and a strong steer that the abolition of child poverty should be a priority. The incoming Conservative Secretary of State for Social Services put his own interpretation on the report, suggesting that since decades of spending on the NHS had been ineffective in reducing health inequalities, the causes of these inequalities must be so deep-rooted that only a programme of public expenditure on a scale that would be impossible to fund might be effective. His introduction to the report therefore bluntly stated 'I cannot, therefore, endorse the Group's recommendations' (Townsend et al., 1988: 31).

The Black Report was later published by Penguin and it went on to become extremely influential in setting the research agenda on the inter-relationship between poverty and health, informing and inspiring a whole generation of researchers, activists and clinicians. Evidence as to the incessantly widening gap in the health of the rich and poor continued to be produced throughout four successive Conservative administrations, from 1979 to 1997. Official efforts, however, persisted in viewing health problems and poverty as individual problems requiring individual rather than social policy or collective solutions.

In 1997 a Labour government was returned to power under Tony Blair's leadership and new strategies were developed in an effort to break the cycle of ill health arising from poverty and deprivation. As part of this effort an 'Independent Inquiry into Inequalities in Health' was commissioned to review the latest evidence under the chairmanship of Sir Donald Acheson, a clinician, epidemiologist and former Chief Medical Officer. In light of this inquiry's evidence, priority areas for the development of policy were to be identified, but with the rider that any recommendations were to be within the government's overall budget, namely, that they should not require any extra funds and should be 'beneficial, cost effective and affordable interventions to reduce inequalities in health' (Acheson, 1998). The Acheson Report (1998), as it inevitably became known, followed its remit and, together with the consultation document *Our Healthier Nation* (Department of Health, 1998), showed the continued existence of inequalities in health. Furthermore, despite falls in the death rate since the 1970s, the difference in rates between those at the top and the bottom of the social scale had widened. Instead of unskilled male workers' mortality rate being twice that of professional men, as in 1971, by the early 1990s this was almost three times the rate (Acheson, 1998: Part 1, second section). This widening gap had arisen because the rates had fallen more in the higher social classes than in the lower social classes, with class gradients getting steeper for life expectancy at birth, life expectancy at 65 years and obesity for women, as well as class differences for women's blood pressure, for women's neurotic disorders and for men's alcohol and drug dependence (Acheson, 1998: Part 1, second section).

The Acheson Report also examined evidence on the socio-economic influences that had been linked to health outcomes by previous research. Since the 1970s, household disposable income per head of population had grown, but the richest households had benefited to a greater extent than the poorest households. The proportion of people with below average income (after housing costs) had increased throughout the 1970s and 1980s, giving another indication of the widening gap in wealth that can be linked to the gap in health.

The Acheson Report's recommendations were numerous and covered an enormous range of government policies, certainly not being restricted to medicine or even just health policy. The report's authors were, however, criticized for not prioritizing the 39 recommendations, which had made it difficult to plan how to put any of them into action (Davey Smith et al., 1998).

Mechanisms causing health inequalities by class

The Black Report had suggested four possible ways that health inequalities in mortality by class might be caused:

1   artefact;
2   social selection;
3   behavioural and cultural influences;
4   materialist or structural influences.

This classification set the research agenda for the subsequent decades and so it is worth describing briefly what each type of mechanism involves. The first possible mechanism is that the consistent association between poorer social class and worse mortality rates is not a real representation of premature deaths, but rather a statistical anomaly that results from the way that data are collected. It was suggested that errors in measurement and definition in the process of collecting social class and mortality data had produced the apparent inequalities. Subsequent to these claims, detailed research has shown that the mortality disadvantage of the most deprived classes is unlikely to be an artefactual outcome of the ways that class is attributed or mortality is registered (Fox and Goldblatt, 1982). Researchers in the field have come to agree that health inequalities are a real reflection of inequitable social relations that can be found the world over, rather than a by-product or artefact of the peculiarities of measurement and definition.

The second possible mechanism in the Black Report is the idea that in their own lifetime people with good health rise up the social hierarchy, whereas poor health results in a tendency to descend to a lower social class; in other words, a person's health determines their social class through a process of health-related social mobility. This idea has now been largely dismissed as population-based health inequality is unlikely to result from people with illness and disability drifting down the social hierarchy, since debilitating illness tends to strike later in life at a time when a person's social status has been established for death certification purposes (Goldblatt, 1989). Artefact and selection are theoretical explanations of health inequalities, but no longer form an important part of the research agenda on health inequalities.

The third possible explanation – that illness is caused by the choices that people make in terms of their diet, smoking, drinking, exercise and occupation – has been extremely influential. This holds that a person's social class determines their health because of class-based differences in health promoting and health damaging behaviours. Many health professionals would nominate the modification of behavioural factors, and most especially cigarette smoking, as the most powerful single means of improving individual health and reducing health inequalities. Behavioural modification for health improvement resonates with the individualist tendencies of post-industrial, capitalist societies and allows the problem of poor public health to be thrown back on individuals. Attempts to explain health inequalities in terms of individual behaviours have consistently been criticized for ignoring the context in which behavioural choice takes place. For instance, a woman living in a deprived area who wishes to improve her family's diet faces considerable structural barriers, which would not face someone living in a more affluent area.

The range of shops available is generally more limited in poorer areas and the range of foods available is also more limited. The difficulty of procuring food in poor neighbourhoods has led to them being described as 'food deserts' (Cummins, 2003) and it has been shown that 'healthier' choices, such as wholemeal bread and fresh vegetables, where found can be more expensive than in affluent neighbourhoods (Ellaway and Macintyre, 2000). The extra difficulty of making health-promoting behavioural choices in poorer areas is illustrated by a study which showed that deprived neighbourhoods in Glasgow were more poorly supplied with parks and sports centres than wealthier neighbourhoods (Macintyre and Ellaway, 1998).

This brings us to the fourth explanatory mechanism listed in the Black Report, namely the influence of material or structural factors, whereby social

Figure 4.1 Living in a poor area may effect health in various ways: ill effects of hard-to-heat, damp or dangerous housing; a lack of amenities such as parks and good retailers to support healthy 'choices'; and a negative effect in psycho-social terms due to being low down in the social hierarchy

class determines health through social class differences in the material circumstances of life. The concern which nineteenth century campaigners showed for the housing conditions, recreational opportunities, diet and stimulant-use of the urban poor remains relevant in terms of understanding poor health outcomes among deprived groups. The merit of disaggregating the independent health effects of various aspects of structural constraint, such as unemployment, living on benefits and living in a poor area, is the subject of ongoing debate among researchers.

The third and fourth possible mechanisms of the Black Report have attracted the majority of research activity, and although theoretically separable many have argued that cultural or behavioural influences cannot be analytically separated from structural or material influences. Material circumstances, such as a limited range of facilities for employment and recreational pursuits, together with compounding cultural factors, such as smoking being widespread, result in the higher smoking rates associated with low social class. The relative contributions of the health-injurious effects of the material environment (such as damp housing exacerbating asthma) and consumption choices (smoking and drinking promoting heart disease) continue to be the focus of interest, because they imply different types of policy response.

Since the Black Report, psycho-social and lifecourse explanations have been suggested to explain class-based inequalities as well as inequalities by other social divisions such as ethnicity and gender. The psycho-social explanation suggests that inequality also takes its toll through the effects of stressful conditions (Wilkinson, 2005). This argument proposes that it is no longer the case that absolute poverty is the only (or even a significant) cause of excess mortality among deprived groups in rich countries, because most people's basic needs are being met in terms of diet and housing. It is also argued that a lack of calories and insanitary living conditions no longer result in high levels of infant mortality, as is the case in much of sub-Saharan Africa. Instead, relative poverty and a lack of social cohesion give rise to the negative sense of being at the bottom of the heap, which in turn damages health via the mechanism of the stress hormones of the endocrinal system (Marmot, 2004). A person's position in the social hierarchy and the control and autonomy that they have in their neighbourhood and at work have an important influence on health in terms of both morbidity and mortality. To illustrate how important a person's relative social status can be for health, Michael Marmot quotes an American study where actors who had won Oscars lived on average four years longer than those nominated actors who had not won this trophy. Marmot suggests that higher social status offers an enhanced degree of control over life circumstances and better opportunities for full social participation, both of which protect health. A criticism of this 'psycho-social' mechanism is that it downplays the ongoing significance of real and systematic deficiencies in people's material needs and implies that

Figure 4.2 The run-down appearance of facilities in deprived areas may belie the good service on offer but a shabby exterior undoubtedly reinforces a neighbourhood's negative reputation and may undermine residents' sense of their own worth

the problem lies in people's attitudes to their situation and so could become another means of blaming victims for their own unfortunate circumstances.

Much research into health inequalities has focused on adult health outcomes measured cross-sectionally, that is, at one point in time. However, there has been increasing interest in a life-course approach that shifts the focus to how, from the moment of conception, humans accumulate 'risk' and 'resilience' in ways that are important to explaining their eventual health status in adulthood. Psycho-social routes and life-course approaches have allowed researchers to consider how inequalities by gender and ethnic group might be explained.

BOX 4.3

Russian evidence

Russian mortality rates have been studied through the 1990s as the country has gone from being part of the USSR with a communist regime, through the political, economic and social turmoil that accompanied the break up of the Soviet Union, to emerging as a capitalist economy where free enterprise and unregulated trade have rapidly taken hold. The variation in mortality rates allows some of the competing, but not necessarily mutually incompatible, explanations for health inequalities to be tested (Notzon et al., 1998). A fall in life expectancy – unprecedented for an industrial nation – occurred in Russia in the 1990s: from 1990 to 1994 an increase in (age-adjusted) mortality meant that life expectancy fell by six years for men and three years for women. The major causes contributing to this decline in life expectancy were cardiovascular disease (heart disease and stroke) and injuries (road traffic, suicide, homicide, and so on).

The disintegration of social cohesion in a swiftly changing and economically unstable society with a rapid rise in alcohol consumption were implicated and thought to be especially important for the younger middle aged. Between 1990 and 1995 the average per capita income declined by two-thirds and as the policy of wealth redistribution characteristic of the Soviet era ended the number of families living in poverty rose from 2 per cent in 1987 to 38 per cent in 1993. An increase in alcohol consumption and smoking, declining standards of nutrition, the deterioration of the healthcare system, a lack of medications, an upsurge in stress and depression associated with increasing unemployment, economic contraction and social discord were all features of Russian society that may have been implicated in worsening health outcomes (Notzon et al., 1998). Russia's case shows how material deprivation and psycho-social strife are likely to go hand in hand. Interventions to address material needs might reduce the sense of social disintegration and therefore the experience of stress that it is suggested may damage wellbeing. In this sense, it may be false to distinguish between material deprivation and psycho-social stress as separate causes of health inequalities.

ETHNICITY AND INEQUALITY

Research in the early 1980s using country of birth data suggested that among migrants to Britain the social class gradients in mortality characterizing the general population in the Black Report and the Acheson Inquiry were absent (Marmot et al., 1984). As discussed in Box 4.1 (see p. 72), the occupation-based class system divides up the population according to men's labour, reflecting the ideal (which may not necessarily have been fulfilled) that men were the main earners within their household, so their occupation was determinate for the standard of living and future chances of the whole household. The normative assumptions encoded in the use of this classification have been criticized and alternative classifications have been devised which better reflect women's position and which include those people without employment. One of these normative expectations is that the population as a whole will be spread across all six of the occupational categories (see Box 4.1, Table 4.2). Before the 1970s the majority of the male population was in the lower categories undertaking manual work – sometimes referred to as 'blue-collar' to distinguish it from white-collar or shirt-wearing office workers – thus giving a pyramid shape to the occupational-class structure. With the shrinkage of unskilled and skilled manual work associated with the decline of Britain's manufacturing industry and the increasing proportion of people employed in the service industry, this is no longer the case. The pyramid has now morphed into a diamond-shape with most people in the middle categories, sandwiched between less of the populace in the top and bottom classes.

For British minority ethnic groups, particularly migrants, occupation-based social class does not sum up life chances in the same way that has approximated those of the ethnic majority. Where a minority has a recent history of migration, expectations of the occupational structure and of the relationship between employment and standard of living may differ from British expectations. A decision to migrate is often intended to disrupt expectations about occupation and standard of living, with many migrants hoping to improve their own and their families' life chances in some way. But migration is not without its risks, and qualifications gained prior to migration do not necessarily translate into money or status after migration, as is shown by the number of taxi-drivers and restaurant-workers working in British cities who had previously qualified in medicine, engineering or dentistry in their country of origin.

Early research on health inequalities among migrants concluded that the expected class gradient (with the higher classes having lower mortality rates) was absent because the relationship between social class and health differed for minority ethnic groups when compared with the ethnic majority (Marmot et al., 1984). More recent research has found that the negative association between lower class and reported poorer health among minority ethnic groups does indeed exist, providing an appropriate means of measuring position within the social hierarchy is used. This association is clearest where a class of households with no full-time worker is defined separately from the other classes, where this class consistently shows the poorest health (Nazroo, 1998). Furthermore, it has been shown that within any given occupational group, ethnic minorities are disproportionately represented in the less prestigious occupational grades, having poorer job security and enduring more stressful working conditions and more unsocial hours. People of minority ethnicity also reported lower incomes than white people in the same social class (Nazroo, 1997).

The socio-economic indicators which overcome the limitations of simple occupational classifications (for instance by including home-ownership, income or ownership of material goods) may nonetheless miss out crucial aspects of disadvantage that pertain for minority ethnic groups in particular. The health consequences of deprivation will accumulate over a lifetime and where individuals have been through dramatic upheavals, such as migration, or periods of extreme poverty, standard measures do not take this into account. The long-term experience of racism which excludes minorities from employment, education and housing opportunities and may also have a psycho-social effect is not measured, and the residential localities within which minority ethnic groups are concentrated differ markedly in ways that could be significant for health (Nazroo, 1998).

AGE AND GENDER

Research reports on health inequalities are usually standardized for age and gender. This takes account of the fact that health tends to deteriorate with advancing age in adulthood, while post-puberty men and women show somewhat differentiated patterns of morbidity and mortality, partly explained by differences in biology and the endocrinal environment associated with sex differences. The degenerative processes associated with aging are normal, but concern has been expressed that morbidity in old age is not treated aggressively enough and that people are denied life-saving and life-enhancing treatments due to prejudice against treating older people (Bowling, 1999).

The morbidity experiences of men and women are difficult to summarize: women have apparently suffered more symptoms than men, but this may be due to their increased visits to the doctor with children, a greater willingness to report illness when compared to men, or the effect of living in a sexist society which psycho-socially and materially disadvantages women. The contrast in mortality rates between men and women is easier to characterize, as in industrialized countries women have consistently lived longer than men with the discrepancy currently standing at just under seven years (Clarke, 1983; Macintyre et al., 1996). Since mortality rates are the result of a lifetime's experience, there is likely to be a combination of factors at work, including the protective effect of female sex hormones against cardiovascular disease and historically lower levels of smoking and drinking. As women's lower rates of smoking and drinking are being eroded, with increasing numbers of young women matching their male peers' drinking levels, this mortality advantage may disappear. Cultural variations in gendered expectations at different stages in the life course may mean that the variations between ethnic groups' gendered mortality and morbidity rates will widen rather than disappear with time.

TACKLING HEALTH INEQUALITIES

To what extent should health and social policy be addressing health inequalities rather than just individual health needs? Should a reduction of absolute or relative poverty be the aim of health and welfare interventions? Universal policies that benefit the whole population (such as child benefit that is not means-tested, free fruit in schools, or free prescriptions for children) may actually increase the gap between rich and poor. The overall wellbeing of the richer classes can mean that they are in a better position to reap the health benefits from extra income, food or healthcare. Initiatives that are targeted at the poorest, most deprived groups in society are most likely to reduce the gap between the upper and lower classes, although a simultaneous brake on the accumulation of wealth by the upper classes is also necessary. The emphasis that different governments give to curbing health inequalities depends on whether inequality in general is seen as an inevitable outcome of capitalist growth. The Conservative governments of the 1980s and early 1990s followed the USA in viewing economic growth as paramount, with social inequality being a price worth paying for its promotion. Continental European states such as the Netherlands, France and the Scandinavian countries have tended to view equality as a social good for which it is worth sacrificing some economic growth.

FUTURE PROSPECTS

At the time of writing, the current Labour government is in its third term of office. Policies, which have attempted to mitigate the worst effects of poverty, continue to be funded by central government, including SureStart (a programme that brings together early education, childcare, health and family support to deliver the best start in life for every child) and various locality-based regeneration packages. Health, and especially the NHS, are key election issues, with all political parties promising that the NHS is safe in their hands. However, closing the health gap between social groups who are defined by class, ethnicity and gender is a long-term enterprise, more long term than the lifetime of most political administrations. Class variations in mortality rates are the result of an accumulation of benefits and insults to health over a lifetime and the effect of this accumulation on mortality rates appears slow in a country that is as wealthy and stable as Britain. Only when upheaval is dramatic and sustained and the ill effects on health are drastic, as in Russia in the 1990s (see Box 4.3, pp. 80–1), does the effect become apparent within a few years. Under more stable conditions there is a time lag between conditions improving and any consequence becoming apparent in mortality rates. This means that any political party elected on a four- or five-year term of office cannot cite improved mortality or morbidity rates as firm evidence of successful public health policies for their re-election. So while health inequalities may remain rhetorically important in national politics, it is difficult to see how this problem will ever get to the top of the agenda for concerted action.

INTERNATIONAL HEALTH INEQUALITIES

As wealthy nations such as Britain address health inequalities within their own borders, there is a danger that the problem has been exported elsewhere.

A rising standard of living does benefit today's Britons, but this increased wealth may be achieved through an economic expansion that is dependent on the exploitation of cheap sources of labour abroad. As British workplaces have become more regulated to prevent fewer industrial and occupational accidents and to disallow the exploitation of workers, manufacturing jobs have been exported elsewhere. Repetitive and sometimes dangerous work is undertaken by cheaper workforces in places such as Vietnam, China and Mauritius, with the potential effect of reducing domestic inequalities but broadening the global gap between rich and poor. Health inequalities by social class, age, ethnicity and gender are world-wide policy issues. A paper by the director of the World Bank's international health policy programme states that while policy has oscillated between concerns about efficacy and equity, the current emphasis is on fairness of provision (Gwatkin, 2000). Changes to the structure of the labour force in Britain mean that there are no longer large numbers of people working in semi-skilled and unskilled man-ufacturing work since production lines are becoming automated and human labour can be found cheaper elsewhere.

The cheapest forms of labour are slaves and children. Slave and child labour has been abolished in Britain for several generations, but is still preva-lent elsewhere in the world. Estimates are extremely hard to make, but on a global scale slavery and child labour may currently involve more people than ever before in history. Global health inequalities are much starker than those within a single nation such as Britain, but the underlying mechanisms and potential solutions are likely to be similar. The political systems which have improved the material circumstances of the richer nations have failed the world's poorest people who face the same health issues as the slum dwellers of Britain's nineteenth century industrialized cities. Historical precedent sug-gests that it is only when the rich identify their own interests as being served by global public health reformation is it likely to occur.

Further reading

Asthana, S. and Halliday, J. (2006) *What Works in Tackling Health Inequalities? Pathways, Policies and Practice Through the Lifecourse*. Bristol: Policy.

A detailed and up-to-date exploration of the processes that give rise to health inequalities across the life course and an identification of key targets for effective intervention.

Marmot, M. (2004) *Status Syndrome: How your Social Standing Directly Affects your Health and Life Expectancy*. London: Bloomsbury.

The author has studied the civil service to show that a higher position in the hierarchy is strongly related to subjective and objective measures of better health status.

Shaw, M., Dorling, D., Gordon, D. and Davey Smith, G. (1999) *The Widening Gap: Health Inequalities and Policy in Britain*. Bristol: Policy.

An accessible account of health inequalities, well illustrated with data that cover Scotland, England and Wales.

Wilkinson, R. (2005) *The Impact of Inequality: How to Make Sick Societies Healthier*. London: Routledge.

This book makes the case that people's sense of their lowly position in a social hierarchy is damaging to health and creates health inequalities.

REVISION QUESTIONS

1 What is meant by 'health inequalities'?

2 Describe the early evidence of health inequalities in industrializing cities.

3 Describe the main reports that updated understandings of health inequalities in the second half of the twentieth century.

4 Which explanations for health inequalities are best supported by research evidence?

5 Can inequalities by social class, gender and ethnic group be explained in the same terms?

EXTENSION QUESTIONS

1 Class and smoking

Men and women in manual socio-economic groups are more likely to smoke than people in non-manual occupations: 20 per cent of men and 18 per cent of women in the professional and managerial groups smoke, compared with 32 per cent of men and 31 per cent of women in routine and manual groups.

- It is regularly claimed that smoking is the biggest single cause of health inequalities. Do the figures given above bear this out? What additional information do you need to come to such a judgement?
- On 1 July 2007 a ban on smoking in enclosed public spaces was introduced in England and Wales, following earlier bans in the Irish Republic, Northern Ireland and Scotland. Is this justified given that smoking is known to be an unusually health-damaging behaviour?

The tobacco industry has historically enjoyed great freedom to promote cigarette smoking, due to its role in the national economy as a significant employer and as a major source of tax revenues. However, more recently arguments about freedom of choice for individual smokers have been rejected in favour of improving public health. Increasing regulation of smoking in industrialized nations seems inevitable as public bodies have to demonstrate their 'duty of care' to consumers, clients and citizens. Tobacco companies have been targeting and developing new markets for their products, allegedly by introducing high-nicotine, extra-addictive cigarettes to China and India.

- Given such aggressive marketing techniques in poorer countries, will banning smoking in richer countries simply widen global health inequalities?

- Does the benefit of economic expansion, for instance through the manufacturing of cigarettes to meet increased demand, ever balance out the health burden of increased rates of smoking?

2 Equity and healthcare

   a. Health inequalities are an inevitable outcome of a competitive economy and providing absolute poverty is not an issue, it is not a matter for statutory intervention.
   b. Health inequalities are an affront to social justice and tackling them should be a priority for the Welfare State and the NHS.

Which of the two statements above do you agree with most?

The extent to which such causes of ill health are considered to be social or individual problems varies with the degree of responsibility assumed to fall to individuals to improve their own lot. The view that people thrive through the pursuit of their own interests within an unregulated marketplace is associated with right-wing politics. This individualistic vision, promoted by Margaret Thatcher's political adminstration, holds that an expanding marketplace which profits traders primarily also benefits the rest of society through a trickle-down effect. There should be minimal governmental intervention to rescue individuals who fail to flourish through their own efforts, since 'safety nets' not only jeopardize the profitability of capitalist enterprise but also remove the incentive for individual effort. In this version of how society should work an underclass is an acceptable price to pay for the accumulation of wealth among the capital-owning classes, and salvation for the unemployed must come via their own efforts ('Get on your bike,' as Norman Tebbit said when he was Secretary of State for Employment). The sick and disabled may be supported by state benefit schemes, but there should be no incentive to remain on benefit, which implies that the support must be minimal and the safety net must remain uncomfortable.

   This version of society does not see an underclass as an unfortunate side effect, since the visible misfortune of the poor, sick and needy acts as a necessary disincentive to keep people labouring hard. A left-wing, communitarian vision of society views the disparities between the wealthy upper classes and the labouring classes as resulting from an iniquitous and unjust

(Cont'd)

social organization which requires political restitution. If the price of reducing the gap between rich and poor is a slowing of economic growth, and therefore a cut in prosperity for some, it is seen as a price worth paying.

Digest the preceding paragraph and justify your agreement with statement (a) or statement (b) in terms of society's obligation to the individual.

- As a key professional group, to what extent should medicine be setting the terms of a national policy on health inequalities?
- What are medicine's responsibilities towards the following groups with regard to health inequalities?

  - individual patients;
  - populations serviced by primary care trusts;
  - people in receipt of benefits;
  - tax payers.

5 *RISK, CHOICE AND LIFESTYLE*

Chapter summary

This chapter describes:

» how encouraging a healthy lifestyle should prevent disease and reduce the burden on the health services and acts as a central plank of modern healthcare policy;

» how choices relevant to health are constrained by structural factors and shaped by cultural interpretations of risk;

» how health competes with other values so choices need to be understood in the appropriate cultural context;

» how the treatment of asymptomatic patients who are 'at risk' on the basis of bio-chemical or genetic indicators has implications for what it means to be ill.

Useful terms for this chapter

horizontal transmission of culture: social learning between peers based on a choice to emulate one another's style of dress, language, communication, often in opposition to family-based vertical transmission of culture

risk: in scientific discourse risk refers to an exposure to a given event and in everyday language this exposure is usually assumed to be hazardous or undesirable

vertical transmission of culture: social learning between old and young, through different generations of people linked by common family and ideas of descent and often justified by ideas of tradition

INTRODUCTION

The previous chapter suggested that a significant portion of the excess mortality associated with low social class involves factors that are beyond the individual's control, for instance the circumstances into which a person is born and the material conditions of upbringing. Three successive Labour governments have attempted to reduce the damaging effects of poverty through interventions in community and healthcare settings to improve the life chances of the most deprived groups. Society's collective responsibility to protect and improve people's opportunities to lead healthy lives holds more sway under Labour than it did under the previous Conservative administrations. However, the individualism and abhorrence for the 'nanny state' that characterized the Tory approach to public health are still very much in evidence in contemporary health advice.

The tension between individual and group interests is a major preoccupation for the architects of health policy. Exhorting individuals to guard their own health is a very cheap option when compared with the provision of hospital services to cope with the effects of chronic conditions such as hypertension, lung and coronary heart disease. Prevention is better and cheaper than cure and so promoting the pursuit of healthy lifestyles can only be a good thing in health terms, except, that is, if equality in health outcome across society is viewed as important. Promoting healthy individual choices can widen health inequalities because wealthier groups stand to benefit more than poorer groups. To simplify the issue: if health policy concentrates on individual-level interventions, the gap between the healthy rich and the unhealthy poor widens.

Doctors deal with people as individual cases, to whom they have a duty of care. However, as explored in the introductory chapter medicine also seeks to promote the population's health through preventative public health measures, which may present some risk to an individual's health. The tension between the particular and the collective benefit deriving from medicine is very much part of clinical communication and decision making. In a nationalized health service, while the individual patient is the focus of much daily work, the doctor's contract is with society as a whole. There are concerted efforts to ensure that the benefits of the health service are shared amongst the widest range of recipients; for instance, a doctor will maximize the number of patients he can see by limiting the length of time of a consultation. NICE (National Institute for Health and Clinical Excellence) guidelines are developed to regulate access to various forms of healthcare so that public resources are shared according to evidence of benefit and to avoid so-called post-code lotteries with differential access by locality. Public health programmes seek to boost participation in immunization and screening so as to promote the population's rather than the individual's health. Thus medicine seeks to promote the health of individuals and of populations, and sometimes these goals do not entirely coincide. A child's best interests may lie in the population being immunized against measles, mumps and rubella, but in not having the inoculation himself. An adult may feel that her mental health problems are assuaged by cigarette smoking and yet society may later have to meet the cost of her treatment for emphysema and periodic pneumonia.

INDIVIDUALS AND THEIR BEHAVIOURS

Preventative medicine has become an important aspect of modern healthcare, and particularly with an ageing population avoiding chronic and degenerative disease has become a priority. We are advised to follow a healthy lifestyle: to avoid excessive alcohol, practise safe sex, stop smoking, take exercise and eat more fruit, vegetables and complex carbohydrates. 'Lifestyle' has come to mean the choices made by a person (although the term used to refer to the social and environmental influences on health) and there is no shortage of official advice on how to establish a healthy lifestyle. The widespread availability and free-flow of information to allow the client, consumer or patient to exercise 'choice' have become iconic to technologically advanced, liberal democracies. Contemporary public health campaigns will seek to avoid the suggestion that people are being coerced into healthy behaviours by being given one-sided information. Liberal democracies promote choice and denigrate fascist or communist systems that restrict information and rely on propaganda to persuade the population how to behave. The problem with this emphasis on informed individuals 'choosing' health is that information about health is never neutral and choice is always constrained by the social and economic circumstances of the person doing the choosing.

This emphasis on following a healthy lifestyle distracts political attention from the constraints that structural inequalities place on individual choice. We know that people living on state benefits struggle to afford the type of varied diet, rich in micro-nutrients, that is recommended in health education literature. Health promotion material presents 'the facts' but it also, implicitly, suggests that everyone has equal access to the health benefits available from making the 'right' choices. This is not, however, the case since wealthier people benefit from making healthier choices to a greater extent than the poor can. For instance, a person with a good diet, warm home and safe working conditions who gives up smoking is likely to benefit far more in health terms than someone who eats poorly, lives in damp conditions and works in a dusty atmosphere. The approach to health education which exhorts individuals to 'choose healthy lifestyles' overlooks how little leeway some people have to modify their own and their family's living conditions. It also fails to address the contradiction that, if healthier choices were adopted throughout the population, health inequalities between the social classes would be exacerbated rather than diminished.

Healthy living advice aimed at the individual inevitably addresses what is assumed to be the lowest common denominator and can therefore be boring

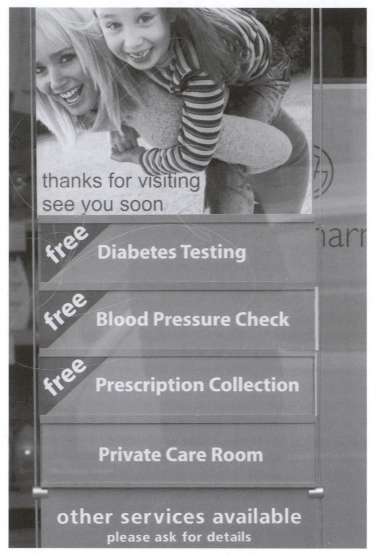

thanks for visiting
see you soon

free **Diabetes Testing**

free **Blood Pressure Check**

free **Prescription Collection**

Private Care Room

other services available
please ask for details

Figure 5.1   Individual responsibility for disease prevention and health promotion is emphasized in public health policy and the 'choice' to take advantage of screening and health checks is promoted through advertisements and target-based incentives for healthcare professionals

and patronizing. The following useful tip came from a booklet on healthy eating produced by the Health Education Board for Scotland (now called Health Scotland), available to download from their website in 2005:

> If you have spare cash on a shopping trip, look for things reduced in price. It is worth buying things you use regularly while they are cheap.

Telling people whose health is compromised by living in poverty that they should shop more cheaply suggests that they are too stupid to work this out

The Chief Medical Officer's Ten Tips for Better Health (Department of Health, 1999)

Don't smoke. If you can, stop. If you can't, cut down.
Follow a balanced diet with plenty of fruit and vegetables.
Keep physically active.
Manage stress by, for example, talking things through and making time to relax.
If you drink alcohol, do so in moderation.
Cover up in the sun, and protect children from sunburn.
Practise safer sex.
Take up cancer screening opportunities.
Be safe on the roads: follow the Highway Code.
Learn the First Aid ABC – airways, breathing and circulation.

Ten alternative tips (Shaw, 2001)

Don't be poor. If you are poor, try not to be poor for too long.
Don't live in a deprived area. If you do, move.
Don't be disabled or have a disabled child.
Don't work in a stressful, low-paid, manual job.
Don't live in damp, low quality housing or be homeless.
Be able to afford to pay for social activities and annual holidays.
Don't be a lone parent.
Claim all the benefits to which you are entitled.
Be able to afford to own a car.
Use education as an opportunity to improve your socio-economic position.

Figure 5.2   Tips for better health: official and alternative

for themselves and raises the spectre of the feckless shopper bringing on (or failing to stave off) her own poverty. Neither is telling people to take more exercise in response to childhood obesity helpful where sports centres are lacking and public parks are not used due to fear of crime. Indeed the effect of such advice may be to increase a sense of inadequacy and anxiety about the health penalties of a lifestyle which cannot be modified.

The contradictions of health advice which people cannot follow are neatly illustrated by the ten official and sardonically alternative tips for improving health shown in Figure 5.2.

By emphasizing individual responsibility for behaviour change official advice can be criticized for avoiding public accountability with regard to the powerful commercial interests in 'lifestyle' matters: what we eat, drink and smoke are matters of global business interest. Politically it is easier to urge people to stop smoking than to curb the tobacco industry's ability to sponsor sporting events which has a proven effect on the brand recall of cigarettes in young people. Urging an increase in the consumption of fruit and vegetables has been seen by government as more expedient than preventing the advertising of convenience foods to children. Industrial accidents such as radiation leaks or chemical explosions are commonly due to profitability taking precedence over safety in the day-to-day running of industry. Disability and death

Figure 5.3 The low cost and widespread availability of alcohol results in a high volume of sales, crucial to the profitability of the drinks manufacturing and retailing sector, as well as constituting a major public health challenge

from industrial accidents are not things that individuals can choose to avoid. The use of industrial techniques in agriculture and food production has led to several problems, some of which have taken years to come to public attention. Beef from cows which had Bovine Spongiform Encephalopathy or BSE (also known as Mad Cow Disease), chickens and eggs infected with salmonella, carrots tainted with dangerous levels of pesticides cannot easily be avoided by the individual shopper, since such contamination is not detectable.

Responsibility for modern industrial diseases such as asbestosis (mesothelioma) and vibration white finger was denied by employers for some time. Prior to recent health and safety legislation there were few options for workers who suspected that their health was being compromised by their work, save leaving their employment. Concern that cattle infected with BSE had entered the food chain and that tainted beef caused human variant CJD (Creutzfeldt-Jacob disease) was also running high in the late 1990s. There was uncertainty over the role of prions (proteinaceous infectious particle or infectious proteins) in causing BSE and the disease was thought to have been at large in cattle for several years. Since there was (and is) no cure for CJD, and nothing can be done to minimize the risk to health from meat consumed in the past, there are very limited behavioural responses to avoid the risk of CJD.

Health promotion literature tends to offer directional advice and does not represent the controversies and unresolved contradictions of the scientific research; for instance, the role of physical inactivity in causing heart attacks is not clear-cut but we are still advised to exercise more. The aim is to persuade behaviour change and not to show how a consensus has slowly emerged from research evidence that may at times be contradictory. In many matters of 'lifestyle', a single approved or advised course of action is emphasized with the implication that there is a correct, health-enhancing way of eating, exercising and drinking. However, this advice can change rapidly which can in turn undermine the public's faith in its authority. For instance, official guidance on how long infants should be fed exclusively on milk before they start on solid food has changed, with mothers of babies born before the mid-1990s being advised that around three months old was the time to introduce solids, whereas by the end of the decade this had shifted to four months, and now official guidance suggests that six months is more appropriate. Should the complex risks and benefits of infant feeding regimens be summarized simply and succinctly and distributed as public health messages? Or do the complexities and particularities of individual babies and their environment make it unsuitable for centralized advice?

Even where the scientific evidence behind public health advice is clear-cut, the contradictions of the risks and benefits for populations and for individuals can still cause difficulties. The measles, mumps and rubella (MMR) vaccination given to pre-school children is a case in point. An NHS website that promotes vaccination, called 'MMR – The Facts' (http://www.mmrthefacts. nhs.uk/), summarizes the research on the combined MMR vaccination as follows: 'The overwhelming weight of evidence proves that MMR is safe, and the number of studies demonstrating this is growing.' This statement would, however, be disputed by those parents, activists and medics who are convinced that the MMR vaccination has a causative effect on the development of colitis or autism. An authoritative, systematic review of the evidence (Demicheli et al., 2005) has confirmed that there is 'No credible evidence of an involvement of MMR with either autism or Crohn's disease' and yet vaccination rates have dropped off to 50 per cent in some areas. Parents are worried enough about the potential side effects of the vaccination to put their children at risk of contracting measles, mumps and rubella. The decision over whether or not to vaccinate one's children is further complicated by the phenomenon of herd immunity, whereby if between 85 and 90 per cent of the population is vaccinated, then non-immunized individuals are also protected from infection. When safety fears were first raised, parents could avoid their own child risking the potential side effects of the vaccination without worrying that they might be infected by measles, mumps or rubella. However, with the vaccination uptake having dropped outbreaks of these infections are predicted. The consequent spread of these childhood illnesses, which had been almost eradicated by mass immunization, may result in a shift in perception of the risks in favour of vaccination once again.

Weighing up the risks to one's child's health or one's own health is an emotive matter and some public health campaigns have played on anxieties to persuade people to behave in specific ways. The notorious 'Don't Die of Ignorance' AIDS information campaign of the 1980s featured tombstones and subsequently icebergs to stress that HIV could strike anyone down, but was rather short on suggestions of how to avoid ignorance or indeed HIV. There are perennial attempts to frighten smokers into quitting, with pictures of dissected, diseased lungs, descriptions of how smoker's good looks will be ruined and, more recently, a television clip of a smoker with lung cancer who, the viewer was told, died shortly after recording his message. Cigarette smoking is known to be the cause of nearly all lung cancers and it is hard for smokers to avoid this knowledge. Smoking reduces life expectancy by an average period of seven to eight years, with one calculation predicting that on average each cigarette shortens the life of the smoker by about 11 minutes (Shaw et al., 2000). Despite the health-damaging effects of cigarettes being well known, this information has not persuaded people to give up smoking. In the 1970s nearly half the adult population of the UK smoked whereas now just over one quarter do so, but the decline in smoking has been heavily concentrated in older age groups and among the professional and managerial occupational classes rather than the manual and semi-skilled classes. A case where the fear of lung disease did, apparently, lead to a mass cessation of smoking was the 50 per cent drop in the number of British doctors who smoked between 1951 and 1964, following the US Surgeon-General's reports of excess cancer deaths among smokers. Over the same time period the decline in smoking in the general population was much less dramatic, suggesting that the doctors' response was unusual.

Influential work by Hilary Graham (1993) has shown that smoking behaviour has become concentrated among the people who can least afford to do it in terms of their health and their personal finances. The statistical chances of being a smoker increase with being a lone mother who is unemployed and looking after a child with a disability. Unemployment, lone mothering and caring for a disabled child are all markers for deprivation and represent severe constraints on women's lives. Graham's work showed that cigarettes for these women were important as small luxuries that could be shared with others and made it possible to cope with the demands of looking after children with very limited resources.

Chapter 3 discussed the range of values that people associate with good health, including maintaining social relationships, which might not always coincide with a medical definition of health. For the single mothers interviewed by Hilary Graham the benefits of 'time-out' with a cigarette outweighed the damage to their health. Young diabetics will risk possible damage to their eyesight by skipping insulin injections to facilitate weight loss. Older people with late-onset diabetes may value their ability to eat and drink freely with friends more highly than keeping their blood sugar level controlled, despite understanding the risks incurred. Dimensions of health, such as strength, fitness and beauty, might be very compelling and

Figure 5.4 Advertising promotes the fun and sociability of drinking, and yet its easy availability means that alcohol-related diseases are increasingly common among groups who were not previously affected, such as women and younger people

sometimes at odds with a narrower definition of health. Body-builders use steroids to maximize their muscular bulk despite concerns about the long-term effects on other bodily systems. Following a calorie-restricted diet may be primarily motivated by a desire to drop-a-dress-size rather than to reduce blood pressure or improve lung function.

Persuading the population to take care of its own health and avoid disease is part of medicine's mission, but is not a simple task. Structural constraints mean that different social classes stand to benefit differentially from health promotion advice and, in some cases, the provision of information about potential health hazards which are difficult to avoid may simply raise anxiety levels. Even where people can change their behaviours to promote their health this may not happen, because although health is highly valued it is often competing with even more compelling considerations. A potential health risk is regularly offset against an alternative gain: using an oral contraceptive, getting drunk and acquiring a suntan all carry potential health risks. The charity Cancer Research UK polled 400 sunbathers in 2007 and found that 90 per cent of them knew the dangers of exposing their skin in terms of increased risk of melanoma, but presumably, as with drinkers and contraceptive users, felt the risk was worth taking. Health risk is not always something that people ignore as minimal or offset against other gains: in some cases the risk associated with a behaviour or a practice is of primary interest to the person involved.

RISK TAKING AND THRILL-SEEKING

Running risks can be exciting: competitive sports and other physical activities such as skiing and mountaineering are gripping partly because, even with appropriate safety precautions, there is a risk of injury. As a society we condone some risks and condemn others: football is high risk for lower limb injuries, but this does not lead to its prohibition; cigarettes remain legal, despite being linked with various health problems, but recreational narcotic-use is illegal. Young people (perhaps especially young men) making the transition from childhood to adulthood often run risks in the course of learning how to drive, drink and enjoy other adult pursuits. Risking their wellbeing while thrill-seeking does not suggest that young people are inviting injury; indeed, it is only a successful rite of passage if the person emerges from a dangerous pursuit unscathed.

Whether or not a 'risky' behaviour is judged socially acceptable is not simply a matter of interpreting the available epidemiological evidence; it is a far more complex mixture of emotion and meaning. An evening in the pub might look like 'binge drinking' to onlookers, or may constitute a quiet night out for a regular drinker, or may be a high-risk act of defiance for a young person whose family has religious and cultural objections to alcohol. Groups with a common cultural background often share a sense of the risks incurred with particular lifestyle choices. Religious affiliations are often associated with prohibitions on particular choices, such as eating meat, eggs or other animal products, drinking alcohol, smoking tobacco or using contraceptives. Culture, including religion, is learned in family groups (vertically transmitted culture), so a Muslim with parents who migrated from Pakistan is likely (but not pre-determined) to be strictly teetotal. However, culture is also transmitted and shared horizontally with peers and colleagues, and the child of migrants from Pakistan may opt to visit pubs and consume alcohol with or without his teetotal parents' permission or knowledge. Many of our assessments of health risks are shared with others in our community and so can be taken for granted: if we all believe that leaving the house with wet hair will bring on a bout of pneumonia, people will tend not to do it. Where assessments of risk are not shared with the population at large, they can became central to the definition of a shared minority culture. For instance, for some Catholics the use of contraception is wrong despite the risk to women's health of frequent pregnancy, and, in some contexts, refusing to use modern methods of contraception has now become part of a Catholic identity. The role of health risk in two cultural contexts will be discussed below in order to consider its cultural dimensions further.

RISKY SEX AND GAY MEN

The arrival of the Human Immunodeficiency Virus (HIV) among gay men politicized an already articulate and distinct cultural group in some European and

American metropolitan centres. Activism around improving research, clinical trials and healthcare for HIV infection and AIDS highlighted the prejudiced attitudes towards a disease that initially seemed to be confined to a gay sub-group of the population. It also made condom use a high profile and political matter that gay men could not avoid during the late 1980s and 1990s. More recently a practice known as 'barebacking', where HIV positive men have intercourse with HIV negative men without using condoms, has been described (Sheon and Crosby, 2003). Such apparent recklessness in failing to guard against contracting HIV has been explained in a number of ways. AIDS fatigue happens when people switch off to public health messages due to over-exposure and may be relevant in circumstances of very low incidence and low prevalence of sero-conversion, so that the risk of contracting HIV is perceived as non-existent. Where the incidence rate is high, AIDS comes to be seen as inevitable and so not worth resisting and where there is good self-help and political organization around HIV support-services, some sero-negative gay men describe feeling excluded from membership of the 'HIV club'. In other cases, contracting HIV from a lover becomes a symbolic aspect of shared life and mutual trust. In San Francisco a shift towards risk-taking sexual behaviour, including non-disclosure of sero-status and barebacking, was justified in terms of the advent of highly active anti-retroviral therapy (Sheon and Crosby, 2003). It is worth emphasizing that while some men who have lived with AIDS in their community for an extended time period may recognize the phenomenon of 'bug chasing' and 'barebacking' (see Box 5.1), there is no evidence that it is a normative or widespread approach to HIV.

BOX 5.1

HIV risk and pleasure

Bug chasers are men seeking to become infected with HIV.
Gift givers are men with HIV who are willing to infect bug chasers.
The gift is HIV.
Conversion parties are group sex parties where bug chasers allow themselves to get infected by gift givers.
Russian roulette parties are barebacking parties with both positive and negative men. Negative men take their chances that they will be infected when having sex with the positive men there. Depending on the circumstances, the participants may or may not know ahead of time who is positive and who is negative.

PREJUDICE AND BLAME

The tendency for cultural groups to denigrate other groups with prejudice against the alien and in favour of the familiar is widespread. To give a simplified characterization, if my cultural group asserts the superiority of brick homes and delights in a dairy-based diet, a neighbouring group who construct wooden homes and eat only vegan food can seem to 'threaten our way of life'. Some gay men identify strongly with a shared culture which has particular values and a lifestyle that are shared horizontally, but not so regularly transmitted vertically. Cultural groups are often defined in terms of their norms of family pattern, religion, language and locality, and usually a mixture of all of these. The tendency to disparage other groups' ways of living, marrying, working, eating and talking can be seen in harmless teasing and stereotyped jokes about the various approaches of the Scots, English, Irish and Welsh, while in today's inner city playgrounds these jokes will feature Punjabis, Bajans, Bengalis, Kurds and Somalis.

Jokes based on stereotypes can be enjoyable, but they can equally indicate a sustained denigration of an alternative way of organizing life. One of the places where this deprecation manifests itself is in the health risks associated with particular behaviours. Risks that are familiar to one cultural group become normalized and therefore acceptable, whereas the risks that other groups run are unfamiliar and so are often seen as betraying a feckless, foolhardy attitude to life and health. Muslim migrants have expressed their dismay at the widespread use of alcohol in Britain, seen as an important cause of social ills such as divorce, prostitution, rape, domestic violence and pre-marital sex and therefore of health problems, including sexually transmitted infections, unwanted pregnancies and violent injury. Reciprocally, some features of Muslim culture have been treated with suspicion by other British groups, with the custom of cousin marriage attracting particular criticism.

COUSIN MARRIAGE AND CONGENITAL PROBLEMS

A preference within South Asian Muslim families for contracting marriages between first cousins offers a means of ensuring the safety and wellbeing of one's daughter. Sending a daughter to be married into the family of an uncle and aunt, where she will be looked after and where contact can be maintained with her, has obvious benefits particularly in a society where women do not have rights to self-determination. Cousin marriage is legal in Britain (and most other European countries) and has, at times, been commonplace among the ethnic majority. However, the raised level of congenital problems in babies of Pakistani-born mothers has been attributed to consanguineous (meaning of the same blood) marriage. A recent review (Bennett et al., 2002) suggests that, on average, the baby of two first cousins has a 2–3 per cent greater risk of birth defects as compared with the general population, and about a 4 per cent greater risk of premature death.

This elevated risk is, of course, undesirable, particularly in families with a history of serious recessive conditions such as thalassaemia. However, it has also been suggested that too much attention has been paid to the undesirable clinical outcomes of close kin marriage given that these affect a minority of families (Bittles, 2005): a much larger proportion of couples who are cousins have children with no identifiable deleterious biological effects. In turn, the assumption that Pakistani Muslim children's congenital problems are due to relatedness between spouses has had negative effects on the care that they receive: parents have felt blamed for their children's misfortune, but have not necessarily understood why. When parents have not understood the principle of recessive inheritance, further affected births may ensue which the parents would not have wished for (Ahmad, 1996; Ahmad et al., 1998). In these cases clinicians have failed to appreciate their patients' points of view and have assumed that a medical model of the transmission of heritable problems and a statistical model of risk will make sense to those who are affected.

The concentration on cousin marriage as the cause of congenital problems has had other unfortunate side effects. It has distracted attention from the effects of poverty from which South Asian Muslim migrants suffer disproportionately. The assumption that 'cousin marriage' is a problem has often meant that the difficult task of establishing the level of genetic relatedness in couples with affected births (sometimes across a language barrier) has been ignored. The term 'cousin' in English is very broad, covering all one's parents' siblings' offspring, with no terms to distinguish, for instance, between the children of an aunt by marriage and the children of an aunt by descent. Other languages have a variety of terms to distinguish, for instance, between one's father's brother's son (or daughter) and one's mother's brother's son (or daughter). The stigma associated with cousin marriage among the ethnic majority has made it hard to establish the prevalence of cousin marriage in the general population, which has made informed comparison between ethnic groups difficult.

RISK AND PREVENTATIVE MEDICINE

The example of cousin marriage suggests that understanding a health risk is more complex than just estimating its epidemiological dimensions: the fear of spiders (arachnophobia) is more common than the fear of dogs (do you know many 'cynophobics'?), but dogs are far more dangerous in terms of numbers of people injured per year. Labradors are the most popular choice of breed for domestic pets in Britain and therefore the risk of being bitten by a labrador is higher than the risk of being bitten by a rottweiler or a bull terrier which might seem to be more aggressive. The relationship between the risk of a harmful outcome and the fear of that outcome is not predictable and the use to which patients put information about risk is beyond the control of the health professional. On being told that he is at high risk for heart disease a person may act to reduce those risks by giving up smoking, taking up exercise and adopting a cardio-protective diet. However, he might instead continue to enjoy smoking, fatty foods and a sedentary lifestyle on the grounds that there's no point in fighting the inevitable, and may point to an 'Uncle Fred' figure who smoked heavily, ate nothing but fried food and died at a ripe old age (Davison et al., 1991).

NEW RISKS, NEW DISEASES – WE'RE ALL PATIENTS NOW?

Risk is measurable whereas other factors that impinge on health relevant decision making are difficult or impossible to measure: public health interventions are often designed around measurable variables. The tendency of medicine to assess a person in terms of his accumulation of 'risks' has been criticized as part of the failure to attend to the social reality of the person experiencing illness. The concept of risk is also a crucial aspect of diagnosis, treatment and patient communication (see Chapter 7) and is essential to understand the epidemiological evidence-base informing good medical practice. Understanding the risks associated with specific disease categories in specific circumstances is a well-established and central aspect of diagnosis and treatment. Medical practice that is informed by epidemiology has invented new risk categories of 'pre-patients' who are asymptomatic but have a statistically elevated risk of developing a disease. Epidemiology measures risk as a property of groups or populations, whereas clinicians apply this risk to individuals, to identify people's risk of particular conditions on the basis of biochemical, genetic or histological markers from screening, lifestyle factors and family history. An individual identified as being at high risk of a particular disease who is then subjected to medical surveillance and prophylactic treatment represents the apotheosis of preventative medicine: treating a disease before it even starts. The problem, of course, is that being at high risk of developing a disease is not the same as having a clear certainty that that disease will develop, even with diseases that are strongly associated with particular risk factors: some smokers do not die of lung cancer and lung cancer can develop in people who have had very little contact with cigarette smoke. Even with Huntingdon's Chorea, caused by a dominant genetic trait, it seems that not everyone with the trait will develop the disease since it does not have 100 per cent penetrance.

Screening is a means of identifying those at highest risk of developing particular conditions in order to target preventative measures. The process of screening carries its own risks: there are the physical costs of taking tissue samples or capturing images using radiation sources, and the psychological penalties of the uncertainty of having one's health status called into question. The anxiety associated with screening may be dispelled if one is found to be at low risk, but some false positive identification is inevitable and prophylactic measures will be needlessly recommended for some people. Some cervical screening services have had high levels of false positives and false negatives, which undermine the value of the service to everyone. Prophylaxis (or preventative strategies) can carry very small associated costs: the use of condoms to reduce the risk of contracting a sexually transmitted disease carries few risks to health (assuming there is no allergy to the latex) but considerable potential benefits. Other preventative strategies, however, carry a heavier cost. Women identified as carriers of the BRCA gene mutations associated with breast cancer can opt for prophylactic surgery. How should the risks associated with major surgery, and the possible psychological consequences of breast and womb removal, be weighed against a BRCA carrier's 55–80 per cent lifetime risk of developing breast cancer? While mastectomy offers no absolute prevention of breast cancer, for women who have nursed their mothers, aunts or grandmothers through the disease any reassurance may be worthwhile. In 2006, three sisters (Joanne Kavanagh (44), Louise Lambert (39) and Michelle King (42)), none of whom carried any evidence of disease but who were all carriers of the BRCA1 gene, each opted to have their womb and breasts removed in response to their elevated lifetime risk of ovarian and breast cancer.

The wisdom and efficacy of bilateral mastectomy and oophorectomy for women who have no signs of cancer, but who carry the gene mutation BRCA 1 or 2, continue to be debated in medical and surgical journals. The surgical removal of breasts and ovaries is a drastic form of prophylaxis. Another example of prophylaxis of debateable value is the promotion of statin drugs that reduce blood cholesterol levels for any man over 45 and any woman over 55. Following a change in licensing permitting Simvastatin to be purchased without prescription, an advertisement campaign featuring a well-groomed, relaxed-looking man and woman, apparently in good health, advocating Simvastatin to reduce the 'risk of a heart attack' in the absence of any other symptoms of atherosclerosis. Prophylactic products can be marketed widely and raising awareness of the risk status for a disease is one strategy to create a set of customers who have no symptoms, but due to age, gender and lifestyle might be considered to be at higher risk of that condition. The possibility of the blanket prescription of statins to all persons over 50 has already been discussed by government health sources as a cost effective means of saving lives.

If medicine is currently extending medical care to perfectly well people, then being symptom free can no longer be trusted as a guide to being in good health and everyone is potentially sick. While NHS doctors have little interest in encouraging the 'worried well' into already over-crowded consulting rooms, the pharmaceutical industry clearly stands to profit by expanding the demand for its products. Is there anything sinister about the way that risks for disease are being used in medical practice? Advising patients on risk management is not a new feature of the doctor's work, as disease has been seen as related to diet and exercise since Hippocrates. The eighteenth century physician George Cheyne (1671–1743), in his 1733 book *The English Malady*, discussed responding to the epidemic of 'nervous diseases' with a diet of milk, seeds and greens and plenty of exercise either on horse-back or on an indoor, wooden chamber horse. What is novel is that modern medicine no longer confines itself to advising on diet, exercise and smoking, since its methods have opened up new areas of medical and surgical intervention. Apart from the huge array of pharmaceutical products to treat old-fashioned diseases, there are now so-called lifestyle diseases which are not life-threatening or pathological but are conditions for which medicine offers treatment. For instance, unexplained infertility would have been regarded as a matter of sadness, regret and perhaps stigma a few generations ago, but not something demanding medical intervention. However, it is now routinely treated with IVF (*in vitro* fertilization) and other techniques of assisted conception.

The architects of the NHS who witnessed the effects of two World Wars did not predict that, with falls in the rates of infectious disease and other indicators of improving health, new diseases and risks of disease would preoccupy patients and professionals. As the population's health and wellbeing have improved expectations have risen apace, so we now expect to live long, disease-free lives with minimal suffering. The enormous promise of scientific medicine to alleviate human misery has been fulfilled to some extent, but the shift in understandings of risk and the expectation of constant wellbeing is one unanticipated consequence. As our children are more likely than ever before in human history to survive childhood without incurring disease or disability, our anxiety about potential hazards seems to be at an all-time high. The exaggerated fear of risks to wellbeing has been described as a characteristic feature of our modern, post-industrial society in which people are deeply 'risk averse'.

RISK, LIFESTYLE MEDICINE – WHAT NEXT?

Should people have unfettered, individual choice regarding the lifestyle choices that they make and the consequent health risks that they run? Such a libertarian view does not call to account the various industries whose economic interests lie in persuading people to follow particular patterns of consumption and the inequalities of opportunity that structure who can benefit from health-enhancing habits. Perceptions of the scale and urgency of health risks are influenced by cultural norms rather than calculated probabilities: acceptable risks are distinguished from unacceptable (and often stigmatized) risk taking by a shared understanding or 'common-sense'. One cultural group's 'common-sense' view of its own risky behaviour as an inevitable part of coping with life's challenges does not prevent it from seeing another group as behaving incomprehensibly irresponsibly: for example, drinking a glass of wine during pregnancy is not unusual in France, whereas in parts of the USA it is seen as highly irresponsible and reprehensible.

Where mortality rates have dropped significantly and consistently over the past century, people have become more averse to taking risks and thus perceptions of risk have changed. Epidemiological risk is a scientifically measured concept that applies to populations and as such it is difficult for clinicians to apply it when advising individuals. The individual's interpretation of a clinician's interpretation of an epidemiological risk introduces subjective dimensions. These subjective elements may not be easily quantifiable but are nonetheless powerfully felt and crucial for identity. The 'risk of disease' is understood to be a negative quality in the sense that there is no such thing as a 'good risk': frequent comparisons to the risks we run when crossing the road are an attempt to remind us of the level of background risk which we encounter every day. Given our aversion to the risk of disease, any action to reduce the risk of disease should be entirely positive, but (perhaps counter-intuitively) disease preventative procedures such as screening and vaccination can feel risky to potential patients and may therefore induce anxiety. Since the nasty symptoms of measles are no longer commonly experienced in populations, the statistically small risk of complications from the MMR vaccination has come to be seen as worse than the disease which the inoculation prevents, and some parents would thus rather risk the infection.

Faced with a daily existence that is low in short-term health risks, the thrill of deliberately risking one's health can be exhilarating and, having escaped unscathed, can feel life-enhancing: this is true for children playing chicken on their local bypass and business executives taking up sky-diving. People who recover from life-threatening disease often describe themselves as more appreciative of life, and with their priorities changed for the better. This chapter has discussed how the experience of risk is part of a cultural identity. In the next chapter, we will consider how the experience of actual illness (and not just its risk-factors) has repercussions for identity.

Further reading

Armstrong, D. (1995) 'The rise of surveillance medicine', *Sociology of Health and Illness*, 17 (3): 393–403.

An influential paper that describes the shift in medical practice from clinical observation of diseased patients to the statistical assessment of indicators of health with a focus on deviation from the average, giving rise to the idea of a risk factor.

Green, J. (1997) *Risk and Misfortune: A Social Construction of Accidents.* London: UCL Press.

This book considers how accidents are understood by health professionals and lay people to account for their patterned occurrence by gender and social class and the inadequacy of statistical explanations for individuals' misfortune.

REVISION QUESTIONS

1 Does everyone have an equal opportunity to 'choose' a healthy lifestyle?

2 In what respect is the promotion of a healthy lifestyle expedient for a nationalized health service?

3 How does epidemiological risk contrast with subjective assessments of risk?

4 What is a pre-patient?

5 What are the benefits and costs of prophylactic treatment?

EXTENSION QUESTIONS

1 Youthful risk taking

Which of the following statements would you defend most readily?

– Unprotected sex, repeated excessive drinking and tobacco-smoking are activities which pose an unacceptably high risk of damaging young people's health in the long term.
– Experimentation with sex, alcohol and cigarettes is part of the normal process of growing up.

Legally there are age limits for smoking, drinking and sex. Do these influence your views on their acceptability?

• Is it acceptable for a 16 year old to have unprotected sex?
   – What about a 15 year old?
   – Is it more acceptable for a young man compared to a young woman?
• Should an 18 year old be permitted to binge drink?
   – What about a 16 year old?
   – Is it more acceptable for a young man compared to a young woman?

2 Rationing and responsibility in healthcare

Take a look at the following papers.

Shiu, M. (1993) 'Refusing to treat smokers is unethical and a dangerous precedent', *British Medical Journal,* 306: 1048–9.

Underwood, M.J. and Bailey, J.S. (1993) 'Should smokers be offered coronary bypass surgery?', *British Medical Journal,* 306: 1047–8.

- Are there any circumstances in which a doctor can justifiably refuse to treat a patient because they have behaved recklessly?
- Who holds the ultimate responsibility for meeting the costs of treating the ill effects of smoking – is it the governments who have benefited from tax revenues, tobacco companies who have actively marketed cigarettes knowing them to be harmful, or smokers who choose to buy tobacco products?

3   Screening our language

'HIV-positive' has become a widely understood phrase. But what about the phrase 'Screening positive for pre-cancerous cervical cells'? This could be a confusing message, since the implications for individual women are extremely negative. Conversely, screening negative is very good news.

   'I am sorry to have to inform you that the result from your breast screening is positive.'

Whose priorities are reflected in the language of screening?
   Imagine that you are a doctor who is giving a person bad news about their routine screening for prostate or cervical cancer. Formulate a phrase that is not only unambiguous in meaning, but also takes into consideration the shocking effect which the news might have. Test the phrase out loud for ease of expression.

4   Risk and the pharmaceutical industry

Vioxx, a painkiller made by US firm Merck & Company, was withdrawn from sale in September 2004 after it was linked to heart attacks and strokes following medical trials.

   - Did the manufacturers sell a defective product, or did they act responsibly in withdrawing the product when the problems became apparent?
   - Who should bear the costs of supporting individuals who have been disabled through the side effects of pharmaceutical products?

6

EXPERIENCING ILLNESS

Chapter summary

This chapter describes:

» how illness is laden with meaning, much of which cannot be addressed by medical science;

» how questions of order and control of the onset of suffering are urgent for patients;

» how illness can mean failure and be experienced as a stigmatized state;

» how biographical disruption, failure and stigma are addressed through the construction of illness narratives.

Useful terms for this chapter

autopathography: a term coined for written accounts of the experience of serious illness

biographical disruption: the disruption between one's former healthy self with the current ill self brought about by the experience of illness

sick role: a reciprocal, unequal set of rights and obligations that structure doctors' and patients' behaviour and expectations

stigma: a condition or attribute that marks the bearer as unacceptable, inferior, polluted, shamed

INTRODUCTION

What does an ill person want? To be reassured, to be relieved of painful symptoms and of onerous responsibilities and to be looked after until recovery arrives. A person experiencing illness often wants answers to questions. Why me? Why now? How can it be fixed? These questions of order and control are asked by a patient as he or she tries to re-establish control over their experience of life that has been disordered by the intrusion of illness (Kleinman, 1988: 29). Where antibiotics cure the infection, analgesics reduce the pain or a plaster-cast immobilizes a fractured bone, these questions may be answered in proximate terms: 'I caught a bacterial infection while abroad', 'I slipped on ice and broke my arm.' But if I regularly travel abroad, or frequently encounter ice, why was I struck down on this particular occasion?

This question is very difficult to answer scientifically: the computation of relative risks for disease or disability does not address questions about order and control. Medicine has developed theories about the causation of disease that give us a good idea about the causes of infections and identify predisposing factors for chronic diseases. This type of causative modelling is useful for understanding disease in populations but cannot explain the cause of one person's suffering. Sophisticated statistical techniques and epidemiological expertise have limited power to explain why a person has developed the symptoms of angina this year instead of last year or next year. Why did I have a heart attack today, whereas my sister with a similar genetic inheritance and lifestyle remains free of heart disease? The urgency of these 'Why me?', 'Why now?', 'What next?' questions for a person experiencing illness and the impotence of medicine to address them can be extremely frustrating for both the patient and the patient's carers.

Medicine aims to alleviate the suffering associated with symptoms, but is ill equipped to help with the distress brought about by the disruption to daily life, the uncertainty and the metaphysical fears that illness presents as a harbinger of death. Illness, like other forms of misfortune, can arrive in the midst of an orderly life without warning, and this is troublesome not only to the ill person but also to those around him, since it is a reminder of the fragility of our daily normality and the finite nature of our lives. Anxieties about human suffering and death can be addressed by religion and other systems of spiritual or metaphysical belief. These may variously explain misfortune as a consequence of an individual's previous actions, as the will of God, or as part of the wider scheme of the metaphysical universe. These approaches are not offered much space in modern medicine, nor are they accorded much authority in the health service. Hospitals provide for a chaplaincy with a space for prayer and contemplation, but a chaplain is not routinely regarded as a key member of a clinical team.

A trenchant criticism of modern medicine has been that its reductive approach to healing, in which mechanical metaphors predominate, serves to suppress the expression of experiential dimensions of illness. A mechanistic view of treating cancer, for instance, would suggest that the job is finished once the tumour is excised, the stray cells are eradicated and the follow-up screening is arranged: if the previously sick body has been returned to normal functioning then medicine has done what it can. This approach takes no account of the complex interactions between mind and body, the moral dimensions of illness and the importance of other people's reactions to a person's illness. One person's experience of living with and being treated for cancer cannot be extrapolated to another's, since the experience of illness and of healthcare is intensely personal. However, since the personal is mediated through culture which structures social, emotional, symbolic and bodily dimensions of illness, there are some general points that can be made about the significance of illness. The rest of this chapter will discuss some of the evidence on the disruption that illness brings to people's social lives and their identities including stigma, and the ways that these difficulties are managed and endured.

THE SICK ROLE

Being ill is both an embodied and a social experience. When painful bodily sensations are suffered in silence and not shared with others, can the individual be said to be ill? Where a person's silent symptoms do not impinge on their work life or home life and are not taken to the doctor, is that person suffering an illness or just suffering in silence? The social, shared dimension of illness means that a person's status as ill depends on how other people react to the manifestation of their symptoms. Suffering has to be named as illness and the naming process involves other people. As described in Chapter 3, a doctor's assessment of symptoms is very important. However, many symptoms are never presented to a clinician, instead being discussed, treated and cured or accommodated in the sufferer's local, non-medical environment.

When a person declares himself ill and, assuming his claim is credible some of the privileges of sickness are allowed: special treatment at home, including bed-rest; light, nourishing food; special drinks; a reduced load of domestic duties; analgesics; other pharmaceutical or home remedies. Being recognized as ill can lead to the suspension of duties outside as well as inside the home: a temporary withdrawal from employment, leisure activities and voluntary service can be justified on the grounds of illness (Parsons, 1951). Withdrawal from normal employment activities can be required, since those who attend work while ill may be regarded as impeding their own recovery, thereby prolonging the illness, and if infectious, they may be jeopardizing others' health. Failing to respond to illness appropriately can attract disapproval, whether this is by exaggerating illness (malingerers and moaners) or by imagining illness (hypochondriasis). Where illness episodes are self-limiting and infrequent a temporary suspension of normal activity will have no serious consequences for one's identity or social role: having flu once a year does not make one unemployable or considered as a bad parent. Normal duties at home and at work can be reprised after a few days in bed taking it easy, and the only consequence is sympathy garnered for the effects of the virus or the bad back that caused the problem. Once symptoms wane, day-to-day activities will re-establish the sufferer in their social roles, as colleague, parent, partner, carer, manager and customer, and will re-make the person's identity as healthy and normal. Order and control will be restored.

But what happens when the illness does not retreat after a limited period of care? Definitions of health described by lay people in Chapter 3 involved a dimension of 'functionality', of being able to get one's work done. So if an illness persists in preventing normal duties from being fulfilled, what happens to a person's identity as healthy or normal? What happens to the role or job that he or she fulfilled in society? And how does the individual adjust to accommodate, or cope with, pain, discomfort or the other symptoms that endure?

SICKNESS AS DEVIANCE

Health and illness are not experienced as mutually exclusive, opposite categories and people with quite serious symptoms can nonetheless see themselves as healthy, as described in Chapter 3. While the experience of health and of illness might not always be clearly distinguished, as cultural categories they are understood as being opposed to one another: sickness/health; disabled/able-bodied; diseased/disease-free; pathological/normal. 'Illness' or 'sickness' describes a state that we recognize as distinct from 'healthy', so while healthy people may have symptoms there is a strong tendency for those who see themselves as healthy to distinguish themselves from those who are sick. This demarcation of the sick from the well, to make them a separate and visible group, has happened down the ages. Sufferers of leprosy in thirteenth century England were gathered in colonies to isolate them from the rest of the population and denied normal social contact: they were unable to marry, forced to dress distinctively and to sound a bell warning of their approach. Physically distancing the sick from the healthy has also been a feature of the organization of twentieth century healthcare, with the committal of patients to the asylum and the sanatorium. Concern over the cost of residential hospital care and contemporary conceptions of 'care' makes the physical isolation of the sick less acceptable. Short hospital visits and community-based health and social care mean that the physical distancing of the sick from the well is no longer the norm.

However, there are more subtle ways that ill people are isolated. Seclusion of the sick can take a mild, caring form, 'Stay in bed, look after yourself', as well as a less therapeutic form, sanctioned by stigma – 'Keep your seizures secret and don't mention your epilepsy to anyone!' The urge to hold the sick apart might have some rationale with infectious disease ('Don't cough on people, keep your germs at home'), but the stigma associated with illness does not depend solely on the identification of an infectious agent to be isolated. Leprosy while transmissible is not highly contagious, and yet sufferers have been highly stigmatized and isolated from society. Other diseases that are not contagious or even transmissible can be nonetheless stigmatizing to the extent that sufferers may be hidden away, mental illness being a prime example.

STIGMA AND ILLNESS

Stigma refers to a condition or attribute that marks the bearer as unacceptable or inferior and renders that person (and perhaps the group with which he is identified) as polluted or shamed. Stigma is a symbolic quality that can be seen in people who are not able to maintain a creditable social identity because of a particular condition. When illness is viewed as potentially stigmatizing it becomes possible to explain some of the difficulties of experiencing illness. There are three types of stigma: stigma of the body from blemishes or deformities, stigma of the character concerning mental illness or criminality, and stigma of a social group such as a tribe or class of people (Goffman, 1963). The first two types of stigma are most important for understanding illness and disability. The third type, whereby groups are stigmatized for some 'tribal' trait, is important when a stigmatized group goes on to suffer disproportionately with a stigmatized illness. Prostitutes, drug users and gay men have been stigmatized as groups and subject to discrimination, and have then had this compounded by being identified as being of higher risk of carrying HIV – a highly stigmatized condition.

Some types of stigma can be managed or hidden to avoid discrediting the bearer's identity: the physical scars of major abdominal surgery can be covered and a prosthetic breast helps disguise a mastectomy, whereas a stutter or blindness is more difficult to hide in day-to-day interactions. A distinction can be drawn between stigma that is *felt* or feared but may not actually happen, and *enacted* stigma which does indeed get played out (Scambler, 1989). People with stigmatizing illnesses may put considerable effort into managing not only the symptoms but also the stigma so as to avoid having their identity spoiled. For example, in one study of HIV positive men one explained that he did not tell his colleagues of his status since 'I don't want the others to look at me any differently. I don't want any condescension, and even less, pity' (Carricaburu and Pierret, 1995). When signs of the illness (such as shingles or herpes) appeared, keeping the disease secret becomes more difficult for men with HIV, but avoiding the stigma was nonetheless important, such that one man told people that diabetes was the cause of his frequent visits to hospital as he felt this to be less stigmatizing than the symptoms of HIV.

Stigma shifts and changes through time. Some of the stigma of illness can be attributed to fear of contagion, but this is not the whole story: leprosy and tuberculosis are treatable conditions, but are nonetheless stigmatized. When Diana, Princess of Wales, was pictured touching people with AIDS in the early 1990s she made headlines around the world and was credited with reducing the fears associated with HIV. But whether the stigma of HIV has actually receded is another matter. On the occasion of his son's death from AIDS, Nelson Mandela appealed to end the surrounding stigma, thereby prompting a member of parliament and former minister Chris Smith to announce his HIV positive status. Despite being Britain's first openly gay member of parliament, Smith had kept his HIV status secret for 17 years. The stigma of cancer has also eroded over the past 40 years, thanks partly to improvements in our understanding of the range of diseases that the term 'cancer' encompasses and advances in treatment making the disease more survivable. Nonetheless the stigma persists, with some people unwilling to utter the word 'cancer' and preferring to employ a euphemism such as 'C' or 'the big C', or to avoid even this oblique reference by holding an index finger and thumb in a C shape in place of the spoken word.

The stigma associated with illness is easier to manage where the ill person is not already subject to some type of class or tribal stigma on grounds of race, religion, behaviour or lifestyle. As a form of stigma, racism discredits young black men as anti-social and threatening, an assumption that is, unfortunately, strengthened by the exhibition of symptoms of a stigmatizing psychotic illness. Groups who view homosexuality as a stigmatized 'condition' have termed HIV a 'gay plague' which, in their view, confirms the polluted and unacceptable nature of the people who suffer it. The possibilities for managing the stigma of HIV are also wider if the carrier comes from a non-stigmatized group: compare the likely reactions to an unemployed, homeless IV drug user and a middle-class, professional haemophiliac, both of whom test positive for HIV. A drug user would be assumed to have contracted the virus through sharing needles or having unprotected sex, whereas a respectable professional person with a blood disorder would be assumed to have received contaminated blood products. Getting ill via voluntary behaviours such as recreational drug-use is blameworthy, particularly when the individual is already part of a group stigmatized as anti-social and feckless, such as the homeless or prostitutes.

ILLNESS AS FAILURE

Blame and culpability for an illness are closely allied to the experience of stigma; however, the stigma associated with an illness is not reducible to the sufferer being held to account for their own ill health, since it also connotes shame and pollution. Pre-scientific thought viewed illness and suffering as linked to the wrong-doing of an individual, his ancestors or community. For instance, in the popular traditions of Chinese medicine social or supernatural factors responsible for illness were seen as punishment for causing offence to one's ancestors, with pestilence and plague resulting from wrong-doing or from ancestral curses. The Judeo-Christian tradition of a vengeful God, together with an epidemiological emphasis on individualized health risks, perhaps reinforce the inclination to see illness as a punishment: the early onset of sexual activity and multiple sexual partners are risk factors for cervical cancer and this can also be interpreted as the punitive consequence for promiscuity. Eating poorly and failing to exercise also carry their own punishment, in the form of obesity and hypertension.

The eighteenth century's Enlightenment thinkers contested explanations of the world based on religion, magic or superstition, placing their faith instead in the explanatory power of rational, scientific reasoning. In the post-Enlightenment world, scientific medicine denies ancestors' curses, fate, God and the supernatural a role in disease-causation, and yet health is nonetheless a form of moral virtue. Hence, as an absence of health, illness can be experienced as a failure of some sort: failure to be well, failure to provide certainty or stability for one's family, friends or dependants. The sense of having failed may intensify the sick person's urge to ask 'Why me? Why now?', and the need to find someone or something beyond oneself to blame. Where an illness occurs without any obvious risk factors (or sins) the question 'What have I done to deserve this?' arises. One 42 year old man is described as being furious when he had a heart attack, since he had already stopped smoking, limited his drinking and lost weight and, after all that effort, felt the injustice of the disease striking 'It's just I'm too young … why me?' (Charmaz, 1994). In the absence of God or a supernatural force to blame, new interpretations of morality may provide an answer to the 'Why me?' question. The character traits of cancer patients have been blamed by some for the development of the disease since, according to a medical doctor, 'No truly happy person ever gets cancer' (Lorde, 1980).

BIOGRAPHICAL DISRUPTION AND ILLNESS NARRATIVES

Stigma, sense of failure at the frailty of the lived body, and uncertainty with regard to the future are all part of the experience of an illness for which there is no medical cure. Nonetheless, these intangible aspects of illness are crucial to people's sense of themselves and are a central part of getting over an acute disease and of living with a chronic condition. The sense of disjuncture between being healthy, with a life story that is unfolding along the lines expected for a healthy person, to being ill with the constraints that chronic illness brings, has been termed 'biographical disruption' (Bury, 1982). Biographical disruption can be 'restored' by the ill person re-telling his story to reinstate a continuum between the healthy self and the ill self. Narrating stories is a widespread means by which people represent and explain difficulties, integrating them into their experience and into an ongoing biography. What have been termed 'illness narratives' are the ways in which people explain the arrival of their illness, its consequent effect on their life, and the ways that they answer the questions of order and control.

Despite each person's story being their own, research that has gathered a range of illness narratives suggests that they can be classified into three types, shaped by the cultural setting and the psychological needs of the story-teller (Bury, 2001). Contingent narratives deal with events around the onset of the illness and are practical and descriptive, dealing with events and their immediate impact. Moral narratives show the narrator as competent, active and socially engaged and try to close the gap between the previous self, before illness, and the current self after the experience of failures. Core narratives describe the course of an illness with plots that might be epic, heroic, tragic, comic or didactic. In some sense we all narrate our illnesses, integrating them into the story of our normally healthy lives through everyday talk. Researchers have translated this type of talk and oral story-telling into written forms through recording and transcribing interviews and have noted that any single narrative might include elements that could be described as contingent and moral, as well as including some of the dramatic plot devices of the core narrative.

AUTOPATHOGRAPHY

Telling the story of an illness can work to realign the stigma and failure of that illness, re-constructing one's biography so that it has hope and a future, whether this is thanks to heroic struggle or comic observation. So-called autopathographies, written by journalists who have cancer (Diamond, 1998; Picardie, 1998; Noble, 2005) or AIDS (Moore, 1996), have addressed their reader's expectations and stereotypes about their disorders. They describe the difficulty of continuing strands of life that they enjoyed when well (parenting, working and keeping up with friends) once they become ill.

As professional writers, one means by which they achieve a continuity of active living is by writing. Reflecting upon one's life in its re-telling can be seen as an opportunity. Having suffered a heart attack two years earlier one man said 'I'm grateful that it happened now, 'cause it changed my life considerably.' Other men in the same study stopped working, changed jobs, retired and adopted healthier habits in response to the experience of illness (Charmaz, 1994). Another heart attack survivor, who also had cancer, described illness as an opportunity albeit a dangerous one: 'Illness … gives you the opportunity to choose the life you will lead as opposed to living the one that you have simply accumulated over the years' (Frank, 1991).

REMAKING LIVES?

The reformative potential of illness narratives should not be overstated, since the disruptive effects of illness, both in social and organic terms, can be overwhelming. A study of people with Parkinson's disease described how the stigma of having trembling, shaking limbs, incoherent speech and constant dribbling had led some people to withdraw from public and seclude themselves (Nijhof, 1995). People can narrate their place in the world and make sense of the arrival and progress of an illness. However, the extent to which these narrations re-integrate their illness experience depends on the cultural meanings of the illness. People have published accounts of their experience of cancer of the breast, brain and lymph system, but there is not yet an autopathography dealing with cancer of the bowel. Perhaps the bowel, and its association with faeces and flatulence, is too taboo to discuss, even in our current times when confession is so widespread.

Research suggests that men who are HIV positive and also gay can present their individual stories in the context of the collective history of gay liberation, which reinforces the homosexual aspects of their biographies. Such an integration of illness narratives in a broader cultural history was experienced as positive but was obviously not a strategy open to the haemophiliac men interviewed in the same study who were not gay (Carricaburu and Pierret, 1995). The therapeutic effect of re-integrating disrupted and chaotic lives is probably still underestimated (Moerman, 2002), but while recasting one's bodily and moral failings is part of maintaining personal integrity, it does not override the embodied experience of illness, to which we turn in the next chapter.

Further reading

There are many accounts available of people's experiences of their own illness, including books by John Diamond, Audre Lourde, Oscar Moore, Ivan Noble and Ruth Picardie, cited above. Oliver Sacks, who has written accounts of his patients' experience of their neurological disorders (for instance, The Man who Mistook his Wife for a Hat and Other Clinical Tales *(1985) London: Picador), has also published his own story of breaking a leg and how he reacted to the pain and symptoms, called* A Leg to Stand On *((1986) London: Pan), which is discussed in the next chapter.*

For a sociological understanding of how these experiential accounts work, the following paper has been influential.

Bury, M. (1982) 'Chronic illness as biographical disruption', *Sociology of Health and Illness*, 4 (2): 167–82.

REVISION QUESTIONS

1 Why might illness be experienced as failure?

2 Describe the three types of stigma.

3 What is the difference between felt and enacted stigma?

4 What is biographical disruption?

5 How do illness narratives address biographical disruption?

6 Describe the types of illness narrative that researchers have noted.

EXTENSION QUESTIONS

1 Stigma and knowledge

Stigma is often seen as arising from a lack of education, which implies, for instance, that once people know that HIV cannot be caught from shaking hands or sharing a cup, the ostracism of people with AIDS will cease. This assumes that disgust and stigma arise from ignorance alone. However, research evidence suggests that public education to de-stigmatize leprosy had the contrary effect of heightening stigma (Navon, 1996).

Consider the following conditions that can be transmitted through sexual contact: genital warts, chlamydia, HIV, syphilis, pubic lice (also known as crabs).

- Are these conditions all equally stigmatized?
- Can you arrange them in order of increasing stigma?
- Which of the following features of the condition influence the strength of its associated stigma:
    - how well known it is;
    - the seriousness of the threat to health without treatment;
    - the ease with which the condition is treated;
    - the efficacy of the treatment available;
    - the ease with which the condition is passed on to others?
- Are head lice more or less stigmatizing than pubic lice? Justify your response.
- Design a public health message that would reduce the stigma of one of these conditions. Consider your public health message in relation to Navon's research (1996). Is there any possibility that your public health message might increase stigma rather than reduce it?

(See Navon, L. (1996) 'Beyond constructionism and pessimism: Theoretical implications of leprosy destigmatization campaigns in Thailand', *Sociology of Health and Illness,* 18 (2): 258–76.)

(Cont'd)

2   Describing disease

A case of microangiopathic hemolytic anaemia was described by the attending doctor in the following terms:

> 34 y/o female, Hb 8.6 g/dL, MCV 104.5 fL, MCHC 32.8 g/dL, platelets 11,000/uL, WBC 59,000/uL. Patient had a history of disseminated non-small cell carcinoma of the lung. She presented in extremis and expired within a few hours of admission.

- What happened to this patient?
- What is missing from this medicalized version of the last few hours of this person's life?
- Write a 50 word summary of this woman's final contact with hospital services that her non-medically qualified parents would be able to understand and make sense of.

7 ILL BODIES IN SOCIETY

Chapter summary

This chapter describes:

» how Cartesian dualism, which divides the physical from the mental, has informed the medical understanding of disease;

» how dualism facilitates metaphors of bodies as machines, which then permit dissection and reparatory surgical intervention on the body;

» how medical metaphors of bodies as machines overlook embodied suffering;

» how mechanistic, pathological views of diseased bodies inform a reductionist view of disability.

Useful terms for this chapter

cyborgs: refers to bodies which combine synthetic and organic material to enhance human performance, although the medical integration of technology with human bodies generally aims to restore 'normal' function, rather than produce super-human abilities

disability: an impaired person's disability derives from interactions between his (or her) individual capabilities and his (or her) social and physical environment

embodied: a way of considering people, and particularly patients, as a mind and body living within a particular environment in a meaningful way that creates experience

impairment: a sensory, cognitive or physical aspect of an individual's functioning which shows some deficit or deviation from the norm

INTRODUCTION

Illness can be a painful reminder that although human beings exist much of the time in a world of culture and thought, where behaviour is governed by socialized expectations, values and aspirations, our bodies exert the constraints of the material world. The experience of illness (as discussed in the preceding chapter) is shaped by the need to keep the bodily effects of illness hidden or contained, so a sufferer can maintain their social presence. Coping with illness means minimizing the negative effects of symptoms and of treatment so as to reduce their impact on one's social role and identity. While the bodily problems of a disease should not be minimized, it is often their effect on social interaction that sufferers find most upsetting. For instance, a pressing concern for people with a stoma is the need to conceal it and the fear that the noise or odour of a colostomy bag in public can disrupt normal social relations because the possibility of embarrassed, disgusted reactions and of social rejection means that concealing the bag and its contents is very important to people with colostomies, to the extent that minimizing the effect of the medical intervention on social life is a key aspect of post-operative recovery (MacDonald, 1988). People with the trembling, shaking or stiffness in their limbs associated with Parkinson's disease describe disguising their condition in public, for instance by buying clothes with pockets in which to hide hands that jerk involuntarily. Parkinson's sufferers may also avoid the potential shame of dribbling or incoherent speech by never speaking or eating in public, since the loneliness of withdrawing from the social world seems less awful than the humiliation and indignity of breaking social rules of comportment (Nijhof, 1995). The responsibility for ill bodies is often shared with parents, spouses, partners, children and other carers: when suffering or impaired bodies become the responsibility of other people this can add to the stigma of a debilitating condition.

BODIES IN SOCIETY

Socialization from a young age schools us in etiquette about bodily conduct and the expression of emotion, to the extent that most of us are unaware of these implicit rules except when they are broken. We manage our bodies and emotions on a daily basis so as to keep certain activities and feelings out of public view: defecation, micturation, menstruation, sexual activity and intimate washing are each carried out in seclusion and cannot easily be discussed. Belching and farting are to be avoided in public, while feeding, sneezing, sleeping and kissing have to be carefully accomplished to avoid the potential messiness of saliva or the embarrassment of snoring or burping. The uninhibited expression of sorrow, anger and joy through loud crying, laughing and shouting is not encouraged in British society, except in very specific contexts such as sporting events. Young children are, however, not expected to follow all of the rules of comportment: a toddler may wear food on her face, wet her pants and have a tantrum in public. On the other hand, errant behaviour, even in babies, may attract opprobrium aimed at their parents.

The British enjoy a reputation for being calm, cool even, with an aversion to demonstrations of physical affection to the point of inhibition, and while this may be a stereotyped half-truth, we do seem to be easily shocked by what we see as the excesses of others. Letting out a resonant belch may be an appropriate and appreciative comment on a good meal in some places, but polite British society views it as a sign of incontinence; loud, continuous ululating indicates profound grief and respectful mourning elsewhere, but in most of Britain it would be deemed unseemly and attention-seeking; disrobing in public is still shocking in many public settings, even to feed a baby, although it is viewed as normal in other cultures. These rules around the appropriate management of one's body and feelings are subject not only to cultural variation, but also to temporal change. Speaking loudly and insistently to oneself in public has been regarded as a sign of madness in our culture, where rational conversation and argument require an interlocutor. However, the sight of people chatting and laughing without company is now commonplace with the spread of hands-free mobile telephone technology. Does this mean that people who converse with themselves out loud no longer seem mad? At the end of the eighteenth century women wore hats and gloves in public and to be hatless was a sign of distress, poverty, madness, or some other problematic disregard for the conventions of respectable society. Covering one's head is still routine for some religious minorities in Britain, but is no longer the respectable norm for the general population.

EMBODIED ILLNESS

Despite the knowledge that taboos on behavioural and emotional management are culturally and temporally specific, adults who fail to conform to the current rules and who behave in excessively noisy, messy or otherwise uninhibited ways are seen as infantile, mad or uncivilized. Illness is, to some extent, a mitigating circumstance for peculiar bodily practice, but ill bodies that shout, scream, vomit or salivate are nonetheless stigmatized. Ill people are often concerned over whether some physical peculiarity or non-conformity will betray their illness, and chronic conditions are often experienced as an unruliness of the body that requires especially stringent surveillance and management. The vigilance over whether his body might betray his

HIV positive status through a visible Kaposi's sarcoma is described by the following man:

> Every morning when I get up, I look at myself to see if I'm OK, see whether I have anything like Kaposi's [He laughs]. I stick out my tongue to see if I have any fungus. (Carricaburu and Pierret, 1995)

HIV has been described as a modern plague which epitomizes our fears of contagion, both moral and viral, and people's reactions to the symptoms of HIV/AIDS have also epitomized the idea that the bodily processes of illness are a form of deviancy. To maintain a stake in civilized society a person must maintain bodily etiquette and control florid symptoms even in the face of infection or other debility. Failure to do so is regarded as a moral weakness and the ill person may be judged as crazy, puerile and possibly contaminating.

DUALIST THINKING

Viewing illness as a bodily process to which the sufferer must attend and mindfully manage rests upon a view that the mind and body are separate and incommensurable. This division of the somatic from the cerebral is referred to as a Cartesian dualism and can be attributed to René Descartes (1596–1650), a seventeenth century mechanical philosopher. Descartes considered the mind or soul to be insubstantial, immortal and the source of consciousness, and the body to be quantifiable and understandable as a mechanism: he also described animals as automatons. Before Descartes, Galenic models of *pneuma*, which understood the vital spirits and animal spirits as animating bodies from which they were inseparable, had held sway for more than a millennium. Cartesian-informed models of bodies as machines made it conceptually and morally possible to dissect them and to operate upon them.

Breakthroughs in anatomy and physiology made by William Harvey (1578–1657), and building on work by Andreas Vesalius (1514–1564), were based on observation and human dissection and paved the way for the march of reason and science that characterized the eighteenth century's Enlightenment. The ascendancy of reason and observation over belief, superstition, religion and other unseen forces of nature was a prerequisite to the development of modern medicine and current understandings of the body as being open to remedial technological intervention.

In a dualist view, the mind tends to be valued over the merely material body. In his historical account of the development of the idea of civilized society, Norbert Elias (1897–1990) describes the importance given to overcoming the coarseness of the body through the mental control of physical functions, such that delicate, restrained eating, rather than a voracious, abandoned appetite became a sign of cultured refinement and high status (Elias, 1969). In a society where the strength of mind to overcome the weakness of the flesh is valued as a sign of good breeding and strength of character, illness is inevitably a failure of 'mind over matter'. Feeble-mindedness becomes a diagnosable condition with strong moral overtones, and stoicism in the face of suffering is noble high-mindedness. A split between nature – the body with which we are born – and nurture – the higher mental functions and capabilities that we develop – has paralleled the mind–body split and is detectable in the justification of familiar prejudices.

Women have been seen as overly subject to the vagaries of their bodies as a result of menstruation and child-bearing, such that physiology has justified the unfavourable comparison of over-emotional women with the superior masculine norm of logic and reason. Women's bodies have been seen as insufficiently ruled by their minds and inherently unreliable and leaky, even when not ill. Black bodies, as with women's, have been seen as closer to nature, more subject to urges and instincts and less ruled by clear thinking and logical reason, when compared to white men's bodies. The presumption that black bodies are less subject to the restraint of reason has been the justification for a variety of abuses under systems of slavery, indentured labour and apartheid, and continues to under-pin stereotypes of 'hyper-sexualised' black bodies, particularly black male bodies.

Cartesian dualism as a model of how the mind and body work together cannot, of course, be held directly responsible for the sexist and racist ideas that have developed in the post-Enlightenment world. However, these abuses do point to a serious conceptual problem with dualist thought that considers the mind and body to be distinct. Our minds and bodies co-exist in complex inseparability: even the most cerebral or spiritual existence must be embodied and even the most physical of people will also show a dimension that we might call mentality, emotion or a psyche. To the extent that dualist thinking has led to the mind being separated from the body in our day-to-day thinking, the Cartesian model is misleading. Despite our daily experience of the inherent inseparability of the mind and body, the organic body has come to be seen as being part of nature, responsible for base functions and acting as a receptacle for the mind, the site of higher, spiritual and academic processes. In this sense illness is part of nature, part of the degenerative processes to which all organic matter is subject. Through the mind and soul western culture (among others) has emphasized the need to transcend the *merely* corporeal through spiritual, cultured and scientific pursuits. Illness is the enemy of transcendence when it jeopardizes the activities that show we are not bounded by our bodies: when illness prevents reading, reasoning and caring for others, it detracts from our nurtured humanity and threatens to reduce us to our bodies alone. The relationship between corporeal suffering and its transcendence by the mind and spirit is central to the Christian religion, with its iconography of crucifixion as salvation.

As the role of organized Christian religion has waned in daily life, it is medicine rather than the church to which people turn in the face of suffering, and great faith is placed in biomedicine's potential to alleviate pain. Medicine is expected to be able to control the organic processes of our corporeal bodies, to liberate our higher selves from pain and degradation. Medicine's concentration on treating bodies as machines that are dissociated from the mind becomes problematic in this context, since suffering is not merely a somatic matter.

BODIES AS MACHINES

Medicine's mechanical approach to the body has tended to marginalize the subjective, experiential aspects of illness around stigma, identity and social role. The metaphor of the body as machine has been important at a time when increasingly powerful automotives, household appliances and computers have transformed everyday life. Viewing the body as a machine that can be fixed with the appropriate pharmacological, surgical or technological intervention has been paralleled by the increasing use of machines as a therapeutic adjunct to the human body. Big machines to which the body is attached, and which perform specific functions, are those which provide ventilation, dialysis or chelation, or take over several functions such as the 'heart-lung' machine or the incubator for premature babies. Small machines can also be attached to the body, for example to diffuse insulin. Machines can be inserted into the body to regulate the heart-beat (pace-makers), to stimulate specific parts of the brain to ease excessively flexed muscles, or to replace worn-out parts (Gore-tex heart valves). If the body is metaphorically a machine, machines perhaps offer the best form of treatment.

This blending of synthetic parts with human bodies to restore function is not new, in the sense that people have long used mechanical aids such as false teeth, wooden legs, eye glasses and ear trumpets to supplement their failing bodies. However, the utility of machines to prolong functional life and to counteract a variety of the disabling effects of illness has increased dramatically. Medical technology, such as the insulin pump or the cochlear implant, can work with the body's own feedback system to imitate an organic function in a way that outstrips the performance of an insulin injection or ear trumpet. Even more dramatic in terms of curative potential is the developing ability to transplant body parts from other humans (cadaver and live donations), or from animals (pigs' heart valves), or by hybrid or transgenic cells where human cells are cultured on animal vectors for subsequent transplantation.

Such transplant surgery could only have developed at a time when the human body is seen as a machine in which constituent faulty parts can be interchanged. The efficiency of the machines that take over breathing, blood circulation and dialysis, together with the harvesting of cadaver organs, has allowed popular and scientific views to shift as to when a body ceases to qualify as alive. Since the late 1960s death has increasingly been defined by the cessation of brain functioning, usually on the basis of EEG (or electroencephalogram) readings. Termination of brain activity has taken over from other bodily functions such as heart-beat or breathing to define death medically, and in some cases legally. In this respect the brain has taken over from the soul as the site where modern notions of the self reside. Our personhood, our worth as human beings, is lodged in the brain and the higher mental functions. The emphasis on the brain as the site of a person's authentic self means that having someone else's heart or kidney is not thought in our culture to alter one's personhood. This point is underlined by the advances made in face transplants: in November 2005 the first partial face transplant was carried out by two French surgeons to replace the mouth and nose of Isabelle Dinoire who had been injured by her own dog. Despite having part of the face of a cadaver donor, Isabelle Dinoire's identity has not been called into question.

A mechanical view of bodies as machines and of organs as replaceable, such that the recipient's humanity is not jeopardized, has, however, had side effects that were probably not foreseen by the pioneers of transplant surgery. Since technological and moral barriers to organ transplantation have disappeared the global demand for organs for transplantation has outstripped the supply. A black-market trade in organs from live and cadaver organs raises difficult ethical issues, as does the large number of transplants carried out in China using organs from executed prisoners.

Despite the world-wide trade in organs, there is no global consensus that brain death constitutes the death of the person. Research in Japan, where brain death is not the accepted definition of social death, shows how important local culture is to the development of biomedicine. Personhood for the Japanese is said to have a communal rather than an individual basis, and death is a process rather than a single event, so that a person's death is not equated with his or her brain's cessation (Nudeshima, 1991; Lock, 2002). Brain death is widely accepted in the western world, although traces of other types of belief about the relationship between organs, bodies and life still persist. For instance, apparently contradicting a mechanistic view of organs as interchangeable body components, cadaver donors' families may express the hope that the spirit of their dead donor relative lives on by passing on a new lease of life. Similarly, some recipients of donor organs have reported changes to their own identities, which they have then related to what they know of the donor's characteristics.

Medicine's models of the human body have informed popular understanding of the body in far-reaching and long-term ways. The long process of the mapping of the inside of the body through dissection and the localization of disease to specific pathology has had a profound effect on our ways of talking about illness. While everyday descriptions of internal anatomy do not coincide precisely or consistently with the representations in a physiology textbook (Boyle, 1970), everyday thinking does locate illness within specific bodily organs in a biomedical fashion. Thus we tend to talk about having a 'bad stomach', a 'sore throat' or 'weak lungs' rather than choleric temperaments or an ancestral curse.

SUFFERING BODIES

Scientific medicine has moved on from hunting illness in organs and systems of the body to searching it out at cellular and sub-cellular level. With evermore powerful means of viewing structures at the sub-cellular level, the whole person has tended to drop out of view in the practice of medicine. Instead, illness is apprehended through scans, graphs, X-rays and print-outs, while the body is rarely looked at as a whole. Some critics have suggested that this disappearance of the patient's body from clinical, and particularly hospital, medicine is linked to alienation from and dissatisfaction with modern medicine (Helman, 2006). In hospital practice a patient's bodily functioning is routinely described as a series of metrics: numbers describing electrolyte levels, rates of organ function, cell counts, and scan results. These strings of numbers are very disconnected from patients' own experience of their bodies and this disjuncture between the embodied experience of illness and medicine's assessment of it in quantitative terms can be distressing.

Written accounts of the experience of receiving the results of T-cell counts (Moore, 1996), cardiograms (Frank, 1991) and brain scans (Noble, 2005) from a doctor are instructive for the ways that medical diagnosis itself can cause suffering. A doctor's description of a person's own pain and suffering in dispassionate, analytic terms seems to be particularly painful and disorienting when the patient is also a physician (Greene, 1971; Sacks, 1978). The intensity and frustration of being treated by medical professionals who pay little attention to how a disease is embodied are described by Oliver Sacks, a physician who broke his leg and who knew that his expressions of distress and upset would be dismissed as irrational by his physicians (Sacks, 1978). The doctors were proved correct in that Sacks's anguish diminished as his leg healed, but this did nothing to diminish the intensity of that suffering as Sacks recalls it in his book.

IMPAIRED BODIES AND DISABILITY

Many patients object to becoming little more than 'the complex fracture in Bed 13' or 'the dystonic' while in receipt of healthcare. To name a person in terms of their impairment ('the epileptic' or 'the diabetic'), pathology ('the acute glaucoma') or excised organ ('the hysterectomy') is to reduce that person to the features of their body that medicine regards as pathological. Where conditions are highly stigmatized, the use of a person's illness as shorthand for his or her total identity is particularly problematic: a negative attitude towards schizophrenia makes it very hard to be known simply as a person with this disease. Almost all disabilities, of whatever type, will carry some negative connotations and people with visible disabilities regularly have to cope with assumptions being made about their intellect, educational level, sexuality, creativity, and overall capacity to lead an independent and worthwhile life.

A challenge to this unfortunate over-determinism of medicalized disability is to draw a distinction between *impairment* and *disability*, which admits another perspective on understanding the effects of bodies' limitations. If the *impairment* is the organic problem, such as partial sightedness or lack of muscle tone, then the *disability* is the restrictions that the impairment implies. The restriction imposed by a disability depends on the social and physical environment in which the impairment is experienced. For instance, with a suitably equipped flat, a good wheelchair and an environment created with the needs of wheelchair users in mind, someone with limited use of their legs might face almost no restriction on their education, employment, leisure, and family life. Thus an impairment can be diagnosed, but this tells us very little about the associated disability implied until the environment in which it will be experienced is described. One important aspect of the environment is the attitudes that people encounter: if it is assumed that seizures disqualify a child from benefiting from an education, then he will find it very difficult to become financially independent later in life. The main impediment for that child is therefore not the seizures, but the prejudice about and discrimination against people who have seizures.

Medicine has a view of the diseased or disabled body which draws heavily on metaphors of machines which are plumbed and wired and which house organs as component parts. Medicine's success in combating certain diseases using this model, including the now routine practice of organ transplant and the re-routing of blood vessels in heart bypass operations, has entrenched the power of such metaphors to condition our understanding. The pervasive power of medical knowledge has costs for those who experience illness and disability because it has become difficult to assert the subjectivities of suffering in medical settings. The reduction of a person to their disease is inevitably stigmatizing. By viewing impairment as separate from the disability it implies the stigma is challenged since the cause of the disability is seen as social, rather than individual. Some of the challenges to medical and individualist views of disability are considered in the next chapter. The challenge of providing effective clinical medicine which keeps the humanity of patients (among other things) in view is addressed in the final section of this book.

Further reading

Davey, B., Gray, A. and Seale, C. (eds) (2001) *Health and Disease: A Reader* (3rd edn). Buckingham: Open University Press.

Section 2, entitled 'Experiencing health, disease and health care', contains a number of brief accounts offering sociological reflections on various illnesses.

Radley, A. (ed.) (1993) *Worlds of Illness: Biographical and Cultural Perspectives on Health and Disease.* London: Routledge.

A collection of research papers that underline the need to understand the patient's own interpretation of the onset, progression and treatment of illness.

REVISION QUESTIONS

1 Which aspects of social existence are threatened by florid or messy symptoms?

2 What is Cartesian dualism?

3 Describe what becomes marginalized when a mechanistic view of the body is adopted.

4 In what respect can the body be said to have disappeared from medicine?

5 Is a person necessarily disabled by an impairment?

6 What does knowledge of a person's impairment tell us about his or her disability?

EXTENSION QUESTIONS

1 Sham surgery, placebo effect

Coronary artery bypass grafting (CABG) is a very successful procedure in that 90 per cent of patients find themselves pain free when it is over. It has never been subjected to double-blind trial, perhaps because the plumbing model of re-routing blood away from furred-up arteries is so very compelling. Another surgical procedure used to treat angina, known as bilateral internal mammary artery ligation (BIMAL), which follows a similar logic to CABG, has been trialled against sham surgery. Bilateral internal mammary artery ligation involves tying off some arteries in the chest, in an effort to increase the blood flow to the heart. In the double-blind trials, patients allocated to sham surgery received the full operation with the exception of the ligation, under general anaesthetic, with the surgeons ignorant of whether the patient was to receive real or sham intervention until they arrived in theatre. After both types of surgery, patients reported significantly less angina pain. The substantial improvements in the patients whose arteries had not been tied off (so had no consequent alteration to their coronary blood supply), throws into question any simple plumbing analogy as a sufficient explanation of the cause of the improvements in the patients who had received the actual surgery. A patient is quoted as saying 'I figure I'm about 95% better' after his sham operation which had left him with scars on his chest.

(This is an extract from a review of Moerman, D. (2002) *Meaning, Medicine and the 'Placebo Effect'* (Cambridge Studies in Medical Anthropology), Cambridge: Cambridge University Press, that appeared in *Sociology of Health and Illness*, 27 (1): 149–61. doi:10.1111/j.1467-9566. 2005.00436.x)

- Why did the man who received the sham surgery feel better?
- Is it ethical to carry out sham surgery?

Moerman suggests that the patient quoted above felt better after sham surgery because he had an explanation for the cause of his angina pain and of the surgical intervention he believed he had undergone, and together with his scars this gave him a meaningful story through which he could explain his experiences. Moerman maintains that in order to heal, patients need to benefit from 'the psychological and physiological effects of meaning in the treatment of illness'.

Compare Moerman's ideas about making medicine meaningful for patients with ideas around 'biographical disruption' and the remaking of illness narratives discussed in Chapter 6.

- Is treatment that is meaningful to patients and makes sense of their experiences compatible with high quality, innovative, scientific medicine?

2   Disability and medicine

In a *Guardian* article, Dea Birkett writes about being the mother of a wheelchair using daughter and discusses whether disability should be relevant to being accepted to a medical education.

- Is it appropriate that policy on the admission of students with disabilities varies between medical schools?
- Should selection to medical schools discriminate against students with:

  - impaired vision;
  - impaired hearing;
  - dyslexia;
  - epilepsy that is well controlled by medication?

- Could any of these disabilities impede carrying out the duties of the doctor?
  An inability to perform CPR or cardiopulmonary resuscitation has been cited as a reason for wheelchair using students to be barred from the study of medicine. It has been argued that with the rise of multi-professional teams of clinicians, a doctor will rarely be relied upon to undertake CPR, given that paramedics, nurses and others are trained in these techniques.

(Cont'd)

- Should wheelchair users be excluded from:

  - medical school;
  - clinical practice in general;
  - hospital practice?

(See Birkett, D. (2003) 'Ready, willing and disabled', *The Guardian*, 7 January, available at: http://www.guardian.co.uk/health/story/0,3605,870003,00.html)

 *THE PROCESS OF
DISABILITY*

Chapter summary

This chapter describes:

» how the onset of impairment during adult life has different implications for identity compared with the effects of congenital disorders;

» how a debilitating impairment does not necessarily lead to the development of an identity as a disabled person;

» how the social model of disability dissociates an individual's bodily impairment from the disabling effects of social, economic and attitudinal barriers to participation;

» how a cultural model denies that an atypical body is necessarily impaired and considers positive aspects of difference;

» how cultural and social models challenge individualist views of disability but overlook the role of stigma and pain and the uncertainty and instability of progressive disorders;

» how designing services that offer people with disability the same quality of care as those without disability is an important principle of equity for the NHS.

Useful terms for this chapter

American Sign Language: a distinct language with its own grammar and syntax, unrelated to spoken languages and different from the sign languages of other Anglophone countries such as British sign language

Asperger syndrome: the main diagnosis associated with autism spectrum disorders, a milder version of autism sharing some features of repetitive or restricted behaviour and impaired social interaction or communication

'Aspies': term claimed by people with Asperger syndrome and associated with an assertion of rights for people with autism

autism: a disorder of the brain's development associated with impaired communication and social interaction and with restricted, repetitive behaviour, often noticeable in children under two years old and thought to be heritable

cultural model of disability: views deafness and the culture associated with signing communities as different from, but equal with, hearing people and their culture

'neuro-diverse': a positive reference adopted by people with neurological conditions such as Asperger syndrome and autism to distinguish themselves from 'neuro-typical' or 'normal' people

social model of disability: the limitations imposed by the physical and social environment, rather than by a body's impairment, are seen to disable people

INTRODUCTION

In Chapter 7 the distinction was drawn between *impairment*, that is the bodily feature that represents a deficit in terms of sensory perception, mobility or physiological process, and *disability*, which is the restrictions that the impairment effects in terms of a person's activity or functional ability. The distinction between impairment and disability has been central to what is known as the social model of disability which emphasizes how social, financial, physical and attitudinal barriers make people disabled, rather than their individual bodily impairment. This model has been used by disability activist groups who, from the 1970s onwards, have lobbied for the needs of people with disabilities to inform the provision of statutory services and for their right to be protected by legislation. In common with civil rights campaigns to gain recognition for women, for gay people, or for black people, disability activists employ strategies that emphasize the collective interests of 'people with disability' and promote their self-determination. The social model of disability focuses on the discrimination experienced by those with visible disabilities and de-emphasizes individual bodies' pathology. Medical treatment of disability, focusing on cures for individuals' problems rather than the adaptation of the environment to accommodate diverse needs, reinforces an individualist view and works against the social model.

Medical progress has had contradictory effects on the genesis of disability, with immunization programmes reducing acquired impairment due to infections such as polio and improvements to the treatment of previously debilitating and fatal diseases such as breast cancer and HIV/AIDS, making them chronic conditions with which people can live. The relationship between chronic illness, impairment and disability is not straightforward, with factors such as the pain associated with a condition and its progression or stability, together with the age and manner at which it is acquired, all influential in the extent to which a person feels and identifies as disabled. It has been politically important to emphasize the shared experience of discrimination among people with disability, yet other aspects of the experience of disability are so varied as to render any such generalization largely meaningless. For instance, some deaf users of sign language reject both the idea that they are disabled and therefore the need for medical intervention to restore or induce hearing, whereas campaigning groups associated with conditions such as spinal injury or multiple sclerosis are highly committed to the search for a medical cure, while the suffering associated with conditions such as advanced motor neurone disease has led some campaigners to demand the right to euthanasia. Such variation is explicable in terms of embodied aspects of conditions which restrict both daily activities and the usual physiological functions, which are both painful and progressive. Furthermore some conditions are highly stigmatized (see Chapter 6), such that people experience a compulsion to hide their impairment from public view.

DISABILITY AND THE LIFE COURSE

Congenital disability refers to developmental problems linked with environmental or genetic causes *in utero*. The rigours of the birth process can bring about the impairment of developmentally normal babies who have suffered oxygen deficit or some other birth trauma. Enormous advances in the medical management of infectious diseases and also of pregnancy and birth (see Box 1.6, Chapter 1, p. 32) have reduced the chances of babies incurring damage before, during and after birth (perinatally), but these advances have in addition made possible the survival of babies born up to 16 weeks early and this prematurity of babies' lungs and eyes at birth can lead to life-long impairment. The long-term study of the development of premature babies is ongoing since the techniques that have enhanced their survival are still relatively new.

The emergence of developmental disorders over the first few years of life is monitored by health checks administered by the health visiting service. If a child has impaired hearing, sight or mobility, there are enormous benefits associated with the earliest possible detection to permit remedial action to support that child's continuing development. While services for children with disabilities command neither big budgets nor high status, there is still this widespread recognition of the need to intervene as early as possible in a child's life. Relatively simple, low-tech interventions, such as providing a child with cerebral palsy with a suitable device to support them sitting upright, can make a considerable difference to a child's ability to learn how to interact and communicate. The recognition that almost every child, regardless of the severity of their impairment, can develop in some measure is an important change in both the medical and the wider culture since the inception of the NHS. Two generations ago it was not unusual for mothers to be advised that their disabled newborns' future was hopeless and, for instance, as recently as the 1960s, babies born with Down's syndrome (referred to as Down syndrome in the USA) were not fed and allowed to die.

For those who have had a stable disability since birth or young childhood, and have received appropriate support, the possibility of establishing an independent life, albeit constrained in terms of mobility or sensory ability or pain, should be good. When a condition is unstable, progressive and/or associated with uncontrollably painful symptoms, then adaptation to the expectations of mainstream daily life becomes more uncertain.

Disability can, of course, arise at any point through the life course as a result of accidental or deliberately inflicted trauma. When people acquire an impairment having already led a 'normal' life there will be another set of challenges in adjusting to the changes to their bodies and to others' attitudes to them, which may be further compounded by the issue of stigma. Whether incurred at birth or later in life and whether or not its cause was avoidable, there is a tendency to regard the onset of impairment as a tragedy for the individual involved and his or her family. Such a blanket presumption of tragedy is unhelpful, given that people with a variety of abilities should have the same chances of a productive, useful, happy life as people without impairments, provided that appropriate support is available. Medicine's approach to disability as an individual somatic problem, and its particular interest in conditions which are subject to medical intervention, have contributed to the general tendency to overlook the social and economic means through which people with an impairment are systematically excluded from mainstream participation. The focus on curing disability has damaged the disability rights agenda, according to some activists. Christopher Reeve (1952–2004), an American actor best known for playing Superman in the feature films of the late 1970s and 1980s who suffered a spinal injury in 1995, was a controversial figure in disability rights organizations, given his high profile advocacy for a medical cure. Up until the time of his death, Reeve actively campaigned for embryo stem cell research and expressed the belief that his own spinal cord injury would eventually be cured. His determination to recover from his injury was portrayed as heroic in the mainstream media, with the pathos of his plight highlighted in contrast to his screen credits playing a man with superhuman powers.

This sense of individualized tragedy perhaps lessens when the onset of disability occurs at an older age: to experience impaired sight, hearing or mobility, or to suffer the onset of a metabolic disorder is regarded as an ordinary aspect of aging. Increased life expectancy and the low fertility rates characterizing western populations have resulted in a demographic aging of the population, as described in Chapter 1. Average life expectancy continues to increase in Britain, for men and for women, as an ever-greater proportion of the population survives into old and very old age. The process of aging has been described as 'a progressive loss of adaptability of an individual organism as time passes' (Grimley Evans, 2001: 406), implying that aging amounts to a rise in the risk of both mortality and morbidity. The likelihood of living with a disability is related to advancing age and, not surprisingly, there are significant increases in levels of disability in populations over the age of 75 years. In some respects disability can be understood as an expected part of the life course, as a sign that a natural lifespan is being approached. However, this common-sense and entrenched association between disability and old age has meant that old people have not always received a good enough service for their chronic illness or rehabilitation. Informal rationing, whereby older people are given lower priority for medical interventions such as cardiac surgery than younger people (Bowling, 1999), is based on the assumption that a young body is more worthy of resources than an older body.

CHRONIC ILLNESS, IMPAIRMENT AND DISABILITY

How can the links between acute and chronic illness, their associated impairments whether temporary or longstanding, and the state of disability be understood? The relationship between disease, impairment and disability is complex and dynamic and also influenced by various factors. Medicine's express aim is, of course, to reduce the morbidity and resultant impairment associated with disease and trauma and, in some cases, its efforts have been highly successful, for example through surgical intervention (hip and knee replacement operations have dramatically reduced impairment through worn joints), cure (childhood leukaemia has become a curable condition) and prevention (immunization against smallpox, polio and measles). A child born today with Tay Sachs disease, an autosomal recessively inherited disorder, is unlikely to live long enough to attend primary school and will experience debilitating symptoms; in the 1950s, a diagnosis of cystic fibrosis held a similarly grim prospect. Nowadays, with improvements in anti-bacterial, anti-inflammatory and airway-clearing therapy, together with mucus-thinners and pancreatic enzyme supplements, people with cystic fibrosis can suffer fewer debilitating symptoms and are routinely surviving into their thirties (and further longevity is predicted), leading lives with the ordinary trappings of education, employment and marriage. Improvements in medical therapy (in combination with changes in environment and lifestyle) mean that the relationship between disease and disability is not fixed such that disease does not necessarily lead to impairment. Diseases such as multiple sclerosis and cystic fibrosis, which in the past were assumed to be universally severe in their effects, have been found to have a variety of forms, ranging from mild to severe, such that predicting prognosis from a diagnosis is less clear-cut than has sometimes been assumed. Leaving aside the vagaries of severity of symptom and medicine's effectiveness in treatment, there is also variation at an individual level whereby a longstanding symptom may or may not become an impairment which then may (or may not) be experienced as a disability.

In Chapter 6 we encountered the idea of biographical disruption, which happens when a person's everyday expectations of their life as a healthy individual are challenged by the experience of illness. The process whereby people re-formulate the narrative of their lives is, of course, dependent on the extent to which highly debilitating symptoms are experienced and on the degree of support available and the possibilities for re-adjustment that a person's life holds. An illness narrative encapsulates the meaning that an individual attributes to the experience of symptoms, and while related to a medical diagnosis and prognosis, this differs in that a narrative covers the meaning and significance of diagnosis and prognosis for a person in a particular familial, social and economic environment. Thus one person diagnosed with, for instance, emphysema, may see this as a bleak predicament and a terminal condition, while another person may, for whatever reason, place less emphasis on the diagnosis and see the emphysema as of minor significance in determining the quality of their day-to-day life. This relationship between a person's identity and the nature of their disease or condition is almost impossible to predict or read from the outside, so one person with a chronic disease such as diabetes mellitus will see themselves as disabled, while another might describe themselves as suffering from an illness and another person might view themselves as in good health, albeit needing to inject insulin.

The complexity of the relationship between the experience of impairment, treatment and support with identity development has been studied by researchers in an attempt to discern any patterns of behaviour. Three elements of the process of a patient responding to chronic illness have been described: coping, strategy and style (Bury, 1991). *Coping* involves the development of a sense of self worth and coming to terms with an altered bodily state and situation. *Strategy* refers to the ways that people manage the chronic condition itself and its impact on their life and their life chances, including getting access to various resources and balancing their need for independence against the benefits of being actively supported by others. The *style* of life adopted by someone who has a chronic illness involves decisions about the extent to which a condition is disclosed in various social settings. Some people will avoid disclosing their condition to anyone, restricting their activities accordingly to allow for this non-disclosure. For some, non-disclosure of a disease is only possible by withdrawing from public life altogether. In other cases, the only realistic option for 'adaptation' may be withdrawal from the public world of work and social interaction, at least over the short term.

For instance, if a person has frequent and severe seizures that cannot be controlled by medication, a choice between risking injury while out and about or remaining in a safe, contained space may make a person housebound. Others will prefer to 'come out' as a person with an impairment in order to integrate an altered identity into their interactions with others in public (Bury, 1991). The extent to which a person can reveal their impairment in public will be influenced by the extent to which a condition is stigmatized: a person with Karposi's sarcoma that is associated with AIDS and difficult to disguise may feel himself to be faced with no alternative but to withdraw from society. If a society has familiarity with particular symptoms the stigma may be lessened, but not necessarily.

For clinicians attending patients in the process of coping with the consequences of trauma or disease, the challenges are considerable. The dimensions that influence a person's coping strategy and style of life tend to emerge gradually, in terms of both the pain and speed of progression of the condition and the support available from their family, friends and colleagues. Clinicians tend to describe the worst case scenario to patients regarding the development of a condition, sometimes accompanied by the risks of various outcomes developing (see Chapter 5). Thus, with the arrival of a condition that is potentially disabling, people often have to cope not only with the difficulties of a changed bodily state, but also with imagining how much worse it could become.

Impairment consequent upon a chronic condition or a trauma is very likely to have some disabling effect on a sufferer, even if its exact nature takes time to emerge. The social model of disability dissociates the assumption that an individual's impairment automatically leads to that person becoming or being disabled, instead seeking to cast disability as a social problem.

THE SOCIAL MODEL OF DISABILITY

Rather than viewing disability as an unfortunate twist of fate resulting from an accidental trauma or bodily abnormality which medicine cannot fix, the social model of disability instead focuses on the barriers that the surroundings may present to people's participation in society. Rather than conceptualizing individual bodies as having deviated from the norm, thereby preventing participation, the social model considers how society disables people through discriminatory attitudes and oppressive ideas. People's inability to participate in social or economic activities is less determined by their own bodies' particular abilities than by physical, attitudinal, economic and social barriers that could, at least in theory, be removed or modified.

The social model of disability developed through activism and has been used and extended through academic research and policy work (Oliver, 1996;

Shakespeare, 2006). The social model has been useful in politicizing disability rights and supplying a single slogan for campaigning, lobbying and analysis. The considerable influence of the model can be seen around us, with legislation requiring that new buildings should be accessible, that pavements should have access ramps and that pedestrian crossings should be marked with bumpy paving for the visually impaired. Given the complexity of the relationship between illness, impairment, and the constraints a condition places on an individual's activities and on his or her identity, the social model's relative simplicity is attractive. But such simplicity, which is politically useful, also means that the model does not apply to the range of conditions that count as 'disability'. Arguably the social model of disability only really explains the situation of people with stable sensory and/or mobility impairments who are not in pain. Shakespeare (2006) comments that the achondroplasia (short stature) that he inherited from his father was not disabling, in the sense that it did not limit his activities. However, when he developed back pain as an adult he found himself highly impaired in a way that the social model of disability could not explain.

If by 'disability' we refer to the full range of people who have a serious mental, physical or sensory impairment, then there are many groups for whom modification of the environment does not offer any sort of solution to their difficulties. For instance, people with learning difficulties do not necessarily have trouble in negotiating the physical aspects of their environment, whereas interpreting text and understanding speech may be more problematic. Shakespeare (2006) points here to the role of information technology in facilitating the participation of a 'neuro-diverse' community in disability rights politics. People on the autism spectrum who experience everyday communication with others as threatening or baffling do not have the disabling effects of their condition eliminated through the alteration of their physical environment. Rather, it has been the ease of access to cyber space that has facilitated communication for those with good cognitive abilities. Another problem with the social model of disability is that certain categories of disability may require conflicting modifications; people with reduced vision could benefit from bright indoor lighting, and open-plan offices without doorways are easier to negotiate for wheel-chair users, but unexpected noises and fluorescent lighting can be irritating or painful for people on the autism spectrum.

The social model of disability has no place for the embodied aspects of disability (see Chapter 7), particularly pain and other forms of physical suffering: no amount of modifying the environment will reduce the severely painful symptoms associated with, for instance, irritable bowel syndrome, migraine, or rheumatoid arthritis. Despite its proven worth as a unifying scheme for disability rights politics, the social model has, according to some, outlived its usefulness (Shakespeare, 2006). What is needed now is an approach that allows an appreciation of the diversity of impairment and of the breadth of experience that is encompassed under the term 'disability'.

THE CULTURAL MODEL OF 'DISABILITY'

For some deaf people, the social model of disability, with its insistence on distinguishing the impairment from its disabling effects, is inappropriate to describe their condition. The deaf community, particularly those people who use American Sign Language, compare being deaf with being a member of a linguistic and cultural minority; deafness is 'no more a disability than being Japanese would be' (Allen, 2007). Deaf activists argue that deafness is not a disability and therefore object to the term 'hearing-impaired', maintaining that the culture and language associated with being a user of sign language are in every sense equivalent to those of the mainstream, hearing world. Membership of the deaf community does not exclude people who have a full sensitivity to sound, and hearing children of deaf adults who are native users of sign language and identify with deaf culture may be considered 'deaf' in the cultural sense. Children who can hear but who have grown up with deaf parents and have been immersed in deaf culture may need speech therapy as they reach adulthood, to familiarize them with spoken language. Deaf communities may welcome the birth of a deaf child, rather than regret that she or he cannot hear. In a much-publicized case in 2002, a deaf lesbian couple in the USA sought sperm from a congenitally deaf donor so as to bring up deaf children in the same cultural and linguistic tradition as themselves. In 2008, a British heterosexual couple speculated that they might wish to use IVF and select an embryo so as to give birth to a deaf child who would share the same characteristics as themselves and their existing child.

A strong identification with deaf culture and language is often associated with an opposition to teaching deaf children to speak and lip read and to medical cures for deafness, in particular, surgically implanted electronic cochlear hearing devices. For people who have been born deaf, who are native sign-language users, and who have been educated at a time when lip reading, speech therapy and adaptation to the auditory world were emphasized, cochlear implants can represent a denigration of deaf culture.

The majority of deaf children are born to hearing parents. While many hearing parents will learn sign language, they are likely to want their children to participate in the hearing world, too, for instance, by learning to speak and perhaps by having a cochlear implant. Cochlear implants do not cure deafness, but offer a prosthetic substitute for hearing. Deaf activism has grown out of the tradition of civil rights which is based on principles of self-determination and autonomy. Children's interests are often assumed to be parents' main concern, but deaf activists have accused hearing parents of failing to understand and promote their deaf children's welfare. The assertion that deafness is not an impairment has led to conflict between deaf activists and the hearing parents of deaf children, with activists pointing out that cochlear implants carry all the usual risks of major surgery and do not work for everyone, especially not for those who have been profoundly deaf from birth and so have no experience of interpreting sound. Furthermore, such implants can cause any residual hearing ability to be lost.

Cochlear implants are expensive, but despite the cost since 2000 the surgery has become increasingly routine, and deaf children with implants have been successfully educated in both oral and sign language in tandem. Opposition to implants persists in the deaf community, particularly in Gallaudet, a US university for the education of the deaf and hard-of-hearing in Washington, DC, where the issues of deaf culture are fiercely debated. As the technology comes to be offered as a routine response to congenital deafness, deaf children of hearing parents will grow up learning how to interpret sound, as transmitted through their cochlear implants from a young age, where previously their acquisition of language was often delayed through a lack of good sign and lip-reading teaching.

This opposition to cochlear implants, on the grounds that an invasive medical procedure is unnecessary and unwanted by deaf people who do not feel themselves to be impaired, offers an interesting challenge to a routine medical understanding of disability. The outright rejection of the medical cure for deafness by some people who do not hear raises the question of whether a cultural model of disability applies to any other conditions. For a fluent user of sign language, who lives in a community of deaf people in a safe environment, there is little disadvantage to not hearing. Perhaps the only potential difficulty is a deaf person's inability to detect the warning sounds of an immediate risk, such as a car approaching at speed, a hostile attack, or a falling object. However, this drawback of deafness probably ranks with the minor disadvantages that many people experience, such as being short-sighted or prone to hayfever, which are not usually classified as disabilities. There are other impairments that are similarly minor in their effects, for instance, having one limb weakened, a reduced lung capacity, being blind in one eye, or having a tendency to experience migraine, the effects of which can be accommodated without great impact on a person's quality of life. In bureaucratic terms such minor disabilities would not be debilitating enough to attract disability benefits. The minor nature of such problems means that a cultural identity is unlikely to develop around them, since they do not greatly differentiate a person's experience of the world from other people's. The cultural model of deafness is in part sustainable, because in specific circumstances being deaf does not present particular disadvantage or social isolation especially where communication independent of sound is developed. Are there other circumstances where the effects of a serious impairment can become minor as a result of cultural or social developments?

There are some signs that the 'neuro-diverse' community is increasingly representing itself as different from, but not inferior to, the 'neuro-typical' mainstream, thereby denying that autism or Asperger syndrome is necessarily constitutive of a disability or even an impairment. There has been public interest in the experience of people with autism since the late 1980s, with the award-winning film *Rainman* (1988) in which Dustin Hoffman played a fictitious autistic man and Tom Cruise his non-autistic brother. Oliver Sacks wrote a non-fictional account of Temple Grandin, an expert on livestock behaviour at Colorado State University, in his 1995 book *An Anthropologist from Mars*. The title of Sacks's book was Grandin's description of how she felt as an autist around 'neuro-typical' people. Public interest has persisted with Mark Haddon's best-selling novel *The Curious Incident of the Dog in the Night-time* (2003) which is told from the point of view of an adolescent with Asperger syndrome. Oliver Sacks, Mark Haddon and the scriptwriter for *Rainman* did not have the condition themselves, but all had worked with people who had autism or other neurological disorders.

People with autism have also met with success when they have written their own accounts of their world-view. Dawn Prince-Hughes (2004) writes lucidly and sympathetically about her experience of Asperger syndrome and how her difficulties interpreting verbal and physical interactions have resulted in impeded social communication. Her experience of social isolation and attempts to overcome it give Prince-Hughes a unique voice in her academic as well as her literary writing. Daniel Tammet (2007), like Prince-Hughes, has autistic traits, in his case combined with extraordinary abilities in mathematics and language and, also like Prince-Hughes, has published a successful account of his world-view. Tammet describes his need for routine and control, the comfort he finds in patterns of numbers, and the excitement he gets from learning a new language or performing a complex mathematical procedure. He relates his extraordinary mathematical abilities to his synaesthesia, whereby numbers resonate with a particular colour. Tammet describes his daily domestic and work life, which he shares with a partner, and the underlying message of his book is that his life is fulfilling: he lives and works independently, within his own limits, and in a loving partnership. These two authors, like growing numbers of others, are asserting the validity of their world-view, in the knowledge that it is contrary to how most people interpret and make sense of daily life.

The networking possibilities of communication in cyber space, which avoid the difficulties of interpreting social interactions, make it possible for a neuro-diverse community to assert the validity of their way of seeing the world. 'I don't see autism as a disability, I see it as another human variation', said Gareth Nelson who has Asperger syndrome and refers to himself as an 'Aspie' (Saner, 2007). The Autism Rights movement asserts the positive aspects of Asperger syndrome, as illustrated by the suggestion that highly gifted individuals such as Albert Einstein may have fulfilled the criteria of a high functioning autist. With the recent surge in research funding for a cure for autism, 'Aspies' object that their condition does not require a cure, merely an adjustment of current attitudes. Concern is expressed by 'Aspies' that research into the genetics of autism will result in the development of ante-natal screening and the selective termination of foetuses with markers for autism. Carers for autists who cannot live independently due to the severity of their intellectual disability point out that Temple Grandin, Albert Einstein and Daniel Tammet are unusual people in terms of their abilities and that only a few autists have special facilities or are academically talented. A larger (albeit disputed) proportion of people with autism have such severe difficulties communicating that their integration into any community, whether neuro-diverse or neuro-typical, is very hard to envisage.

The fear of selective abortion of foetuses with markers for impairment also seems entirely justified, given that approximately 80 per cent of pregnancies which test positive for Down's syndrome are currently terminated. An effect of the reduction of levels of disability in the community at large is that many people have no first-hand experience of people with congenital impairments. One response to this lack of knowledge has been to establish a website (http://www.antenataltesting.info/default.html), aimed at women undergoing ante-natal screening who receive the news that their pregnancy is affected by a genetic condition. The website includes profiles of people at various ages living with conditions which, when detected ante-natally, can result in the decision to terminate a pregnancy, including cystic fibrosis, Turner's, Down's and Klinefelter's syndrome. The information on this website, while not anti-abortion, attempts to balance out the implicit assumption that a pregnancy affected by a potentially disabling condition should be aborted.

SPECIAL OR UNIVERSAL NEEDS?

A political view of disability which emphasizes the social rather than the individual origin of the difficulties that people face offers a strong challenge to a medical approach which focuses on fixing and normalizing disabled bodies. The social model of disability challenges us to distinguish between individually impaired bodies and the shared social attitudes that discriminate against people with a disability. The cultural model of deafness views people who don't hear as a community defined by language rather than impairment, and is similar to the view of 'Aspies' as a group defined by the positive aspects of the autism spectrum. Social and cultural models are important for challenging our assumptions about disability, since they show that conditions which medicine assesses to be highly impairing are not necessarily experienced as such by the affected individuals. The problem with the social and cultural models is that they do not explain the painful and debilitating embodied aspects of conditions, nor do they address variations in the experience of stigma. The cultural model of disability is applicable only in special circumstances where a form of communication, such as sign language or internet-based discussion, overcomes the effects of the impairment.

As a society we need to focus on the universal needs of users of the NHS, rather than seeking to diagnose the special needs of minorities. Everyone needs access to good quality healthcare, well integrated with other social and educational services and characterized by skilful, patient-centred communication. Evidence that people with disabilities are routinely less likely to receive such a service is a reflection on the mainstream assumptions of the service providers. As the population ages, we can all expect to live some portion of our lives with significant impairments, so it is in the majority of the population's interest to recognize the universality, rather than the particularity, of the needs of people with disabilities.

Further reading

Shakespeare, T.W. (2006) *Disability Rights and Wrongs*. London: Routledge.

An assessment of the changing meaning of disability in the contexts of health and social care and more widely in British culture.

REVISION QUESTIONS

1 Explain the difference between an impairment and a disability.

2 How are chronic illness, impairment and disability related to one another?

3 How does the social model of disability differ from an individualized view of bodily deficit?

4 What is meant by the 'cultural model of disability'?

5 What evidence do people with autism draw on to deny that they are disabled?

EXTENSION QUESTIONS

- Would a pregnant woman's decision to abort a foetus on the grounds of suspected deafness (for instance, due to a German measles infection) be acceptable in your view?

    - Would your response be different if the grounds for termination was suspected blindness?

    - Or mental disability?

- Look at the website of the 'Little People of America' (http://www.lpaonline.org/)

    - Do you consider that short stature or dwarfism constitutes a disability?

(Cont'd)

- Is it ethical for a parent to consent to his or her profoundly deaf child having a cochlear implant?

  - Does it make any difference to the ethics of the parental consent if the parent is hearing or deaf?

- 'I don't want to get to be an old man and know that there will be no more people like me being born', says Gareth Nelson (Saner, 2007) to explain his objection to the possibility of the termination of pregnancies on the grounds of autism.

  - How should the views of people with disabilities be represented in the formulation of ethical clinical practice?

PART 3

Getting healthcare

9 DOCTOR–PATIENT RELATIONSHIPS

Chapter summary

This chapter describes:

» how much illness provokes help-seeking from non-medical informal quarters;

» how doctors and patients frequently disagree over the appropriate process for a medical consultation;

» how the nature of the relationship between doctor and patient has been analysed as

- unequal but socially functional;
- inherently conflictual;
- based on negotiation;
- becoming more consumerist in nature;

» how doctors maintain control of consultations in terms of how the discussion is conducted and recorded in medical notes.

Useful terms for this chapter

internetitis: derogatory term to describe the condition of patients who bring information garnered from internet sites, as well as their symptoms, to medical consultations

medical dominance: the authority and autonomy of medicine that permit its domination of other occupations involved with healthcare and confer an advantage over patients and an expertise that extends beyond the institution of medicine

therapeutic network: the totality of a person's relationships that maintain his or her health and wellbeing, including means of accessing medical expertise and the therapeutic aid of friends, family, colleagues and neighbours

INTRODUCTION

Most people, most of the time, do not visit a doctor with the onset of symptoms; self-medication and seeking informal advice or support are more usual first responses. The 'therapeutic network' is a term used for the way that people get advice and help with illness from family, friends and colleagues, self-help groups, spiritual and religious healers and alternative healing systems. Feminist work has described how women bear the burden of maintaining these networks and offering informal, non-professional care through their roles as mothers, wives, girlfriends, daughters, and so on. Therapeutic networks are not only a first port of call for those experiencing symptoms, but are part of the ongoing, everyday process of maintaining health within which, once sought, medical advice and treatment are discussed, criticized, compared and weighed up.

SELF-CARE

Responsible self-care for minor symptoms is promoted by public health campaigns that encourage appropriate responses to indications of illness. For instance, around 1942 the Ministry of Health advised the population that 'Coughs and Sneezes Spread Diseases' (poster held in Imperial War Museum) and that a clean handkerchief should be used to prevent the spread of illness. Nowadays advice is available from the Department of Health on the appropriate course of action following the contraction of flu: 'Stay at home and rest; take plenty of non-alcoholic drinks to replace the fluid loss from sweating; eat what you can' (Department of Health, 2005). Looking after one's self without recourse to medical services is a crucial aspect of a publicly funded health system which struggles to cope with the level of demand for its services. However, it is not just minor symptoms which people tend to keep to themselves: health diaries show that, for instance, only one in 14 occurrences of chest pain prompted a visit to the doctor (Banks et al., 1975). A reluctance to 'bother the doctor' or to acknowledge the implications of serious symptoms means that people suffer in silence when medical intervention could be effective. Stoicism is highly valued among men and other groups who esteem the ability to withstand suffering with dignity. But experiencing symptoms without seeking healthcare is not confined to the super-stoics: morbidity surveys show that a high proportion of the general population tolerates serious symptoms without necessarily defining themselves as ill or seeking professional help. This phenomenon is sometimes called the symptom iceberg (Hannay, 1979) and acknowledges that despite a primary care network, NHS Direct (a 24-hour, nurse-led telephone helpline, launched in 1998 in England and Wales), NHS24 (in Scotland), and a growing number of walk-in clinics where no appointment is needed, health professionals will probably encounter only a minority of the treatable illness experienced in the whole population.

APPROPRIATE CONSULTATION

Alongside the evidence of under-consultation for some serious symptoms, clinicians consider that patients frequently bring inappropriate symptoms for consultation. GPs estimate that between one- and two-thirds of their consultations are inappropriate, either because the underlying problems are caused by poverty, stress at work or relationship problems and so cannot be addressed medically, or because the problems are too trivial to require medical expertise (Cartwright and Anderson, 1981). Similarly, in emergency medicine, hospital professionals describe more than half of their clients as 'normal rubbish', saying 'It's a thankless task seeing all the rubbish, as we call it, coming through' (Jeffery, 1979). Worried mothers bringing their children for assessment are often seen as using the health service inappropriately, as described by the following doctor: 'Anxious mothers, I sometimes think they haven't got the sense they were born with' (Roberts, 1992).

The friction between a mother trying to persuade a doctor to take her child's symptoms seriously ought to be the exception rather than the rule, given that, for the most part, both the parent and the health professional should have the child's best health interests at heart. Arguably, parents and health professionals operate with similar reasoning in deciding how to treat children's symptoms: parents often err on the side of caution with young children's symptoms, as do health professionals when faced with medical uncertainty, especially in the very young. However, when permitted to elaborate the background reasons for bringing a child into hospital parents' actions are often appropriate in medical terms. Where there is tension between doctor and parent, research suggests that it is due to the professional's inattention to the carer's views and a failure to understand their predicament (Roberts, 1992). Although the disgruntled patient who resorts to the official complaints procedure is still relatively rare, where it occurs the largest proportion of complaints is made about poor communication style and the unhelpful attitude of the doctor rather than any problems with treatment, tests or diagnoses (Mulcahy, 2003). This suggests that even patients who complain will tend to comply with doctors' judgement about medical matters, but will object to the manner in which they are treated.

From a doctor's point of view, how would a model patient behave? Ideally a patient should use his judgement about when it is appropriate to consult a doctor, but once the consultation is under way he should defer to both the doctor's judgement and interpretations about the meaning and significance of the illness (Bloor and Horobin, 1975). To put this another way, patients must be informed enough to know when to present their symptoms for medical attention, but should not present their own analyses of the meanings of these symptoms, since this oversteps their expertise. Patients who offer their own diagnoses risk being labelled as worriers or hypochondriacs, or being diagnosed as suffering from 'internetitis'.

COMPLIANCE, CO-OPERATION, CONFLICT

When the doctor–patient relationship emerged as a topic of research and policy interest in the 1950s, the hierarchical organization of social relations was more widely accepted than now and professionals were routinely shown greater deference. Deference shown to a doctor during a consultation, does not, of course, amount to an unquestioning acceptance of his or her advice. From the 1960s, as the practice of medicine shifted towards a scientifically informed evidence-based enterprise, concern about the degree to which patients complied with their doctors' orders became a focus of research. The noted tendency for patients to follow their physicians' advice, treatments and medications in a selective, experimental or idiosyncratic fashion was not a new phenomenon, but jarred with the faith that scientific medicine placed in the stability of disease and the unequivocal nature of the evidence base.

The uptake of prescribed medicine is one aspect of a patient's response to a doctor's orders that is fairly easily monitored and measured. Systematic comparisons of prescriptions issued by doctors with those issued by pharmacists have suggested that about 7 per cent of prescriptions written are never taken up by patients. But of course, obtaining medication does not necessarily mean that patients are using it according to the doctor's orders. Research using techniques such as urine testing to monitor patient compliance suggests that between one-half and one-third of patients do not take all the medication according to the terms of the prescription (Stimson, 1974). Anecdotes from general practice suggest that a proportion of people consult doctors on other people's behalf (by describing, for instance, their partner's symptoms) in order to obtain a prescription by proxy. The failure of patients to seek medical advice appropriately and to abide by that advice once it is obtained is seen as a lack in the public's understanding which should be addressed by education campaigns, for instance urging the public to use antibiotics appropriately (Department of Health, 2006). Professionals' condemnation of 'over-consulting' and 'non-compliant' patients who use health services inappropriately expresses their frustration that patients do not understand the rules of engagement. When a patient behaves in an apparently irrational way that impedes medical recovery, it may be that benefiting his own health is less compelling than a competing goal, such as autonomy and freedom from the constrictions of a demanding therapeutic regime.

Figure 9.1 Patients are viewed as taking up prescriptions without proper consideration: a problem that is tackled through public information campaigns exhorting people to use medicines properly, as advised by professionals

Patient non-compliance has been researched as part of a wider interest in deviance against the social order and the doctor–patient relationship has been idealized as a functional albeit unequal relationship. The inequality between the authoritative doctor who gave expert, unbiased advice and the passive receipt of care by the acquiescent patient was understood to be socially functional (Parsons, 1951). Talcott Parsons (1902–1979) formulated the view that the contract between doctor and patient was a means of regulating illness and preventing self-induced illness, malingering and psychosomatics. The impartial nature of the doctor's application of knowledge and expertise in the patient's best interests compensates for the patient's powerlessness in the asymmetrical relationship with the professional. In return for giving up autonomy, the patient is reassured of the doctor's beneficent intent. Parsons viewed the unequal but reciprocally functional roles played by doctor and patient as essentially functional and consensual, in that patients voluntarily enter into an asymmetric relationship because they need the services of a doctor.

Another approach to understanding the relationship sees doctors' and patients' interests as inevitably in conflict (Freidson, 1970). Doctors are seeking to treat patients according to the best-practice protocol, and to balance this with the interests of all the other patients who have a call on their time and the other medical resources at their disposal. Meanwhile, patients are likely to see the significance of their illness from their own point of view, and so will want urgent care, tailored to their personal needs. In this model doctors and patients are in constant conflict, albeit latent, with patients trying to get more from the relationship than doctors are prepared to give.

As an alternative to functional consensus on the one hand and conflict on the other, a negotiation model is perhaps the most realistic approximation for the way that both doctor and patient will actively seek to influence a shared consultation. In some cases the negotiation between doctor and patient may be well balanced but research has suggested that for much of the time patients are not treated as full players or competent experts in consultations (Tuckett et al., 1985).

Models of an encounter as complex as the doctor–patient relationship are inevitably simplified and not equally applicable to all branches of medicine or types of relationship. Each model highlights a particular aspect of the relationship and how the balance between doctors' and patients' interests is maintained. Parsons's idea of an unequal consensus is clearly part of what happens during a consultation, but since he was writing in the 1950s much has changed. For instance, with the possibility of a more actively consumerist approach on the part of patients and with doctors becoming more mindful of litigation, this relationship is now more likely to become a matter of negotiation. The rise of consumerism and the awareness of patients' rights mean that conflict between doctor and patient is likely to be resolved through the relationship taking on a contractual nature (Bury, 1997).

INVERSE CARE LAW

There are systematic variations between the social classes in terms of the service they receive, such that the middle classes are apparently more successful in their negotiations with doctors than the working classes. Inequalities in health outcomes (see Chapter 4) are compounded by the better quality of service received by the wealthiest classes when compared with more deprived groups. The phenomenon of the neediest groups receiving the poorest service was noticed early in the history of the NHS, when Richard Titmuss wrote:

> We have learnt from 15 years' experience of the Health Service that higher income groups know how to make better use of the Service; they tend to receive more specialist attention; occupy more of the beds in better equipped and staffed hospitals; receive more elective surgery; have better maternity care; and are more likely to get psychiatric help and psychotherapy than low income groups – particularly the unskilled. (Titmuss, 1968: 196)

Some of the inequalities between the higher and lower income groups are due to area effects: prosperous residential areas tend to be served by well-resourced, maintained and staffed healthcare institutions as compared to impoverished areas where, as with other community resources, healthcare services are absent or of poor quality. This observation has been summarized in the inverse care law which states that 'the availability of good medical care tends to vary inversely with the need of the population served' (Tudor-Hart, 1971). This law plays a role in the persistence of the inequalities described in Chapter 4 between social classes and between ethnic groups, as well as maintaining area-based inequalities.

EVIDENCE ON MEDICAL CONSULTATIONS

Inequalities can be demonstrated to operate at the level of one-to-one interactions between doctor and patient as well as at the level of class. Research shows that the time devoted to and information imparted during consultations will vary with socio-economic class and education, favouring the more privileged classes (Waitzkin, 1991). Inequalities in treatment and outcome have been found along class and racialized lines for various specific conditions from coronary heart disease to schizophrenia. Despite the profession's assertion that doctors work in their patients' best interests, taking each case on its own merit, other values also clearly influence the exchange between doctor and patient. For instance, a tendency to withhold healthcare intervention from older people constitutes a form of informal rationing, while racialized ideas have informed what is considered an appropriate medical intervention for black psychotic men, black multiparous women and Asian women in labour. It is, of course, no surprise that medical professionals are subject to the same prejudices that structure everyone's day-to-day exchanges. However, medical autonomy, self-regulation and medicine's dominance over other health professionals have rested on the claim to exercise expertise altruistically for the benefit of others in clinical and therapeutic work. Patients' preparedness to put their lives in doctors' hands rests, in part, on these altruistic, professional values.

Inequalities between doctor and patient are often played out during consultations and can be seen to structure the procedure of an interaction. Audio-recording the communication between doctors and patients has established some consistent features about the way that doctors and patients talk to one another during consultations. These features concern what is said (the content of the discussion), as well as the way that conversation is conducted in terms of its structure of turn-taking between doctor and patient and those lines of thought that are followed up and those which are ignored. In the course of a consultation, the patient's feelings, worries and symptoms are discussed and interpreted with reference to medical understandings, but it is consistently the medical interpretation that is treated as more reliable and important than what the patient reports. Within limits this is appropriate, since a patient will have consulted in order to access medical expertise. However, the depth of the assumption that patients' evidence is less reliable and less valid than medical evidence is demonstrated in the following, widely cited study of pregnant women at routine ante-natal appointments. In the first case, the doctor's mis-reading of the woman's case notes is taken as more reliable than her own account of her previous pregnancies.

> Doctor: Ah, I see you've got a boy and a girl.
> Woman: No. Two girls.
> Doctor: Really, are you sure? I thought it said … (checks in case notes) Oh no, you're quite right, two girls. (Oakley, 1980)

This doctor's attempt to question the woman's knowledge of the gender of her own children could be dismissed as an absurd mistake. Or it could be seen as an example of the way that patients' accounts of their own condition are routinely treated as less reliable than case notes, test results and other medical evidence. Another example shows the same tendency, where the doctor only accepts the woman's account of the duration of her pregnancy when it is confirmed by the evidence in her notes.

> Doctor: How many weeks are you now?
> Woman: Twenty-six-and-a-half.
> Doctor: [Looking at case notes] Twenty weeks now.
> Woman: No. Twenty-six-and-a-half.
> Doctor: You can't be.
> Woman: Yes, I am; look at the ultrasound report.
> Doctor: When was it done?
> Woman: Today.
> Doctor: It was done today?
> Woman: Yes.
> Doctor: [reads report] Oh yes, twenty-six-and-a-half weeks, that's right. (Graham and Oakley, 1986)

Since pregnant women are not patients and their condition is not an illness for which they are seeking a cure, ante-natal care (particularly where the woman's pregnancy is normal) makes the peculiar ways in which medical consultations are structured appear even more stark. The fairly mild resistance that the women quoted above raised to their doctors' incorrect assertions shows how deferential people tend to be when in consultation with doctors. Doctors are in control, not only of the content of the consultations in terms of the types of knowledge that will be admitted as evidence, but also of that knowledge's structure.

In a standard consultation, the doctor invites the patient to describe his or her problem, determines the structure of the discussion, which elements of the problem to follow up, and when the session should close. Close analysis of the mechanics of speech in transcriptions of audio-recordings of consultations shows how doctors control the interaction by various techniques (Strong, 1979). These techniques include asking questions rhetorically: if a doctor asks 'You're happy with this treatment aren't you?', a patient's silence can be taken as agreement. By posing a series of questions, without explaining why such information is necessary, a doctor can maintain control of an interaction. The interruption of a patient's speech in order to finish their sentence for them or to ask a new question effectively blocks the description of matters that the doctor considers irrelevant. Cutting off a parent's talk by starting a new line of questioning with a child or by talking to a medical student has the same effect. The closure of a consultation is in the doctor's hands and can be effected by issuing a prescription, suggesting a follow-up appointment, or turning away from the patient to write up notes. It is extremely difficult to persist in the description of one's symptoms when the professional's attention is focused on updating computerized or hand-written notes. The medical control of consultations has been described as 'systematic, all pervasive and almost unquestioned' (Strong, 1979).

The version of the consultation which influences future care is in the hands of the doctor as she or he chooses which aspects of the interaction to write up and how to note them. Describing a patient as 'very emotional' may be accurate and at the same time may also be a means of labelling that patient's concerns as an over-reaction. A clinical judgement on what constitutes 'excessive' emotion in a patient can then become part of a diagnosis, particularly in matters of mental health, and can be used further to justify more interventionist treatment.

COMMUNICATING ACROSS THE DIVIDE

A narrow range of evidence is admitted in coming to a diagnosis and people suffering symptoms for which a single underlying cause cannot be identified, such as chronic fatigue syndrome, Gulf War syndrome, or chronic back pain, often express frustration that their own evidence is seen as medically irrelevant. People suffering long-term back pain have described how they repeatedly returned to their healthcare providers, despite tests and examinations finding no underlying cause (Rhodes et al., 1999). Repeated X-rays or MRI scans may have eventually turned up an explanation to legitimate the pain (a trapped nerve or ruptured disc), but for others no such external 'proof' of their pain was forthcoming and the search for a solution was coloured by the feeling of not being believed, as was described by the following man in his forties with lower back pain.

> And the doctors … kind of left me with the impression that it was not real …
> For years now I've been living with … 'It's all in your head'. (Rhodes et al., 1999)

Doctors' reluctance to take seriously the evidence or insights offered by patients about their own conditions has been well described by physicians who fall ill and find that their status as trained doctors does not protect their views from being dismissed (Sacks, 1978; Pensack and Williams, 1994).

In an idealized version of the doctor–patient relationship the authority which doctors wield over compliant patients is not seen as problematic, since it is assumed that both parties are working to the same ends and have the same expectations of the consultation. However, a clinician's concerns about a patient's case will routinely differ, and differ markedly, from a patient's own concerns. This divergence of expectation is perhaps most obvious at the moment when unwelcome diagnoses and prognoses are delivered. In the face of bad news about illness, which renders their future uncertain, patients often look to health professionals for reassurance. The patient's most urgent question on receipt of a diagnosis might be very precise, but not strictly medical, for instance 'Will I see my daughter get married?' or 'If I die, who will care for my cat?'

A widely promoted method for breaking bad news to patients (Buckman, 1992) follows a sequence of questions which will lead a clinician to find out how much a patient knows about their own condition and prognosis before giving any new information. While such communication guidelines are to be welcomed, essentially they are techniques to monitor how much medical information a patient has absorbed. But the infirmity, anxiety and pain which will have triggered the consultation will render a patient vulnerable and will routinely compromise the ability of that patient (and their carer) to communicate. Vulnerability is not conducive to active participation in communication, as was described by the following patient:

> Yes I was able to ask [questions], but not much came to mind at the time … the situation of being told half naked, lying down – I can't speak to a strange man easily. (Audit Commission, 1993)

Where the patient is a child, or very elderly, or mentally ill, or not speaking his first language, the difficulties of communication may be further compounded. Offering reassurance and succour to sufferers is not an explicit aim of communication in modern medicine: the ethos is better characterized as transferring information where possible and keeping patients aware of their options.

The gulf between a patient's concerns and the medical understanding of disease management is more than simply a question of training doctors in good communication. While sensitive, humane and reflective communication with healthcare providers is an ideal, it does not surmount the problem that medicine does not have the answers to the metaphysical questions which disease, disability and the experience of suffering and uncertainty present.

Consider the problem of communicating risk information to patients. Imagine that you are a patient and have just been told that you have significantly raised levels of blood cholesterol. Your doctor has to help you to consider whether a pharmacological treatment is appropriate. She might explain the options as follows:

> If 100 people like you are given no treatment for five years, then 92 will live and eight will die. However if 100 people like you take this cholesterol-lowering drug every day for five years, then 95 will live and five will die. I do not know whether you are one of the 95 or one of the five. (Editor's Choice, 1998)

It is the last sentence that sums up the real problem in communicating epidemiological risk based on population statistics; it does not easily translate to address the concerns raised during individual clinical consultations. If communicating risk in health education campaigns is about trying to make individual people feel vulnerable, and to thereby induce behavioural change, what is happening when communicating risk in the clinical setting? Probabilistic information does not, by definition, deal in certainties and this can be difficult when patients are seeking reassurance and directional advice from a consultation. Medical uncertainty is troublesome in various ways to clinical practice (and this is a theme to which we will return in Chapter 11). Communicating uncertainty to an angry, pained person with whom a language might or might not be shared represents an enormous challenge. Offering routine consultations characterized by good communication and leading to good outcomes that tackle rather than compound a person's health problems represents an even greater challenge. What is more, this challenge must be met consistently not only by the doctor but also by the range of professionals that a patient meets, from the podiatrist to the sonographer and the hydrotherapist to the prosthetist. Research into the 'doctor–patient relationship' is part of the wider study of 'practitioner–client' relationships, reflecting the team-working of contemporary medicine.

CO-OPERATION AND CHALLENGE

We have considered some of the ways in which patients are disadvantaged in the doctor–patient relationship due to inequalities of class, gender and ethnicity. A reluctance to consider the patient's values or experiences means that patients' questions are unanswered and sometimes unanswerable during medical consultation. In this view, the under-use of health services by people suffering from serious symptoms and the non-compliance by those who are patients within these services are surprising, not so much for their occurrence but because they are not more widespread. The high level of co-operation between patients and medical professionals could be viewed as surprising given the invasiveness of the interventions that patients permit doctors to perform. Unlike most other professional relationships, doctors are allowed to examine body parts usually kept private, to ask questions that would usually be considered impertinent, to cut and pierce the skin, to penetrate orifices, to remove blood and other tissue, and to dispense medicine with unpleasant side effects. The ever-increasing demand for medical services, despite the invasive and sometimes brutal aspect to the methods employed, should perhaps be subject to urgent research: why do people continue to consult doctors with such regularity and why does society continue to treat medicine as an authoritative institution, given the ways in which patients' interests are not always served on a one-to-one basis? This question has been of interest to sociological research over the last 20 years as various challenges to medicine's authority have been considered (and we turn to this in Chapter 11).

This chapter has considered the imbalance that characterizes the doctor–patient relationship and the ways that it favours doctors. Whether the evidence points towards an essentially conflictual, consensual or co-operative realationship between doctor and patient has also been evaluated. Strong critics of the medicalization of childbirth or the role of psychiatry in oppressing minority ethnic groups would suggest patients' interests are consistently in conflict with those of medicine. Commentators have pointed to the increased access to medical knowledge available among lay people via the internet and self-help groups, and that this combined with a consumerist approach to accessing healthcare further supported by the Patients' Charter seems to have given patients the upper hand in the conflict. (Chapter 11 considers challenges to medicine's power.) A co-operative or consensual model of the doctor–patient relationship is promoted by initiatives such as the expert patient programme, suggesting that patients' knowledge of their own chronic conditions can and should become part of the clinical process. Significant limitations to the power of medicine have also come from management and funding structures rather than individual patients, and some of these are discussed in the next chapter.

Further reading

Bury, M. (1997) *Health and Illness in a Changing Society*. London: Routledge.

Offers an over-view of the various models that sociologists have used to make sense of the doctor–patient relationship.

Penhall, J. (2000) *Blue/Orange*. London: Methuen.

Shaw, B. (1946 [1906]) *The Doctor's Dilemma*. London: Penguin.

Both of these plays deal with the complexities of how doctors negotiate with one another and with patients, balancing out the different players' interests in coming to diagnoses and decisions on treatment.

REVISION QUESTIONS

1   What is meant by the symptom iceberg?

2   Describe Talcott Parsons's model of the unequal reciprocity of the doctor–patient relationship.

3   What is the inverse care law?

4   In what sense are doctor and patient in conflict with one another?

5   How can a doctor maintain control of a consultation?

6   How is a patient disadvantaged when attempting to assert his or her priorities in a consultation?

EXTENSION QUESTIONS

1   Service users' accounts

At the following website, www.dipex.org/, you will find a large number of interviews where patients talk about their experiences of various illnesses. Under the heading 'Living with dying' look at the interviews in the age category 51–60 years. Listen through to interviews LD35 and LD37.

- Summarize the interviews by noting the key points that are made.
- Note the contrasting accounts of patients expecting to receive a serious diagnosis.
- What are the implications of these patients' views for the doctor–patient relationship?

You can read about the background of the DIPEx project in the following book chapter:

Herxheimer, A. and Zeibland, S. (2004) 'The DIPEx project: collecing personal experiences of illness and health care', in B. Hurwitz, T. Greenhalgh and V. Skultans (eds), *Narrative Research in Health and Illness*. Oxford: Blackwell. pp. 115–31.

- How might the DIPEx website be useful to patients?
- How might the DIPEx website be useful to doctors?

2   Patient choice

A paper in the *British Journal of Cancer* suggests that screening for prostate cancer (the commonest male cancer in the UK) using the PSA blood test has led to large numbers of men receiving unnecessary surgery. Using statistical modelling techniques the researchers calculate that even without treatment only about 1 per cent of men aged 55–59 diagnosed with

(Cont'd)

low-grade cancer would die within 15 years. Given that the side effects of prostatectomy include incontinence and impotence, this excessive surgery has significant costs both for individual patients and for the NHS which supports them. 'Watchful waiting' or 'active surveillance' is instead suggested as an alternative treatment regimen.

A man, aged 59, is diagnosed with a low-grade cancer of the prostate.

- What questions would you want him to ask his doctor in deciding whether or not to opt for surgery?
- How should advice be balanced with information in the consultation?

(See Parker, C., Muston, D., Melia, J., Moss, S. and Dearnaley, D. (2006) 'A model of the natural history of screen-detected prostate cancer, and the effect of radical treatment on overall survival', *British Journal of Cancer*, 94 (10): 1361–68. Also available at: doi:10.1038/sj.bjc. 6603105)

3 Describing a patient as 'non-compliant' suggests that he or she is not following medical advice in a way that a professional views as appropriate. However, if partnership with patients is to be meaningful then this term is meaningless. If that patient's views and experiences are part of the process of treating disease, then any 'non-compliance' suggests that the treatment plan needs to be revised. 'Concordance' between patients and doctors in decision making implies the active participation of patients and careful discussion with a doctor about acceptable and beneficial treatment options.

- Some reasons why a patient might not adhere to a treatment regime are listed below:
  - complex dose regime;
  - unpleasant side effects;
  - unwillingness to discuss problems with a treatment regime;
  - unwillingness to appear ungrateful.

Suggest how a doctor who is seeking to achieve concordance in deriving and monitoring a treatment regime might address these reasons for non-adherence with a patient.

10

HEALTHCARE ORGANIZATION

Chapter summary

This chapter describes:

» how the NHS is worth studying because it:

- provides universal healthcare at a low cost;
- is a major employer;
- is where healthcare providers negotiate their own professional interests;
- is the market for providers of services, medical technology and pharmaceuticals;
- is an important symbol of a British way of life to which great loyalty is shown;

» how the NHS is somewhat unresponsive to patient needs and changes in clinical practice;

» how reforms that have sought to address this have resulted in a power shift towards general practice and management.

Useful terms for this chapter

clinical governance: a systematic approach to maintaining and improving the quality of patient care within the NHS by defining standards and having a system of audit which measures the attainment of those standards

INTRODUCTION

The British National Health Service (NHS) is the biggest employer in the country and there are few people who are not touched by some aspect of organized healthcare at some stage of life. The NHS has been extensively studied as a means of funding and organizing a national system of healthcare and has been compared with alternative models from other countries. As well as an economic and organizational structure, the NHS is the location where various health professions assert their rights in competition with one another for material resources and for the power to interpret the meaning of illness. The NHS is a crucial site for the production of medical knowledge and its transmission to doctors and it is one of the places where patients and their carers are given diagnoses of disease and disability and begin to make sense of this information. The NHS is not only a setting where a variety of health work is accomplished, but also an important part of the machinery that generates research and profit for the pharmaceutical and biotechnology industries. It is also the setting for the provision of contracted services such as catering and cleaning. Furthermore, it is a crucial partner in the education system that trains, assesses and validates healthcare professionals and is part of the system of academic research.

A single NHS healthcare setting such as a hospital or clinic can be analysed in terms of the interests of patients, of various groups of clinical staff, of management, of government, and of the industries supplying services and products. The NHS is thus more than just an employer of medics and a provider of hospitals in terms of the role it plays in the economic, political and educational life of Britain. This chapter will consider the structure and funding of the NHS and then introduce various critical perspectives on inter-professional rivalries and co-operation and on the interests of capital within healthcare provision.

WHAT'S SO SPECIAL ABOUT THE NHS?

While the seemingly endless series of funding crises make the description of the NHS as 'the envy of the world' (by Enoch Powell, Minister for Health, in 1962) questionable, the structure and funding of the NHS are unquestionably of ongoing national and international interest. The principles that under-pinned the NHS from its inception – universal coverage, financed from general taxation, with the capacity for national planning of provision – remain in place and distinguish the British system of health service provision from alternative models. The NHS provides for the entire population, is financed by central government which owns most of the facilities and funds most of the staff, yet doctors remain independent and, while receiving most of their income from the state, reserve the right to practise independently (Field, 1973).

Socialized medicine

The significance of these features of the organization of the NHS can be appreciated in contrast to the organization of health services in other indus-trialized nations. A fully socialized healthcare system, of the type associated with the former socialist states of the USSR, operated where most employees (including doctors) were salaried state workers and most facilities were state owned. The failure of these universally available systems has been attributed to under-funding (only 2 per cent of gross national product in Russia) and corruption (Field, 1995), and since the fall of Communism they have been opened up to market forces and privatization and have evolved into systems that depend on health insurance.

Insurance system

In a health insurance system the state does not directly finance services via general taxation and individuals and employers are required to pay insurance against future health costs which in turn funds healthcare provision. This model, often supplemented by tax-funded welfare provision for the uninsured, does not depend on the state owning the healthcare facilities and can co-exist with alternatives in a pluralist model of provision. Thus facilities may be owned privately as well as by the state or by regional government, and services may be purchased via one-off payments as well as via insurance schemes.

Pluralist socialized system

The state-owned and state-run British NHS is a socialized system of healthcare in which doctors enjoy considerable autonomy and where the state-owned system co-exists with private insurance schemes and privately owned and run profit-making hospitals and clinics. The NHS was not designed and operationalized as an ideal type of health service, but was instead taken over from existing municipal and charitable facilities with various compromises made in order to keep all of the players on board (as described in Chapter 1). The compromises between the medical profession and the policy makers, brokered by Aneurin Bevan, have been described as resulting in a service that was and still is

> split rather than unified, free but with private practice and including both elective and appointed systems: all in all an odd administrative structure, especially when viewed against earlier attempts at a simplified but comprehensive administration. (Wilcocks, 1967: 19–20)

Bevan, commonly lauded as the architect of the NHS, has also been portrayed as a jobbing builder who happened to get some of his tenders accepted (Cartwright, 1977). Nonetheless, the largely state-owned character and government-funded nature of the NHS represent an economical means of funding healthcare compared with other systems operating in comparable nations. The 6.5–7.5 per cent of gross national product that Britain has historically spent on the NHS is lower than other countries (for example

9.6 per cent in France, 10.5 per cent in Germany, 13.9 per cent in the USA, and 8.5 percent in the Netherlands), but measures of life expectancy and mortality are similar (OECD, 2003). The main difference in the funding structure of the UK when compared with other countries is that private expenditure makes up a far smaller proportion. The NHS constrains health-care spending more effectively than alternative systems, so that while the NHS may no longer be the envy of the world it may still nonetheless be the envy of the world's finance ministers (Abel-Smith, 1994).

EVALUATING THE NHS

The Beveridge Report which predated the establishment of the NHS assumed that expenditure on healthcare would decline once existing ill health had been addressed. This turned out to be a misguided assumption: in its first full year of operation from 1948 the running costs of the NHS came to £43 million, which was already more than parliamentary estimates had allowed and provided cause for concern. By the early twenty-first century it had risen to an estimated £74 billion, which in real terms (allowing for inflation) suggests that the cost of the NHS has increased seven-fold (Ham, 2004). Unfortunately for economic planning, disease and disability do not exist in a fixed quantity which can be addressed and eliminated through medical inter-vention. Rather, the demand for healthcare services seems to be potentially infinite. The increasing proportion of older people in the population and the new opportunities for diagnosis and treatment offered by technological innovation, as well as the ongoing expansion in the number of conditions which medicine can treat together with rising expectations about quality of service, all suggest that this increase in demand is set to continue.

Overall mortality rates are a crude but still useful summary measure of the health of a nation. However, in terms of evaluating the performance of the NHS favourable mortality rates cannot be wholly or even greatly attributed to the quality of the health service, since social and economic factors play such an important role (as discussed in Chapter 4). There have been various attempts to construct measures to gauge the effectiveness of the NHS that are more sophisticated than mortality, but the methodological difficulties in developing such measures are considerable. For instance, an efficient health-care system might be expected to get people off their sickbeds with some speed, yet if this is done too speedily, the system may well be creating future hospital admissions. So the methodological problem is whether the same individual admitted with a new episode of illness should be counted as a new case or the continuation of a previous one. For many audit purposes there is a time limit, so that once a stipulated period of time elapses, say 30 days, then the problem is deemed to be a new case.

Despite methodological difficulties in measuring the performance of the NHS, there is agreement on the criteria that should, ideally, be in use. To judge whether the NHS represents a good means of delivering health services its efficiency, accessibility, equity, social acceptability and relevance to health needs (Maxwell, 1984) should all be measured. These dimensions of quality of healthcare are reflected in the domains of the NHS performance assessment framework, introduced in 1998.

REFORMING THE NHS

The desire to 'improve efficiency' is never far down the management agenda for the NHS. International comparisons show that the NHS carries low administration costs, compared to systems based on insurance which need to bill for each healthcare intervention. However, in 1973 when oil producers quadrupled their prices, western economies that were (as now) highly dependent on oil products as fuel were plunged into economic crisis. As a result, public services were drastically cut back as a means of reducing government expenditure. The re-organization of the NHS in 1974 aimed to address the problems of iniquitous access to, and excessive costs of, services by introducing new levels of management and administration. In retrospect, it is widely agreed that the replacement of one layer of management with three, together with a doctrine of 'consensus management', compounded the delays and increased bureaucracy without any great gain in the unity of the service (Berridge, 1999).

The excessive managerialism of the post-1974 service was addressed with a further re-organization undertaken in 1982. This reform abolished one tier of administration and established 192 district health authorities, which were the location for the reforms of planning and service provision. The introduction of professionally trained general managers at regional, district and hospital level replaced consensus management. General practice remained outside this management structure and also escaped the financial constraints imposed on hospitals, as budgetary limits imposed on health authority spending attempted to prevent the compensation of inflation.

Interventions of the 1980s and early 1990s attempted to introduce marketplace competition as a means of 'driving down' unnecessary costs. An 'internal' or quasi-market was introduced in healthcare by engineering a division between purchasers of services and providers of services as separate roles within the single public body responsible, such as the health authority. Economists predicted from experience in free markets that any actual or potential competition between providers of services would result in 'efficiency savings' as well as improved performance in public services. What was less well predicted was the extra administrative and management cost incurred by the new requirements for audit information and the need to negotiate contracts in the newly created internal market. Any positive or negative effect of the quasi-markets was highly attenuated by the ongoing force of central directives, for instance to reduce waiting times. The constraints placed on any market forces that were introduced meant that competition between different service providers could not disrupt the status quo for better or worse to any great extent. However, one lasting impact of the drive to make healthcare subject to market forces has been the shift in the balance of power away from hospital providers and towards general practitioners and, to a lesser extent, in favour of healthcare managers.

GPs have long been gate-keepers to the more expensive tertiary services that help-seeking patients must get past. By making GPs into fund-holders in the 1990s, it was hoped that services would become more responsive to the needs of patients by ensuring that 'the money followed patients' rather than patients having to present themselves at whichever location had sufficient capacity. While the extent to which patients were influencing service provision has remained fairly limited, the power exerted by primary and community-based services over the provision of tertiary services has increased. The successor to fund-holding GPs in England and Wales was primary care groups which have evolved into primary care trusts, bodies which commission primary, community and hospital services for their patients. In this respect the split between purchaser and provider has persisted in the NHS in England, whereas in Scotland a partnership model has replaced NHS trusts, and Wales has seen various organizational changes with a new structure introduced in 2001 after the establishment of the Welsh Assembly.

CLINICAL GOVERNANCE

Another long-standing effect of the introduction of internal markets to healthcare has been the exposure of the inequities in the system in terms of measures of the quality of healthcare, such as the frequency of intervention, the length of stay, the type of intervention available and drug prescription. The rationing of resources which clinicians had performed implicitly on an individual basis came under scrutiny with the production of new information required for management systems. The deficits in both professional self-regulation and clinical audit became apparent with the instigation of a public inquiry into the practice of surgeons at the Bristol Royal Infirmary. The need for consistency and regulation in the availability and quality of services across geographical areas has been addressed by the establishment of the National Institute for Clinical Excellence (NICE) in 1999 (now called the National Institute for Health and Clinical Excellence, but retaining the acronym NICE). This public body makes available the evidence on the effectiveness and cost effectiveness of treatments and interventions with guidance on their suitability for use within the NHS. The watchdog for these guidelines, with a statutory duty to assess the performance of healthcare organizations, is the Healthcare Commission (formerly known as the Commission for Healthcare Audit and Inspection or CHAI, which took over from the Commission for Health Improvement or CHI). Among other duties the Healthcare Commission seeks to ensure that trusts, including primary care trusts, have implemented 'clinical governance' which refers to the ongoing improvement of clinical services at an individual and professional level.

International surveys of healthcare systems have consistently shown that the NHS is a low-cost health service that offers a good degree of equity of service across the population, but that its service is somewhat unresponsive. The lower expenditure compared to other countries has meant less in the way of expensive technology being purchased, such as scanners, and consequent delays in diagnosis and treatment. This may underlie the short-fall shown in terms of some measures of the quality of service in the NHS, such as cancer survival rates. The weakness of the NHS is a consequence of its strength, with the centralized control of costs leading to capacity constraints and therefore impeded responsiveness and access (Ham, 2004). In terms of improved quality of care and improved health outcomes, the consequences of sustained increases in NHS funding administered under Labour remain to be assessed in the long term. An important plank of the rhetoric of healthcare reform at the outset of the twenty-first century has been the suggestion that a greater degree of patient choice in the timing and location of treatment should be achieved. There is a concerted effort to increase the degree to which the NHS is 'patient-led', yet much of the initiative comes from senior NHS management rather than from patient groups. Whether it will prove possible to achieve patient choice without expanding NHS costs beyond a level that taxpayers will tolerate is not yet clear. Also unaddressed is how a patient-led NHS should respond when patients and clinicians are in conflict as to the most advisable course of action, as in the dispute over MMR vaccinations for children (Bury, 2008) (see Chapter 5).

The NHS is not, of course, a homogeneous system that can be easily characterized or quickly modified. The NHS is highly valued by the public, as shown by successive opinion surveys, and despite evidence of increasing dissatisfaction with regard to certain aspects, the population's commitment to a universal tax-funded service remains strong. The three major British political parties share a common ground in being committed to maintaining the NHS, with their disagreements being limited to details of the interface with private practice and charging policy for specific services such as eye tests, prescriptions and dental services. Whatever the ideology of the politicians responsible for health policy in the future, priority-setting or rationing is likely to remain a major issue.

The establishment of NICE to address inequities and issue guidelines on best practice has made rationing a higher profile issue although not necessarily in predictable ways. Considerable press coverage of a number of women's attempts to get NHS funded-prescriptions for Herceptin, a drug developed for particular forms of early stage breast cancer despite it not yet being licensed for NHS-use by NICE, led to ministerial intervention to over-ride official policy. There was criticism that broadening the availability of Herceptin, an expensive drug, would inevitably limit the budget available for other treatments. The ongoing process of medical and pharmacological innovation means that there is always going to be upwards pressure on resources and hence on the level of taxes needed to meet spending priorities.

MEDICAL DOMINANCE

Commentators mostly agree that the NHS will continue in something close to its current form for some time to come, since pressure to reform continues but no major forces are seeking to abolish the NHS. For doctors practising in Britain the ongoing vigour of the NHS is crucial, since it remains the main forum in which the profession's interests have been pursued.

With the creation of the NHS in 1948, doctors fought hard to defend their own interests, maintaining control over their working conditions and, for GPs, their status as independent contractors. The agreement struck between the medical profession and the post-Second World War government has been long-lasting and has ensured medicine's position at the centre of NHS management's decision making. Medicine's triumph has been to ensure that management has been thoroughly medicalized and that central issues of policy have been claimed as being of medical significance (Klein, 1989). Doctors participate in policy making in the NHS executive and the Department of Health, and their views are represented via regional NHS executive offices and health authorities, with all NHS trusts having a medical director on their board.

Doctors' success and their dominance over other medical professions can be seen in the ongoing lower pay available for other categories of staff, such as nurses, when compared with doctors. Medicine's achievement in gaining a state control monopoly to practise and its claim over a distinct body of knowledge has not been matched in nursing, which has been subject to medical management and viewed as a caring, rather than an expert, therapeutic occupation.

THE ROLE OF THE HOSPITAL

Although more recent changes have prioritized primary care, high technology, science-based, interventionist, hospital medicine has represented society's hopes for a better, prosperous and healthy future in large measure. The transformation of the hospital from a charitable foundation which isolated the sick poor, to a modern institution characterized by a complex division of labour and a technologically sophisticated approach, is an important part of biomedicine's success. Hospitals have been the site where much of the hope placed in medicine has been fulfilled, but they have also been criticized on the grounds that they are designed around the needs of various professions rather than patients' needs. There is historical evidence that hospitals were primarily designed to serve the interests of business, including the business of medicine. Originally the hospital's key role was to remove the sick from society, with any therapeutic role a secondary matter. The development of the lunatic asylum throughout the eighteenth and nineteenth centuries served the needs of capital by providing a place in which to sequester those who would not or could not fit into a market-led economy. People who were incapable of being economically productive were removed from society, allowing capitalism to develop smoothly. The substantial increase in numbers of asylum inmates through the nineteenth century followed the 1845 Lunatics Asylums Act, which gave medicine a monopoly on the diagnosis and treatment of madness. At this time the medical profession also needed to ensure a clientele for the services of their asylums (Pilgrim and Rogers, 1993). Regimes of psychiatric care in asylums in the twentieth century prioritized the needs of the institution rather than the patient. Critics began to note how patients' individuality was undermined as they became 'institutionalized' by participating in timetabled group activities to fit in with the running of the institution.

The physical layout of general and psychiatric hospital wards reflects institutional and professional priorities, rather than those of the individual. The lack of privacy in a medical ward allows the surveillance of a large number of patients by a small number of healthcare professionals. This may offer no health benefits, but certainly allows unruly patients to be quickly controlled while keeping staff costs down. Hospitals are familiar workplaces for healthcare professionals and yet for patients they are not just unfamiliar, they can also be experienced as positively hostile and far from therapeutic. At the point of admission, when facing the unwelcome effects of illness, surgery or disability, people can find themselves in a ward with almost no privacy, making sleep difficult, and attended to by a bewildering array of staff following unfamiliar routines. Hospitals have tended to treat patients as the passive recipients of healthcare interventions, which reduces the labour and organizational costs of providing healthcare but at the cost of ignoring some of the patients' needs. People's need for reassurance, information and communication has been side-lined in hospitals which have sought to maximize the through-put of patients, and this 'emotional labour' has either remained undone or been taken on in addition to contracted work by cleaning or nursing staff.

Appraisals of the negative impact of institutional care on people were one of the influences favouring the shift towards care in the community, which has been under way since the 1990 NHS and Community Care Act. The then

Conservative government needed to cut public expenditure to cope with economic recession, and had an ideological commitment to enforcing family responsibility for caring roles which coincided with a raised awareness of the damaging aspects of institutionalization. As the care for many individuals with mental or physical impairments has been moved from hospitals or asylums to smaller dwellings located in residential or urban areas, problems with the policy have been noted. The concept of 'care in the community' implies that former institutional inmates will be absorbed in a 'community' which may, in practice, not welcome their presence (Prior, 1993). The term also suggests that some care will be available in a community setting, which has not always been the case as people with complex or multiple needs can slip through the networks of the different agencies involved, such as social work, local authority housing and mental health services. More recent initiatives emphasize the need to work in partnership with patients and to consult their expertise. There are good arguments that a patient who is well informed and carefully consulted is likely to benefit from treatment to a greater extent than a patient who feels marginalized, anxious and uncertain. However, it is doubtful whether these ideas have been incorporated into the core medical mission.

It is not only long-term care that has been moving out of the hospitals and into the community, as minor surgical procedures and dialysis are increasingly available in primary care settings. The advantages of treating chronic conditions in the settings where they are experienced have led to the employment of larger numbers of nurses, physiotherapists and other health professionals in the community and to the re-location of specialist consultants' clinics such as those for diabetes and ophthalmology (Morgan, 2003). These changes suggest that the roles of hospital- and community-based professionals and the boundaries between primary, secondary and tertiary care, which have been carefully demarcated in the past, may now be tending to blur.

COMMERCIAL AND INDUSTRIAL INTERESTS IN THE NHS

While the majority of NHS activity is publicly funded, it is a pluralist system which includes the provision of private sector services. BUPA, a provident association, and various private hospital groups co-exist with the NHS, with the legal and policy regulation of their activities varying over time. The early 1980s saw planning controls relaxed, which together with contractual changes for NHS consultants and tax changes to encourage raised levels of private health cover brought about an expansion in the provision of private healthcare. Increasing the private provision within the NHS has been seen by government as one means of meeting the ever-increasing demand for healthcare. The expansion of private provision has raised the possibility of the emergence of a 'two-tier' system where those with money or insurance can queue-jump for diagnostic tests or elective surgery. When those with influence and finance can demand and receive a better quality of health service than the rest of the population through formal channels, as well as the informal means discussed in the previous chapter, it seems likely that health inequalities will be compounded and will widen further. Apart from the speed of response, it is not clear whether the private provision of healthcare is any better than NHS provision. Private care is undoubtedly more comfortable and convenient, but in other respects the quality of the service offered by the private sector is similar to that on offer within the NHS.

While often described as if they were separate the private and public sectors do overlap, where, for instance, private hospitals rely on doctors and nurses trained in the NHS who are often working simultaneously in both sectors. Co-operation between the two sectors, where NHS patients are cared for at public expense in private facilities, has been used as one means of reducing waiting lists. Private Finance Initiative (PFI) was a Conservative policy of the early 1990s that uses private companies to design, build and run hospitals for payments from public money. Despite ideological objections subsequent Labour governments have pursued PFI funding, since it permits the renewal of building stock and the expansion of capacity at reduced cost in the short term as the capital investment is not levied through taxation. Critics point out that hospitals which have used PFI have often had to reduce their bed numbers and devote an increased proportion of budgets to service high interest rates, thereby reducing the funds available to hire clinical staff.

Within NHS facilities the provision of goods, equipment, services and staff is undertaken by commercial enterprises, committed to making a profit for share-holders or owners. Manufacturers of medical equipment and supplies, companies that tender to supply laundry, cleaning and catering services, agencies that offer bank nursing and locum medical staff, and manufacturers and suppliers of pharmaceuticals, are all pursuing profits within the NHS. The drugs industry is a major UK employer which contributes significantly to exports, and commands a powerful position within the national and international economy, accounting for 10 per cent of total NHS expenditure. Prior to the 1960s, when faith in the beneficence of pharmacological innovations was higher, there was very little government regulation of the safety or efficacy of the medicines produced, with the pharmaceutical industry being trusted to carry out appropriate safety tests and act accordingly. After the effects of thalidomide on the unborn children of women who took it as a sleeping or anti-nausea aid became apparent, such an unregulated approach became impossible. This has been seen as a key moment when the potential of new pharmaceuticals to damage as well as enhance life was dramatically recognized. New regulatory mechanisms were introduced; however, whether

Figure 10.1 Private finance initiatives have facilitated the renewal of NHS building stock, but critics suggest that the long-term cost may outweigh the benefit

the right balance between the public's interest and commercial interests was then, or is currently, achieved continues to be debated.

The 1968 Medicines Act made the Department of Health responsible for the safety of new products and, advised by the Committee on the Safety of Medicine, regulated their release onto the market. The independence of this regulatory mechanism has been queried on the grounds that its workings are closed to public scrutiny and its overall effect has been to safeguard the industry's interests (Abraham, 1997). Manufacturers' submissions to the Committee remain confidential, so that information about adverse drug reactions can be kept away from both public and legal scrutiny. Committee members can also be share-holders in pharmaceutical companies, which does suggest that business interests rather than public safety are prioritized. In the early 1980s regulation of the drugs industry was relaxed once again under the ideology of freeing up markets favoured by the Conservatives, and the amount of toxicological data that had to be submitted prior to clinical trials was reduced. Ongoing campaigns by consumer groups to release into public view the processes by which regulatory agencies assess trials evidence have not yet been effective, despite further instances of products with unacceptably high levels of side effects being withdrawn from the marketplace, including Ativan, Opren and Seroxat.

Apart from the granting of licences, there are other moments where pharmaceutical products are regulated before their arrival with the consumer, and medicine plays a key role in this. Medical practitioners are given the job of assessing whether licensed drugs are safe for use by particular patients and of choosing which companies' version of a drug to prescribe. The pharmaceutical company puts their resources into reminding doctors of the brand-name and clinical benefits of particular drugs. From the industry's point of view, drugs which can be sold directly to the consumer and that bypass the rationing effects of medical prescription are ideal products. Viagra epitomizes this ideal product because knowledge of its existence is so widespread and demand is so high that it can be sold directly to the paying public. Where drugs can be sold 'over the counter', that is, without a prescription, the pharmaceutical industry will advertise directly to the consumer via the internet, newspapers, television and radio, to create a demand for those products. The advertising campaign to encourage men over 45 and women over 55 to buy a brand-name, Simvastatin, for the prophylactic reduction of their 'risk of a heart attack' in the absence of any other symptoms of arthereosclerosis is another case in point. As discussed in Chapter 5, drug treatment for 'risk factors' rather than more tangible symptoms opens up the possibilities of marketing products for 'pre-patients' who, by definition, are more numerous than those who will go on to experience the disease. Those who pay for the drug and do not develop the disease will be satisfied customers, although only a proportion of those with the recognized risk factors would ever be likely to develop the disease.

THE CONTEXT OF CARE

This chapter has sketched some of the funding and policy considerations that have informed the development of the NHS and the commercial interests that surround the activities of doctors and their patients. While these matters may seem far from the concerns of clinical work, they have a direct effect on the conditions experienced by service users and providers in the NHS.

The importance of the political and economic context of healthcare delivery should never be under-estimated. The desire to ensure good healthcare for oneself and one's family is more or less universal. However, access to good healthcare is unequal, both in national and global terms. In the UK context, party politics is highly pertinent to the working conditions of medical practitioners. The salience and urgency of access to healthcare for British voters together with the business interests involved in the NHS mean that politicians are reluctant to make swingeing changes to the NHS structure or funding, unless these can be portrayed as uncompromisingly beneficial. The increasing resources and attention devoted to the NHS, as well as the escalating involvement of senior ministers in NHS policy decisions, show how healthcare is a major part of the process of government and this seems unlikely to change. The political and commercial interests in the NHS mean that the case for doctors to maintain an educated interest in the democratic process is perhaps more compelling than for any other public sector workers. Doctors' professional as well as individual and communitarian interests are intimately bound up with the politics of healthcare.

Further reading

Ham, C. (2004) *Health Policy in Britain: The Politics and Organisation of the National Health Service* (5th edn). Basingstoke: Palgrave Macmillan.

Klein, R. (2006) *The New Politics of the NHS: From Creation to Reinvention* (5th edn). Oxford: Radcliffe Medical.

Together these two books give a comprehensive account of the development of today's NHS.

REVISION QUESTIONS

1 What are the principles that have underpinned the NHS since its inception?

2 Describe three models of healthcare organization.

3 What have been the overall effects of reform in the NHS?

4 What criticism has been levelled at hospitals as institutions?

5 What are the two key moments of regulation for pharmaceutical products?

---

1   Doctors' interests, patients' interests

Doctors' defence of the terms and conditions of their work since the inception of the NHS has been successful in many respects.

- To what extent are patients' interests served by having their medical professionals well re-numerated and working in good conditions?
- Can and should these benefits be offset against other categories of NHS expenditure, such as the costs of employing nursing staff, paying drugs bills or maintaining buildings?
- Are there any instances where NHS doctors' interests are diametrically opposed to their patients' interests?

2   Pharmaceutical industry's interests

An advertising campaign encourages men over 45 and women over 55 to buy a brand-name drug, Simvastatin, over the counter (that is without a prescription) to prophylactically reduce the 'risk of a heart attack' in the absence of any other symptoms of arthereosclerosis.

- Is the pharmaceutical industry's campaign to create new categories of patient or 'pre-patient' a cynical means of maintaining profits or is there real public health merit in distributing statins more widely?
- Should access to statins be regulated by the ability to pay for them?
- Who is most likely to buy statins?
- Who is most likely to benefit from the effects of statins?
- What might be the effect on health inequalities of the marketing of these drugs: will inequalities by class, gender and ethnicity get wider or narrower?

11 CHALLENGES TO MEDICINE

Chapter summary

This chapter describes:

» how the context and content of medical practice have changed over the past 100 years and the pace of change does not look like slowing;

» how medicine remains a socially valued practice and a powerful professional group which dominates the way that healthcare is delivered;

» how the public's commitment to medicine and its beneficent potential is matched by critical commentary on the effects of medical practice;

» how medicine's response to criticism has often been to reform medical practice, yet there is a great tendency to dismiss non-medical critique;

» how new viral infections and drug resistant bacteria represent a non-human threat to medicine, the scale of which is hard to quantify.

Useful term for this chapter

majority world: instead of referring to the 'undeveloped' or 'Third World' the term 'majority world' draws attention to the fact that the countries where most people live in the world have very little of the world's wealth, but by contrast the 'developed' or 'First World' which controls most of the world's resources includes a minority of the global population

INTRODUCTION

Healthcare is a social good to which everyone should, ideally, have equal access according to need. The devotion of increased resources towards improving the health services via the NHS continues to be politically popular and there is no sign that the need for healthcare is about to abate. The demand for healthcare remains strong notwithstanding evidence that powerful causes of ill health lie in socio-economic circumstances that are not easily addressed by medical methods and despite the sometime expression of dissatisfaction with the clinical encounter by both patient and clinician alike. Medicine, and the prospect of the prevention of disease and restoration of good health that it holds, is highly valued. Medicine's importance to society is reflected in the degree of commentary and criticism that the practice and policy of medicine attracts and these criticisms are the subject of this chapter.

CHANGING MEDICAL PRACTICE

Doctors' pivotal position in the healthcare market can be traced back to the 'golden era' of hospital medicine when the scientific potential of innovative techniques and therapies seemed almost unlimited and, along with the trust placed in the patrician practitioner, medicine was vindicated by clear-cut successes leading to the expectation of 'a pill for every ill'. Expertise, resources and technology became concentrated in hospitals where highly specialized medical practice was taught, researched and accorded status. However, the idealized practice of medicine when patients were respectful and doctors enjoyed an unfettered autonomy may not have been the experience of doctors at the time, and may indeed be mythical. Nonetheless, it is important as the backdrop against which current changes to medicine's role are experienced and understood.

The balance of power between generalists and specialists and between hospital and community practitioners continues to ebb and flow, yet the power of the profession as a whole persists, despite suggestions of its demise. The impressive buildings that make up the Royal Society of Medicine, the General Medical Council and the British Medical Association in London speak of medicine's ongoing command of resources. The authority of medical explanations of problems that might be better understood in social, political or moral terms, and the legitimacy of the medical solutions for the same problems, indicate the ongoing influence of medicine. Conditions associated with deprivation, such as obesity and depression; forms of deviancy, such as delinquency and drug addiction; features of the lifecycle, such as menstruation and the menopause; all these have become medicalized as both diagnosable and treatable by a relevant branch of medicine. 'Diagnostic creep' is the spreading of a definition of disease to include people who fall into 'at risk' categories because of their lifestyle, class or inheritance, and who may be altogether asymptomatic yet can still be subject to medical attention. Medicine continues to accrue ethical and moral responsibilities as, for instance, clinicians designate who should qualify for assisted conception and who is too old to benefit from interventionist surgery.

As described in Chapter 2, medicine also plays an important role in the absolution of full legal responsibility for people's actions through a medical diagnosis such as 'oppositional conflict disorder', 'severe and enduring mental illness', or alcoholism. A diagnosis of severe psychosis at the time of killing someone can lead to a person being found guilty of manslaughter instead of murder, which in some countries can incur a penal sentence rather than the death penalty. As well as looking to medicine for arbitration on individuals' responsibility for their behaviour, society depends on the promise of biomedical research and clinical innovation to solve some of the most feared global threats to humanity: the spread of HIV and the potential of an epidemic of Avian flu. In the western world we count on medicine to resolve the conditions that our affluence has rendered commonplace: stem cell research could offer new treatments for Alzheimer's and diabetes, while spare-part surgery may prevent the suffering incurred when specific body parts fail.

In the face of this type of evidence of medicine's influence in the contemporary world, how should we then interpret the suggestion that medicine's standing has been undermined? Is there evidence that medicine has lost its autonomy to the extent that its healthcare provision has been compromised? Given that medicine draws much of its authority from its clinical relationship with patients, is there any indication of a dissipation of trust between doctors and patients? Is it the case that the relationship between medicine and society has fundamentally shifted to the extent that the contract between doctors and patients has to be renegotiated?

As described in Chapter 9, the role of the paternalistic doctor in determining patients' healthcare needs has been predicated on the ideal of a disinterested professional ethos that safeguards the patient's interests. A number of trends have been identified which militate against this notion of the idealized, consensual doctor–patient relationship prevailing and it has been further suggested that doctors and patients are inevitably in conflict, albeit latent rather than overt. The social and economic context in which doctors and patients meet has changed dramatically since 1948, when the NHS was established, with the rise of chronic illnesses, an aging population, and a consumerist approach to healthcare leading to a more contractual relationship. The doctor–patient encounter is embedded in the context of commercial, administrative, bureaucratic, academic and educational interests. With the possible exception of the Indian railway system the NHS is the largest global bureaucracy, and doctors' success in defending their professional autonomy and dominance in the face of other groups' claims has been considerable. The phenomenal development of a world-wide market for healthcare and its associated products and services was not anticipated in the post-Second World War years, when the universally accessible service offered a relatively affordable means of responding to what was assumed to be a finite set of health needs. The range, efficacy and productivity of global biomedical business mean that today's doctor has countless more products compared to the simple equipment and analgesics available to the early twentieth century's family physician. The relative powerlessness of the family physician of the 1920s meant that expectations of a cure among patients were limited and thus there was a premium on interpersonal skills and bedside manner. The prospect of 'magic bullets' to target human ailments and twenty-first century patients' raised levels of education, of knowledge about specific health issues and of expectations of their quality of life, all create greater demands on doctors. Economic changes have seen markets fragmented and reconfigured to attend to (and create) customers' demands, while the rhetoric of consumer power has been used to gain leverage over medical dominance in NHS reform as was epitomized by the Patient's Charter published in 1991. Patient 'choice' continues to be pursued by political parties as a goal for NHS services and is becoming an economic reality as individuals buy hip operations in Germany and plastic surgery in South Africa, and also pay for alternative and complementary therapies to supplement orthodox biomedical services. That consumerism is more than just a convenient political rhetoric is suggested by the apparent increase in patients' willingness to make formal complaints and to pursue legal cases when treatment fails (although this varies considerably by medical specialism and locality).

DISAPPEARING DOCTORS, DISAPPEARING PATIENTS

Improvements in the efficacy of many medical interventions, including preventative measures, may have fuelled unrealistic expectations of medicine: if smallpox and polio can be eradicated, why not the common cold and influenza? If some cancers have become chronic diseases that are survivable, why isn't this true for all cancers?

Paradoxically, medicine's success may have had a negative effect on the doctor–patient relationship as patients' expectations exceed what clinicians can offer. In some instances the kindliness and compassion of the physician is no longer necessary: polio immunization works regardless of the mood of the clinician administering it and the diagnosis of tuberculosis from a lung X-ray does not require empathy. Indeed, it has been argued that one aim of a modern medical education is to achieve the alienated view of disease processes which allows trainees to practise the more invasive aspects of medicine and surgery. How can doctors otherwise overcome deeply ingrained taboos during surgery, and mutilate another's body in the name of healing and repair? By teaching histology, biochemistry, epidemiology and anatomy and with the dissection of a real cadaver still an important rite of passage, it is hardly surprising if doctors tend to develop a less than holistic view of human suffering and the process of healing.

During medical training, students are taught to substitute their intuitive, interpretive skills, learned from birth, with scientifically measurable and replicable means of assessing the parameters of human life that are inevitably reductionist. The mechanical model of the human body that informs much medical school teaching simplifies and perhaps facilitates student learning, but it can be badly misleading. The body is a complex adaptive system in which any input to the system has an unpredictable and potentially far-reaching consequence. How such complexity and adaptiveness can be communicated in medical curricula that are routinely taught and assessed without the input of far greater resources is not clear. Much medical practice has always been taught via a form of apprenticeship, where novice doctors learn on the job. Reform to reduce the number of hours that trainee doctors work (the European working time directive) means that fewer hours of apprenticeship are being accumulated, and so by the time a doctor qualifies he or she may have witnessed and participated in a smaller number of 'critical incidents' during their clinical practice.

Modern medicine works with relative risks, with tissue samples and biochemical indicators, focusing downwards on ever smaller constituent parts of the human organism towards a sub-cellular level. This 'geneticization' of medicine promises that every human ill is traceable to the level of DNA, and it is at this level that a cure will be effected through the use of pharmacogenetics.

The scientific progress that has underpinned medicine's development could in time perhaps do away with the doctor's role altogether. Doctors as diagnosticians could be negated by analytic computer software, digitalized imaging and modelling which could recall and compare more cases than any human being could experience in a lifetime. Furthermore, the possibilities of telemedicine mean that even where a doctor is needed to conduct diagnosis and treatment he does not have to be at the patient's bedside: diagnosis and surgical procedures can all be delivered remotely through the use of digital imaging technology and remote kinesis.

As the doctor disappears from some clinical encounters, the patient's body is also gradually disappearing from day-to-day clinical work in the sense that the whole humanity of a person, including his or her suffering, has dropped out of the clinical purview. Arguably the human body has been reduced to sets of scanned images, lab results and relative risks as it figures less and less in the process of diagnosis and treatment. Does any of this matter? After all, in some respects innovation in medicine continues to reduce pain and suffering: anxieties and depression can be treated with selective serotonin reuptake inhibitor (SSRI) antidepressants; the stigma of visible disability can be addressed by sophisticated plastic surgery; pre-natal diagnosis avoids the births of babies with serious impairments; disruptive behaviour and social non-conformity can be treated with methylphenidate-based drugs such as Ritalin and Daytrana; congenital heart problems can be remedied with surgery *in utero*; keyhole surgery makes intervention less invasive and recovery faster. And yet, despite these indisputable advances, the sense of there being something wrong with medicine persists in the minds of dissatisfied doctors and patients.

One index of concern over the loss of humanity in medicine's methods has been the reform of medical education. Problem-based learning, which encourages students to integrate knowledge and information while addressing a real medical problem as it would be encountered in practice, has become a fairly widespread feature. Inter-professional learning, where medical students are taught together with, for instance, trainee nurses or physiotherapists, encourages the co-operative team-working necessary for multi-disciplinary practice. Service users' perspectives and expert patients with whom doctors are encouraged to work in partnership also feature in medical school teaching, particularly where teaching takes place in community healthcare settings led by clinical staff. These reforms to medical education are aimed at producing a collaborative style of practice involving decision making that is shared between professionals and patients.

Do such reforms to medical education effectively address the sense of dissatisfaction and even alienation that patients say can compound the suffering and disorientation associated with the experience of illness itself (discussed in Chapter 9)? The disappearance of a personal and embodied style of medical practice has been held responsible for various developments in patients' behaviour. The presentation of growing numbers of the 'worried well', the anxious and the depressed in primary care may, paradoxically, suggest that medicine's methods are failing to respond appropriately to expressions of suffering. The expansion in the uptake of alternative therapies such as acupuncture and homeopathy can be attributed to people failing to have their symptoms alleviated by medicine and so they will search for a more benevolent relationship with a healer in which their own experiences are taken seriously. The therapeutic effects of the old-fashioned bedside manner, no longer cost effective in the NHS, are thus being used in alternative settings. Payment for aromatherapy, chiropractic or psychotherapy allows patients who can afford the fees to tell their individual story about symptoms, illness and suffering, relatively unconstrained by time and by the narrow expectations of biomedicine.

The frustration that patients feel with the reductionist, disease-focused aspects of medicine where evidence from service users is ignored has propelled the establishment of interest groups to campaign for, support and inform patients and carers. Charitable foundations, focused on a particular disease (the Muscular Dystrophy Society, Alzheimer's Society, Multiple Sclerosis Society), condition (Sense, Scope [formerly the Spastics Society], the Royal National Institute for the Blind), or syndrome (Gulf War Veterans, ME action), lobby for the interests of sufferers. Some of these organizations, such as Cancer UK and the Asthma Society, command considerable resources, being able to commission, fund and disseminate their own programmes of research and to lobby at high levels in government and medicine. Such groups support people by putting them in touch with others in the same position and by offering specialized counselling and/or information to those carers and sufferers who may be unsupported by statutory services, thereby relieving the professionals of a considerable burden of care. Other groups, such as JABS (Justice, Awareness and Basic support, a self-help group for accine-damaged children), effectively promote the views of a minority of doctors against the more orthodox medical line. The degree to which these groups campaign to radically reform medical practice, or more moderately seek to promote the interests of one condition within the existing medical context, varies.

The reluctance of patients to rely solely on orthodox medical advice from the GP is further illustrated by the enthusiastic uptake of alternative routes to biomedical advice, including the NHS Direct phone-line in England and Wales, the NHS24 phone-line in Scotland, walk-in NHS centres in England and Wales, and the internet, where health sites proliferate, offering information, chat rooms, hospital reviews, doctors' commentaries, picture libraries, patients' stories and blogs. People's desire to access health information that is independent of their family doctor should not, however, be interpreted simply as a withdrawal of trust in medicine: information is often used in a way that complements medicine, for instance by being presented to the doctor for discussion. The marketing of various publications, vitamins, herbs, gadgets, food, clothes, diagnostic testing and other products through old and new media attempts to persuade patients to behave more like consumers of healthcare. Health has become not just a personal obligation of self-care, but a lifestyle choice, an entertainment and a leisure-time pursuit.

Medicine has in turn had a rather tetchy attitude to those patients who bring information and ideas to consultations, with disparaging diagnoses of 'internetitis' implying patients who are exploring medical internet sites have too much time on their hands and are unlikely to be equipped to sift the available information. This updated version of hypochondria (traditionally levelled at any condition which does not fit medical categories) contrasts with the rhetoric of patient partnership and the expert patient that has been adopted in national health policies. The defensive attitude of some members of the medical profession suggests a discomfort with not being able to maintain a monopoly over a body of knowledge and expertise.

Another cultural change affecting the practice of old-style medicine is the 'risk-averse' climate and its impact on public and private life. The emphasis on risk avoidance as a rationale for various policies (from banning cigarette advertising and river-swimming, to restrictions on behaviours permissible within schools) has had particular implications for healthcare professionals. The culture of risk avoidance, monitored by clinical governance and measured by specific outcomes, has arguably intruded on the ability of a doctor to follow his own clinical intuition. Evidence-based practice subject to clinical governance assumes that best-practice can be defined, applied more generally, and its application monitored. Risks can be calculated and steps taken to minimize them, and the language of risk management implies that such practice can avoid adverse events altogether. Medical technology appears to manage, minimize and perhaps negate those risks: high dependency patients will have machines, monitoring breathing, pulse and heart-rate, to warn of a downturn in their vital signs. The apparent medical management of misfortune means that when it does strike people are less likely to respond with fatalism ('When you're number's up, you've just got to go') and more likely to look for recompense, public apologies, and undertakings to change future practice. The public's intolerance of mistakes or misfortune, combined with a 'blame' culture in the NHS whereby an individual scapegoat shoulders the culpability for a mishap, make the discussion of medical uncertainty and error very difficult. The role of medical uncertainty in adverse events is difficult to discuss because the medical profession has upheld a vision of an idealized, fault-free medical practice, where it is assumed that only professionals with an inadequate scientific knowledge or training will make errors.

DOCTORS' DIFFICULTIES

The rise in a consumerist attitude to health services, such that patients expect both fault-free practice and decisive reassurance from health professionals when faced with the uncertainties of illness, puts doctors in an unenviable position. This is even more unenviable when these contradictory patient needs are played out in the context of a general scepticism about authority, experts and the stability of scientific knowledge. Patients are increasingly likely to assert their own desire for certainty within the clinical relationship and, at the same time, will be aware of the insecurity that abounds in a secular, post-modern age. Doctors are, in many respects, poorly qualified to contend with the uncertainty that disease visits upon us, since biomedicine has made a virtue of its objectivity in naming and diagnosing diseases, and treating these as stable entities which can be unproblematically and repeatedly recognized in humans. Clinical diagnosis has been reduced to a comparison of a prototypical textbook case of an injury, pathology, condition or disease against a real case with all its individual peculiarities, assuming that enough information will lead to a correct diagnosis. When first introduced, the medical textbook was an innovative means of pooling experience that had been difficult to share in a largely oral teaching tradition, but the prototype described in the standard text has become the archetype which defines a truth. A textbook has become more than a teaching tool or an *aide memoire* to help recognize constellations of symptoms: it is the model against which observation is measured.

The business of diagnosis is, of course, much less certain than matching symptoms to a textbook description and this is manifest, according to some doctors, in over-diagnosis accompanied by unnecessary tests and procedures in an over-invasive attempt to reach diagnostic certainty. In some cases, such as a simple fracture, both diagnosis and treatment are unambiguous, but these are not the mainstay of medical practice which is better characterized as an undertaking fraught with uncertainty. While the diagnosis of conditions such as hypertension or diabetes may be clearly defined, the appropriate course of treatment is not. In other cases diagnosis is explicitly uncertain, as with the large proportion of women who receive a diagnosis of 'unexplained fertility' after hormonal and gamete testing, and yet this uncertain diagnosis does not prevent IVF treatment taking place in a large proportion of cases.

Clinical uncertainty can be addressed in various ways: experienced, confident practitioners may rely on a clinical sense of the patient's situation to a greater extent than the generalized and evidence-based rules would suggest. However, those lacking such confidence may, in checking their own practice against other doctors', tend towards the norm for the protection that it offers against accusations of deviancy. There are various examples of rates of surgical interventions (an easily measured aspect of clinical decision making) rising without any apparent increase in need, for instance grommets for glue ear, hysterectomy and Caesarean sections. This increase in the rate of intervention has been interpreted as a response to uncertainty in diagnosis rather than as an increase in the incidence of the conditions being treated.

REGULATING MEDICINE

Training for medical uncertainty takes place implicitly as part of a professional socialization into dealing with the 'problems' of medicine rather than viewing uncertainty as an integral component of medical knowledge and practice (Fox, 1957). The scientific view of a concrete world of knowable facts that underpins medical education remains unchallenged by a clinical education which promotes a reliance on personal experience as the response for coping with medical uncertainty. Far from undermining faith in the certainty of medical knowledge, the turn to individual experience is a means of recreating certainty and avoiding a consideration of the limits of medical knowledge (Atkinson, 1984). Medical certainty can be reinforced by casting an individual clinician's doubt as ignorance and currently unresolved areas of professional knowledge as awaiting further research for their ultimate resolution. The inadmissibility of uncertainty in medicine is a serious source of difficulty in medicine's relationship with other professionals, the public and for its contract with society. Since fact-based scientific certainty is a central object of medicine, those patients, carers, nurses or practitioners of alternative therapies who challenge medicine with evidence of iatrogenesis or ineffectiveness are met with a reiteration of 'the facts'. And since a successfully completed medical training is the only means by which access to the rarefied means of ascertaining 'the facts' can be gained, non-medical objectors' views are, by definition, excluded from consideration.

Cases of malpractice and mismanaged care that have received media attention have been a strong challenge to medicine's ability and right to define fact in medical terms. Devastatingly poor decision making at the Bristol Infirmary during the early 1990s – where the treatment of babies' heart conditions and the posthumous retention of their organs clearly served medical interests at the expense of patients and families – made the case for clinical governance and outside regulation unavoidable. The reluctance of doctors to question their colleagues' poor practice has also been highlighted in a variety of other cases, including the murderous GP Harold Shipman where other GPs have been called to account for their counter-signing of the death certificates of his victims. Despite physicians having urged their colleagues to acknowledge mistakes for years (Hilfiker, 1984), individual doctors who have attempted to break professional ranks and become 'whistle-blowers' have found it very difficult to have their allegations taken seriously, and if they do succeed to find employment in the UK subsequently. The discussion of medical errors has been kept within the profession, withheld from patients and the wider public: being privy to the discussion is part of the process of becoming a doctor (Bosk, 1979).

Dame Janet Smith, the High Court judge who chaired the investigation into the case of Harold Shipman, noted that the GMC had failed in its duty towards patients, tending to protect its own professional interests in preference to considering the public's safety or best interests (Smith, 2005). This preoccupation with the profession's interests had been noted more than a decade earlier in a sociological study of the GMC (Stacey, 1992). Smith's report details 'lessons from the past and proposals for the future' in recommending a new approach to primary care complaints in England. Her recommendations, described as 'revolutionary', have produced ample reaction from doctors, some of which suggests that any reform arising from the case of a murderous doctor will be resisted, on the grounds that Shipman's intent to murder could not have been tempered by any amount of professional re-validation or outside regulation. Another theme of the response has been that Dame Janet Smith cannot understand the nuanced complexity of the clinical process since she is not a doctor, reinforcing the idea that non-doctors cannot begin to appreciate and therefore regulate medicine. Smith is, of course, a lawyer and so is representative of the only non-medical profession that regularly arbitrates on medical matters when disputes go through the courts.

The respective parents of Charlotte Wyatt and of baby MB (whose anonymity has been lawfully protected) have both resorted to legal action when agreement with doctors over appropriate treatment for their child eluded them: these parents wanted more aggressive treatment or resuscitation than doctors felt was warranted. In Charlotte Wyatt's case the judge imposed a 'Do Not Resuscitate' (DNR) order, in line with doctors' views, although it was subsequently lifted when the child survived longer than had been expected. Doctors wanted to withdraw life-sustaining treatment from Baby MB on the grounds that he was suffering intolerably. But the judge ruled in favour of the parents, who argued that their son's life was worth living. Innovation in medical technology and clinical care has meant that very sick children can be kept alive and so we are likely to see more cases of parents and professionals disagreeing about treatment plans. The complex and emotionally fraught nature of these cases turns on defining what is in the sick child's best interests and who should define it. While such cases do not often end up in the courts in the UK, when they do, lawyers are providing something akin to a mediation service rather than behaving as a regulatory body. This type of legal intervention is, however, unlikely to develop into the type of aggressive litigation that has impaired medical practice in the USA. Medical posts there apparently remain unfilled in those specialties and localities particularly prone to tort litigation, and some physicians have refused to treat lawyers or their families so as to avoid the risk of being sued. The aftermath of the Shipman Inquiry, in terms of the threat of external regulation of medicine, has yet to be determined and the legal profession may still become more involved in regulating medicine in Britain.

REFORM FROM WITHIN

Medicine's right to self-regulate has been crucial for its development as a powerful profession and the prospect of this ending marks a significant change. The danger of self-regulation is that criticism from outside the profession can be ignored, but one of the remarkable features of medicine has been its ability to adapt to changing demands through accommodation.

Nurses have demanded increased autonomy from medicine and designated nurse practitioners and midwives are currently permitted to diagnose and prescribe for a limited range of conditions. The European working time directive required a reduction in the hours that junior doctors worked, creating a pressure for nurses to take on some of the tasks that trainee doctors had performed (Rees Jones, 2003) and therefore granting extra autonomy to nominated nurses occurred at a strategic moment. Non-medical therapies popular with the public, such as aromatherapy, talking therapies and acupuncture, far from threatening medical dominance are being subsumed within the medical project. Some primary care trusts offer the services of counsellors and aromatherapists, thereby freeing up doctors' time. Hour for hour, a doctor's time is more costly than most alternative therapists' and so their employment can represent a saving to trusts in economic terms. Where marshalled by medicine, complementary therapies may make medicine more difficult to challenge from without, since by absorbing alternative therapeutic methods it has responded to criticism of a reductionist, disease-centred style of practice.

The discontents with medicine and its methods expressed by patients and other healthcare professionals do not, at present, seem to constitute a challenge to medicine's institutional power. This is not to say that patients, or indeed doctors, are content with the situation, but that medicine as a practice and as a body of individual and institutional interests can modify certain procedures to answer its critics without jeopardizing the overall project. The challenges that might seriously alter medicine's role in society come from the state, the legal system and, crucially, from within medicine itself.

Contravention of conventional medical wisdom has been very successful when undertaken by a physician and the examples are numerous. Obstetrician Grantley Dick-Read (1890–1959) published *Childbirth Without Fear*, in which he suggested that doctors created much of the fear and pain experienced by women during childbirth and recommended antenatal education including breathing and relaxation techniques. His ideas were promulgated by the National Childbirth Trust that was established in 1956 and these were central to campaigns to rescue birth from high-tech hospital routinization. French gynaecologist Fernand Lamaze (1891–1957) published *Painless Childbirth* in 1956, and Frederique Leboyer (born 1918) who was *Chef de Clinique* in the Paris Faculty of Medicine published *Pour Une Naissance Sans Violence* (Birth Without Violence) in 1974. Their ideas were taken up by Michel Odent (born 1930), an obstetrician who has been influential in encouraging women to give birth in a comfortable position and in an environment that is soothing, warm and welcoming to the newborn. *The Common Sense Book of Baby and Child Care,* published in 1946, was written by paediatrician Dr Benjamin Spock (1903–1998) and stressed the freedom and relaxation of medically endorsed and regimented childcare regimes. This sold over 30 million copies and was hugely influential on the post-war generation's childrearing habits.

The Swiss-born physician and psychiatrist Elizabeth Kübler-Ross (1926–2004) wrote *On Death and Dying* in 1969, which drew attention to the taboos around death and encouraged their frank discussion. Cicely Saunders, a British nurse and physician (1918–2005), developed the hospice movement, founding the St Christopher's hospice in 1967 as a means of encouraging 'good' deaths, free from pain and fear. Leading anti-psychiatry campaigners, themselves practising psychiatrists – Thomas Szasz (born 1920) in the USA, and R.D. Laing (1927–1989) in the UK – routinely appealed to the public against their own colleagues and profession.

Medicine's ability to cohere as a discipline and a profession, despite the disruptive effects of the work of such visionary reformers, is remarkable. Reforming physicians have fundamentally changed how medicine is viewed and practised, using ideas that were drawn from beyond what, at the time, constituted conventional medicine.

NON-HUMAN THREATS

Medicine's good standing in society has been maintained by its responsiveness to change, which is often driven by physicians who are highly critical of medicine. The challenge that could prove most trying for medicine, however, may come from the microbial world rather than human society. One of medicine's big twenty-first century challenges is the question of whether medicine can keep up with the speed of evolution of viral and bacterial life forms that can evade the human immune system and produce symptoms that challenge medical therapeutics.

Over the past 25 years the numbers of new viral infections have increased dramatically: the Lassa, Ebola and Hanter viruses and HIV have each appeared by crossing the species barrier from a natural host to humankind. Viruses that may provoke no symptoms in their monkey or pig host can cause severe symptoms and premature death in infected humans. Rapid urbanization and intensive farming methods have together brought about ideal conditions for the emergence of new strains of influenza and other viruses which have the potential to spread extremely rapidly, given the speed and accessibility of long-distance travel. HIV spread from its host – monkeys in Africa – to almost every country in the world within two decades. New strains of bacteria, such as E.coli that causes gastroenteritis, MRSA that is responsible for necrotizing fasciitis, and the bacterium causing tuberculosis, have all emerged in recent years and existing medical methods have struggled to cope (Crawford, 2000). There is evidence an Avian flu virus can cross from domestic poultry to humans and a suspicion that a transfer between humans has already taken place. Should a mutation of the Avian virus permit efficient human-to-human transfer, an epidemic is possible because in many parts of the world humans and poultry live in very close proximity. Outbreaks of SARS, an atypical and highly contagious strain of pneumonia-causing virus, were contained in local epidemics in 2002–2003 and did not become pandemic, but the disease could recur. Clostridium difficile, a bacterium that occurs naturally in the human gut, may be evolving drug-resistant strains which could prove more problematic in the future. Research also suggests that the SARS infections, as with many previous epidemics in human history, were blamed on immigrants, and this blame was then associated with racialized abuse (Eichelberger, 2007).

In 1969 the US Surgeon-General Dr William Stewart prematurely announced that the book of infectious diseases was closed, since, in his view, western development had conquered epidemics. It would now seem that microbial challenges to medicine are in part a consequence of medicine's own methods, for instance the emergence of antibiotic resistant (and so, to humans, virulently anti-human) strains of tuberculosis and diphtheria. The need for very specialized research and clinical experience to treat new microbial infections also raises the possibility of medicine fragmenting as a single discipline. In global terms the hazard to humanity of HIV potentially outweighs any other disease, as it removes virtually a whole cohort of parents of working age in various African countries. HIV's effects in India, China and other countries remain to be seen, not least because its presence has been denied for an extended period of time. The global inequalities that a disease like AIDS opens up also present another potential hazard to medicine. Will doctors working with AIDS patients in the majority world, without the funds to supply retroviral therapy, continue to see themselves as part of the same profession as surgeons in Europe who are developing the use of a machine to keep cadaver hearts beating during transplantation? Or are the diseases of the rich world so different from the diseases of the poor world that the medical professions that treat them will, inevitably, diverge?

PROSPECTS

'For centuries the medical enterprise was too feeble to attract radical critiques' although it always had its mockers, suggests Roy Porter (1997) concluding his history of medicine. There have been anxieties about medicine and its methods in the past which have not (yet) accurately predicted the demise of the profession nor its removal from its esteemed position in society. The number and strength of medicine's critics within and beyond the profession could be seen as an indication of the general commitment to maintaining medicine's relevance and vitality as both a practice and a science in contemporary society: criticism is rarely consistently levelled at institutions regarded as simply irrelevant. Assuming that medicine continues to respond to critics constructively, then perhaps it will address issues such as medical uncertainty and the place of sorrow and human suffering in a therapeutic regimen.

While reform has transformed medical practice from within, the great challenge to medicine today is how to admit non-medical evidence and respond to it constructively. The microbial world presents a challenge of a different order to the practice of medicine. Humanity has always lived with the threat of fatal infections, but the eradication of smallpox and polio and the reduction of the threat from others has altered our expectations. The death toll from HIV infection still continues to rise and the possibility of serious pandemics of SARS or a new form of flu reminds us of the impressive speed and diversity of microbial evolution. It seems unlikely that humanity will ever be able to congratulate itself on the total and lasting defeat of viral and bacterial infection. Despite medicine increasingly treating chronic disease, and despite the allure of the high technology approach to medicine, infectious disease management looks set to remain part of the medical mission.

Further reading

Kelleher, D., Gabe, J. and Williams, G. (eds) (2006) *Challenging Medicine*. London: Routledge.

An interesting set of essays covering a range of potential influences on medicine's institutional standing.

Bury, M. (2008) 'New dimensions of health care organisation', in D.Wainwright (ed.), *A Sociology of Health*. London: SAGE. pp. 151–72.

An up-to-date survey of the government initiatives regulating the provision of healthcare towards a 'patient-led NHS' and the resulting shifts in the relationship between providers and recipients of services.

REVISION QUESTIONS

1 What factors have raised patients' expectations about their healthcare?

2 Name some of the sources of information that people will use in addition to their family doctor.

3 What are the major microbial challenges facing medicine at present?

4 How is medicine regulated and how might this change in the light of Dame Janet Smith's reports?

EXTENSION QUESTIONS

1 Who should regulate medicine?

The following excerpt comes from an editorial written by Richard Smith (when he was editor of the *British Medical Journal*) during a furore over the absence of a doctor on the panel of the independent inquiry into the practice of paediatric heart surgery in Bristol.

> Doctors in Britain have been insufficiently regulated for too long. It has been too easy for doctors to sink into poor and dangerous performance without anybody doing anything. Now in response to a storm of publicity about bad doctors we may be in danger of overregulation. The dangers of overregulation may be less obvious than those of underregulation, but in the long run they may be just as damaging ... Those who put their fingers into the hearts and brains of others to try and save their lives are qualitatively different from those who don't: it requires a special kind of courage and a mixture of compassion and detachment that most find difficult to muster. Only another surgeon can understand fully the difficulties that the Bristol surgeons faced. (Smith, R. (1998) 'Regulation of doctors and the Bristol inquiry', *British Medical Journal* (5 Dec), 317: 1539–40).

- Do you concur with the respect that Smith accords to surgeons?
  Interventionist work that carries a high risk of death and disability for the patient, and that also holds out the prospect of dramatic improvement, is sometimes termed 'heroic

medicine'. Respect for 'heroic medicine' where the doctor is the main hero, as expressed by Richard Smith, is widespread. So too was condemnation of the disregard for patients' dignity that was shown by the Bristol Royal Infirmary surgeons.

- Do the high risks of surgery for patients, particularly paediatric patients, mean that the practice should be regulated solely by other surgeons, or does it make it more important that non-surgeons and non-doctors participate in regulation?
- Should medicine be regulated differently, according to the activities involved – for instance, can success and failure in community paediatrics, renal surgery and obstetrics all be judged by similar criteria?

2 Diagnostic and therapeutic medicine

In an article in the *Observer* newspaper, Charles Rodeck, a specialist in foetal medicine who has pioneered ultra-sound screening, comments that:

> Our diagnostic abilities have outstripped our therapeutic skills … We now screen more women and can identify a huge variety of abnormalities, but we still can only treat a minuscule fraction. Very often all we can do is give parents two options: to keep or terminate their pregnancy …

because, as the journalist points out, 'Other options, such as attempting an operation in the womb, are still very rare'.

(See Hill, A. (2007) *The Observer*, 15 July, available in full at the following link: http://observer.guardian.co.uk/focus/story/0,,2126656,00.html)

- Is it responsible for medical practice to develop sophisticated diagnostic techniques for conditions that cannot be treated?

3 In fiction (for example *Bodies* (2002) by Jed Mercurio and *A Vicious Circle* (1997) by Amanda Craig) the death of patients at the hands of inexperienced or uncertain doctors has been described.

- Is medical error an inevitable part of medical practice?
- How can trainee doctors learn without making mistakes on patients?
- How has medical uncertainty been dealt with in your training to date?

4 Is it ethically appropriate to fund medical research into obesity and coronary heart disease, when dysentery and malaria remain such serious health threats on a global scale?

12 CONCLUSION

Chapter summary

This chapter describes:

» how criticism of the institution of medicine and the organization of healthcare is a professional rather than an individual responsibility;

» how individual practitioners have to develop a style of practice that alleviates the symptoms of disease and also the wider difficulties that patients and colleagues face;

» how some minimal and initial steps towards this can be suggested in terms of communication style and content, the treatment of medical uncertainty and an understanding of each patient's context.

INTRODUCTION

This book has rehearsed a number of criticisms levelled at medicine and the dominant role it plays in defining health and in the organization of healthcare. These criticisms have been influential in the NHS and in the reform of the healthcare system which have sought to emphasize the patient's concerns and priorities. Such reform notwithstanding, medicine continues to be the most powerful player in healthcare provision and this can be seen in national negotiations about the terms and conditions of healthcare workers as well as in day-to-day interactions between individuals. For the most part, patients and their carers welcome the confident expertise of doctors, while the occupational division within the NHS relies on medical authority. Although medical power can be seen as functional in many ways, medicine's focus on pathology as a means of diagnosing and treating disease leaves little room for patients' embodied suffering and their priorities in healthcare. Attempts to change the balance of power in healthcare provision have been made, with the promotion of managers' role in the NHS, reforms to make 'the money follow the patient' in the 1990s, and the current emphasis on primary care trusts in England as the means of reflecting local community priorities.

The NHS, like medicine, is a big, complex and fractured institution, and there is every danger that at the end of a medical training those students who become fully-fledged doctors may feel that they have little influence over the shape and direction of their profession. This final, short chapter will try to persuade the reader of the possibility and necessity of doctors continuing to reform medicine and will offer some initial suggestions on the development of a style of practice that might facilitate this.

CHANGE AND CONTINUITY

In the UK, where the majority of medical practice is the provision of statutorily funded services, the state has played a key role in the regulation and facilitation of medicine. However, despite the political and statutory structures within which medicine works and the power of other professions, particularly the law, the medical profession continues to be self-regulating and any influences from beyond the profession remain tempered. During the 1970s when doctors felt that their professional status was threatened they were prepared to withdraw their services in order to see their own conditions (and therefore their patients', so they argued) improved. Arguably, the effectiveness of that strike in maintaining doctors' rewards and autonomy meant that people are still keen to start a medical training and so the profession remains buoyant. Medicine continues to expand as a profession, with new specialist areas emerging. Patients clearly benefit from clinical innovation, with the availability of a wider range of treatments with improved effectiveness. But can critics from within and beyond the profession be answered in a way that ensures the public's trust in the profession of medicine?

Critics have suggested that reforms to the NHS leading to contractual relationships between the providers and recipients of services, and between the various providers themselves, have eroded trust. High levels of trust between clinicians, patients and managers are seen by many commentators as crucial for a responsive NHS (Annandale, 1998). Can medicine address patients' negative experience of health services, such as depersonalization and alienation, to reduce the unwelcome effects of institutionalization? Can medicine work so as to alleviate, rather than compound, the inequities that patients face in the wider world?

EFFECTIVE CARE: COMPETING PRIORITIES

A doctor may have a decade or more training in a highly specialized area such as rare forms of cancer or complex child development disorders, and from an organizational view this doctor is best deployed by applying these skills to the largest possible number of NHS patients. Therefore this doctor should delegate much of the care and communication work to more junior doctors or other allied professionals who do not have his specialized, technical skills. This is how hospital medicine is organized, with, for instance, consultant surgeons maximizing their time in theatre and less experienced doctors running clinics on their behalf. From a patient's point of view, trying to make sense of an illness, reconstruct a life-story and adjust his identity, there are serious disadvantages to this delegation of care and communication: there is a sense of dislocation when a clinic consultation is held with a doctor who did not carry out the surgery or recommend the treatment plan. This is a genuine dilemma in healthcare organization: the conveyor belt approach to medicine might get more hip replacements completed in a shorter time. However, is a gain in throughput outweighed by the disorientation of the patient being processed with all due speed? This is a question for the medical profession, rather than the individual practitioner of medicine.

Can individuals, and especially trainees, act to influence the direction of the development of the medical profession? If you have read the preceding 11 chapters of this book, you will appreciate that medicine can be seen as being embedded in a political, economic and social context. What is the significance of an appreciation of the context of medical practice for individual practitioners? For a sociological analysis, the significance can be summarized in one word: power. Trainee doctors will very often feel powerless within the day-to-day business of medicine, in terms of meeting the multiple and sometimes conflicting demands of their superiors, the representatives of other professional and occupational groups, patients and the patients' significant others. Trainees are, of course, the next generation of superiors, but in the shorter term, what can the responsible medical student do? The answer is she or he can use what limited power is available to him or her in a way that is careful and attentive.

THE POLITICS OF COMMUNICATION

One very simple means of addressing some of the de-humanizing effects of medicine's approach to the patient is the style of communication. As part of the high-throughput approach to medicine, some professionals do not waste time introducing themselves, or using patients' names. During a course of treatment a patient is likely to meet many health professionals, and since it can be difficult to tell the difference between a midwifery assistant, a hospital visitor and a paediatrician, it helps a patient to know what to expect from a professional if the role as well as the name is given in an introduction. For instance: 'My name is Dr Ray and I am here to discuss the result of the scan you had last week and your treatment options.'

Using a patient's name is an important check on their identity, but also has the effect of acknowledging an identity other than that of 'patient'. If names are unfamiliar then Mrs Sareshwallah or Miss Ngugi may correct your pronunciation, giving them momentary authority. The pace of social change in British society and the ease of international travel mean that one cannot assume shared values or culture let alone a shared language when encountering a patient. This means that all communication should be geared to avoiding offence and cues should be taken from the patient.

Although informality increasingly characterizes British communication, with first name terms between colleagues becoming a widespread norm, this does not suit everyone. When a doctor uses a patient's first name in a consultation this is generally meant to indicate a friendly lack of hierarchy or equality. However, informality is not universally interpreted as friendly and the use of a first name may give an impression of impertinence, disrespect or of being inappropriately over-familiar.

A systematic approach when meeting a patient is to check their full name and ask how they wish to be addressed as follows:

Doctor. 'Good-morning. [Consulting notes] Um you are Mrs Gladys McCormick?'
Patient nods.
Doctor. 'Good. Can I call you Mrs McCormick?'
Patient nods again.

Having been addressed formally in the first instance, Mrs McCormick could say 'No, please doctor, call me Gladys.' However, if the doctor had said 'Can I call you Gladys?' only a very confident patient would request greater formality: 'Please don't use my first name, only my husband and sister use that. Call me Mrs McCormick.' Some cultures also tend to use full names for everyone: it is a Quaker tradition to avoid titles and their self-aggrandisement by using first and second names to identify people. In the Sikh tradition, men have Singh as a second name and women have Kaur. In the British context some women will have adopted their husband's surnames, but just because 'Gurinder Kaur' is married to 'Kiran Singh' it does not necessarily mean that she is known as 'Mrs Singh'. So a safe bet is to use the full name, as written on the notes, rather than guess at a title: 'Good evening Fatima Abdullah!' is safer than 'Good evening Miss Abdullah!' when you discover that the patient has been married for 10 years and feels offended at being demoted to her unmarried status.

Why does any of this matter? Names are only names aren't they? Surely it's the treatment that counts? But addressing people by an appropriate name is important because firstly it makes sure that the correct notes are available. Secondly, it also gives a strong signal to the patient that he or she is being talked to with some measure of respect and in their own right. Talking to the patient in a way that notes their social status brings a medical consultation in line with other forms of social interaction. Failing to do this is unprofessional. For instance, the routine, sloppy practice of addressing children's women carers as 'Mum' perhaps avoids the need to get a person's title wrong: Mrs, Miss or Ms can prove a tricky choice. However, an adult woman who is not the child's mother is in an awkward position – foster mothers, older sisters, aunts, lesbian partners and young-looking grand-mothers can all be assumed to be 'Mum'. More respectful alternatives would be to take the time to consult the child's notes and to ask the woman accom-panying Muhammed Qureshi whether she is in fact 'Mrs Qureshi' and whether she is the child's mother.

Having established a suitable name, it should have become clear whether the doctor and patient have any language in common. It is useful to do this before getting into more clinical matters. Where a patient does not speak English and the patient and doctor don't share another language, there will be a major problem. Ideally, an interpreter who is trained to work in medical set-tings and in whom the patient trusts should be present. Ideally also, the doctor should be trained in how to work with an interpreter. Despite an official com-mitment that the quality of service should not be compromised by language, the coverage of NHS clinical settings by adequate translation services is cur-rently poor. Doctors should insist that their hospitals and clinics are served by local or remote telephone translation services. This would reduce the chances of people who don't speak English receiving inappropriate care, or experienc-ing delays in their care, or having their confidentiality breeched.

Assuming that a common language can be established, another important feature of a consultation is that a doctor listens to a patient. 'The patient will tell you the diagnosis' is a longstanding aphorism passed on to medical students and yet, on average, doctors tend to interrupt their patients after only 18 seconds. Is this a fear that if not re-directed a patient's speech will continue *ad infinitum*? If so, it is ill founded since, if allowed to proceed, a patient's full story lasts only 28 seconds on average (Svab and Katic, 1991). People are willing to report very stigmatized, painful problems including domestic violence and rape to doctors because they are trusted professionals and because such problems can have devastating effects on their health. However, this means a doctor listening to the clues that a patient might be offering in the hope that they might ask the right question. Abuse is also very often experienced as the victim's own fault so that feelings of shame makes admitting to its occurrence difficult. Allowing the patient's own story to come out in full, in their terms, at the start of a consultation, is not only cour-teous, there is also some evidence that the ability to tell one's own story may be therapeutic in and of itself.

A patient's understanding of his or her condition will develop and change, especially over the course of a chronic problem. Some people will want to be aware of and involved in decisions about their treatment, and others will prefer to delegate all aspects of their care to their family or to healthcare staff.

How is a doctor to ascertain a patient's knowledge or preferred style of clinical care? Often patients will be quite clear about what they want, but where this does not happen the style of communication recommended by clinicians who regularly have to break bad news is useful. This involves regularly checking what the patient knows by persuading them to talk as much as the doctor does. A consultation might open with 'Tell me what you know about your illness' and the answer may give an impression of the patient's understanding and priorities. When giving complex and emotive information, a preparedness to repeatedly check the patient's interpretation of what the doctor has just said avoids situations where patients nod or say 'Yes' simply because they feel it is expected of them.

UNCERTAINTY

None of the suggestions made so far will transform clinical practice into a simple, straightforward, consistently mutually satisfying encounter. Medicine is shot through with uncertainty and yet this is not often reflected in doctor–patient interactions. Medical educators have long been criticized for teaching students to strive for an unrealistic, error-free practice (Mulcahy, 2003). Teaching students to cope with both error and uncertainty as part of their clinical reasoning might help a patient's evidence on their illness to be taken more seriously. It has also been suggested that a better tolerance of uncertainty in clinical communication would benefit patients from minority cultures (Gerrish et al., 1996): rushing to a diagnosis based on misunderstood or missing patient evidence may give the impression of certainty, but it will in fact cover up what remains unknown. Allowing some queries to ride from consultation to consultation may, in some cases, be a professional and appropriate response to issues that cannot be rapidly or satisfactorily resolved.

CONTEXT

Developing a respectful and reflective style of communication is part of establishing a practice that acknowledges power differentials and seeks to build trust. Medicine has traditionally worried about communication as a means of enhancing compliance: 'If we make our instructions clear enough, patients will conform to our orders.'

Communication style is also, as has been suggested, an important indication to the patient of what his or her role will be in treatment: patient-centred care can only become a practice (rather than a rhetoric) if patients have a sense of being part of the process. If patients are routinely spoken to in a dignified manner, it is much harder to dismiss them carelessly during treatment.

Style of communication is central to giving patients a dignified role in the process of healthcare. However, as this book has discussed much illness causation, incidence and recovery occurs outside the healthcare system. Some of the limitations of medicine's consideration of community-based experience of illness can be addressed by considering a patient's social context as part of a diagnosis. A major contributory factor to illness is poverty: any condition is likely to do better when the sufferer has sufficient food, a decent home that is heated and furnished, and where there are adequate resources to care for children and other dependants. The complex procedures for claiming benefits, grants and tax credits from local and national agencies means that a considerable portion of the funds set aside by government to alleviate deprivation remain unclaimed. Hospital social workers bear some of this workload, but as in-patient stays become shorter this is less likely to be a site where social problems can be resolved. Some primary care trusts work alongside benefits advisers from the Citizens Advice Bureau so that patients, particularly those with disability and/or small children, can get good quality advice in a primary care setting. The advantage for the doctor is that once complex social, housing and financial problems have been addressed, the medical problems may be easier to understand and to treat. Illness is experienced in terms of its impact on daily life, but medicine tends to view a disease as a collection of symptoms and signs. However, unless medical treatment has a positive impact on the individual patient's daily life, can it be considered successful? Medical therapy is only as good as its outcomes.

This chapter has suggested that one means of improving outcomes is to practise what is known as 'person-centred care', whereby every intervention is considered from the point of view of the person experiencing it. If the idea of putting the patient's body and identity at the centre of medical concern were to be taken seriously, it would lead to services organized around patients' needs, rather than the convenience of the professionals or the demands of the organization. It would also mean that the boundaries between different professionals within health and social care would be dissolved, so that patients did not have to make sense of such professional divisions. Some of these changes towards 'joined-up services' delivered by a team of professionals are happening, but progress is inevitably limited by the requirements of budgeting and political agendas together with the inertia of organizations.

The number of reorganizations in the NHS has doubtless sapped professionals' willingness to co-operate and has contributed to cynicism. But since health policy is under direct political stewardship, there is a need for public sector professionals to resist cynical disengagement and to participate in the democratic process to safeguard the future of the NHS. The General Medical Council has focused much of its efforts on formulating education for tomorrow's doctors. Perhaps an equally important message for the profession is that trainees are the day-after-tomorrow's patients.

REFERENCES

INTRODUCTION

Illich, I. (1976) *Limits to Medicine: Medical Nemesis: The Expropriation of Health*. London: Boyars.

O'Neill, B. (2000) 'Doctor as murderer', *British Medical Journal* (5 February), 320: 329–30.

CHAPTER 1

Klein, R. (2000) *The New Politics of the NHS*. New York: Prentice Hall.

McKeown, T. (1979) *The Role of Medicine: Dream, Mirage or Nemesis*? Oxford: Basil Blackwell.

Porter, R. (1997) *The Greatest Benefit to Mankind: A Medical History of Humanity from Antiquity to the Present*. London: HarperCollins.

CHAPTER 3

Blaxter, M. (1990) *Health and Lifestyles*. London: Routledge.

Bradby, H. (1997) 'Health, heating and heart attacks: Glaswegian Punjabi women's thinking about everyday food', in P. Caplan (ed.), *Food, Health and Identity*. London: Routledge. pp. 211–33.

Cornwell, J. (1984) *Hard-Earned Lives: Accounts of Health and Illness from East London*. London: Tavistock.

Currer, C. (1986) 'Concepts of mental well- and ill-being: the case of Pathan mothers in Britain', in C. Currer and M. Stacey (eds), *Concepts of Health, Illness and Disease: A Comparative Perspective*. Leamington Spa: Berg. pp. 181–98.

Helman, C.G. (1978) '"Feed a cold, starve a fever": folk models of infection in an English suburban community, and their relation to medical treatment', *Culture, Medicine and Psychiatry*, 2: 107–37.

Herzlich, C. and Pierret, J. (1984, 1987) *Illness and Self in Society*. Baltimore: Johns Hopkins University Press.

Pill, R. and Stott, N.C. (1982) 'Concepts of illness causation and responsibility: some preliminary data from a sample of working class mothers', *Social Science and Medicine*, 16 (1): 43–52.

Scambler, A., Scambler, G. and Craig, D. (1981) 'Kinship and friendship networks and women's demand for primary care', *Journal of the Royal College of General Practitioners*, 31: 746–50.

CHAPTER 4

Acheson, Sir Donald (1998) 'Independent inquiry into inequalities in health report'. London: The Stationery Office. (Also available from: http://www.archive.official-documents.co.uk/document/doh/ih/ih.htm)

Bowling, A. (1999) 'Ageism in cardiology', *British Medical Journal* (20 November), 319 (7221): 1353–5.

Clarke, J.N. (1983) 'Sexism, feminism and medicalism: a decade review of literature on gender and illness', *Sociology of Health and Illness*, 5: 62–82.

Cummins, S. (2003) 'The local food environment and health – some reflections from the UK', *American Journal of Public Health*, 93 (4): 521.

Davey Smith G., Morris J.N. and Shaw, M. (1998) 'The independent inquiry into inequalities in health', *British Medical Journal* (28 November), 317: 1465–6.

Department of Health (1998) *Our Healthier Nation*. London: The Stationery Office. (Also available at: http://www.archive.official-documents.co.uk/document/doh/ih/ih.htm)

Ellaway, A. and Macintyre, S. (2000) 'Shopping for food in socially contrasting localities', *British Food Journal*, 102: 52–9.

Fox, A.J. and Goldblatt, P.O. (1982) *Longitudinal Study: Sociodemographic Mortality Differentials 1971–1985*. London: HMSO.

Goldblatt, P.O. (1989) 'Mortality by social class 1971–85', *Population Trends*, 56: 6–15.

Gwatkin, D.K. (2000) 'Health inequalities and the health of the poor. What do we know? What can we do?', *Bulletin of the World Health Organisation*, 78 (1): 3–17.

Macintyre, S. and Ellaway, A. (1998) 'Social and local variations in the use of urban neighbourhoods: a case study in Glasgow', *Health and Place*, 4: 91–4.

Macintyre, S., Hunt, K. and Sweeting, H. (1996) 'Gender differences in health: are things really as simple as they seem?', *Social Science and Medicine*, 42 (4): 617–24.

Marmot, M. (2004) *Status Syndrome: How your Social Standing Directly Affects your Health and Life Expectancy*. London: Bloomsbury.

Marmot, M.G., Adelstein, A.M. and Bulusu, L. (1984) *Immigrant Mortality in England and Wales 1970–1978*. London: OPCS/HMSO.

Nazroo, J.Y. (1997) *The Health of Britain's Ethnic Minorities: Findings from a National Survey*. London: Policy Studies Institute.

Nazroo, J.Y. (1998) 'Genetic, cultural or socio-economic vulnerability? Explaining ethnic inequalities in health', *Sociology of Health and Illness*, 20 (5): 710–30.

Notzon, F., Komarov, Y., Ermakov, S., Sempos, C., Marks, J. and Sempos, E. (1998) 'Causes of declining life expectancy in Russia', *Journal of the American Medical Association*, 279 (10): 793–800.

ONS (2003) *Deaths: By Age and Sex, 1971–2021: Social Trends 33*. Newport: Office for National Statistics. (Also available at http://www.statistics.gov.uk/StatBase/Product.asp?vlnk= 9794&More=Y)

Townsend, P., Whitehead, M. and Davidson, N. (1988) *Inequalities in Health: The Black Report: The Health Divide*. London: Penguin.

Wilkinson, R. (2005) *The Impact of Inequality: How to Make Sick Societies Healthier*. London: Routledge.

CHAPTER 5

Ahmad, W. (1996) 'Consanguinity and related demons: science and racism in the debate on consanguinity and birth outcome', in S. Samson and N. South (eds), *Conflict and Consensus in Social Policy*. Basingstoke: Macmillan. pp. 68–87.

Ahmad, W., Darr, A., Jones, L. and Nisar, G. (1998) *Deafness and Ethnicity: Services, Policy and Politics*. Bristol: The Policy Press in association with the Joseph Rowntree Foundation.

Bennett, R.L., Motulsky, A.G. and Bittles, A., Hudgins, L., Uhrich, S., Doyle, D.L., Silvey, K., Scott, C.R., Cheng, E., McGillivray, B., Steiner, R. and Olson, D. (2002) 'Genetic counseling and screening of consanguineous couples and their offspring: recommendations of the National Society of Genetic Counselors', *Journal of Genetic Counseling*, 11 (2): 97–119.

Bittles, A. (2005) 'Background summary'. Available at: http://www.consang.net/ (accessed 19 March 2005).

Davison, C., Davey Smith, G. and Frankel, S. (1991) 'Lay epidemiology and the prevention paradox: implications for coronary candidacy and health education', *Sociology of Health and Illness*, 13 (1): 1–19.

Demicheli, V., Jefferson, T., Rivetti, A. and Price, D. (2005) 'Vaccines for measles, mumps and rubella in children', *The Cochrane Database of Systematic Reviews*, 4. (Art. No.: CD004407. DOI: 10.1002/14651858.CD004407.pub2.)

Department of Health (1999) *Saving Lives: Our Healthier Nation*. London: The Stationery Office.

Graham, H. (1993) *When Life's a Drag: Women, Smoking and Disadvantage*. London: HMSO.

Shaw, M. (2001) 'Try our alternative slant on the "Top 10 tips for better health"', *Health Service Journal*, 27 September: 20.

Shaw, M., Mitchell, R. and Dorling, D. (2000) 'Time for a smoke? One cigarette reduces your life by 11 minutes', *British Medical Journal*, 320: 53.

Sheon, N. and Crosby, G.M. (2003) 'Ambivalent tales of HIV disclosure in San Francisco', *Social Science & Medicine*, 58 (11): 2105–18.

CHAPTER 6

Bury, M. (1982) 'Chronic illness as biographical disruption', *Sociology of Health and Illness*, 4 (2): 167–82.

Bury, M. (2001) 'Illness narratives, fact or fiction?', *Sociology of Health and Illness*, 23 (1): 263–85.

Carricaburu, D. and Pierret, J. (1995) 'From biographical disruption to biographical reinforcement: the case of HIV positive men', *Sociology of Health and Illness*, 17 (1): 65–87.

Charmaz, K. (1994) 'Identity Dilemmas of Chronically Ill Men', *The Sociological Quarterly*, 35 (2): 269–88.

Diamond, J. (1998) *C: Because Cowards Get Cancer Too*. London: Vermillion.

Frank, A. (1991) *At the Will of the Body: Reflections on Illness*. New York: Houghton-Mifflin.

Goffman, E. (1963) *Stigma: Notes on the Management of Spoiled Identity*. New York: Doubleday Anchor.

Kleinman, A. (1988) *The Illness Narratives: Suffering, Healing and the Human Condition*. New York: Basic.

Lorde, A. (1980) *The Cancer Journals*. London: Sheba.

Moerman, D. (2002) *Meaning, Medicine and the 'Placebo Effect' (Cambridge Studies in Medical Anthropology)*. Cambridge: Cambridge University Press.

Moore, O. (1996) *PWA: Looking AIDS in the Face*. London: Picador.

Nijhof, G. (1995) 'Parkinson's disease as a problem of shame in public appearance', *Sociology of Health and Illness*, 17 (2): 194–205.

Noble, I. (2005) *Like a Hole in The Head: Living With a Brain Tumour*. London: Hodder and Stoughton.

Parsons, T. (1951) *The Social System*. New York: Free Press.

Picardie, R. (1998) *Before I Say Goodbye*. London: Penguin.

Scambler, G. (1989) *Epilepsy*. London: Routledge.

CHAPTER 7

Boyle, C.M. (1970) 'Difference between patients' and doctors' interpretations of some common medical terms', *British Medical Journal*, i: 286–9.

Carricaburu, D. and Pierret, J. (1995) 'From biographical disruption to biographical reinforcement: the case of HIV-positive men', *Sociology of Health and Illness*, 17 (1): 65–87.

Elias, N. (1969) *The Civilizing Process, Vol.I. The History of Manners*. Oxford: Blackwell.

Frank, A. (1991) *At the Will of the Body: Reflections on Illness*. New York: Houghton-Mifflin.

Greene, R. (1971) *Sick Doctors*. London: Heinemann Medical.

Helman, C. (2006) *Suburban Shaman: Tales from Medicine's Front Line*. London: Hammersmith.

Lock, M. (2002) *Twice Dead: Organ Transplants and the Reinvention of Death*. Berkley and Los Angeles: University of California Press.

MacDonald, L. (1988) 'The experience of stigma: living with rectal cancer', in R. Anderson and M. Bury (eds), *Living with Chronic Illness: The Experience of Patients and their Families*. London: Unwin Hyman. pp. 177–202.

Moore, O. (1996) *PWA: Looking AIDS in the Face*. London: Picador.

Nijhof, G. (1995) 'Parkinson's disease as a problem of shame in public appearance', *Sociology of Health and Illness*, 17 (2): 193–205.

Noble, I. (2005) *Like a Hole in the Head: Living With a Brain Tumour*. London: Hodder and Stoughton.

Nudeshima, J. (1991) 'Obstacles to brain death and organ transplantation in Japan', *Lancet*, 338: 1063–4.

Sacks, O. (1978) *A Leg to Stand On*. New York: Viking.

CHAPTER 8

Allen, C. (2007) 'Identity Politics Gone Wild: The Deaf culture wars at Gallaudet University', *The Weekly Standard*, 12 (28), 4 February. (Available at: http://www.weeklystandard.com/Content/Public/Articles/000/000/013/458tonjc.asp).

Bowling, A. (1999) 'Ageism in cardiology', *British Medical Journal*, 319: 1353–5.

Bury, M. (1991) 'The sociology of chronic illness: a review of research and prospects', *Sociology of Health and Illness*, 13 (4): 451–68.

Grimley Evans, J. (2001) 'Ageing and medicine', in B. Davey, A. Gran and C. Seale (eds), *Health and Disease: A Reader* (3rd edn). Buckingham: Open University Press. pp. 405–10.

Oliver, M. (1996) *Understanding Disability: From Theory to Practice*. London: Macmillan.

Prince-Hughes, D. (2004) *Songs of the Gorilla Nation: My Journey Through Autism*. New York: Harmony.

Saner, E. (2007) 'It Is Not A Disease, It Is A Way Of Life', *Guardian*, G2 Comment & Features, 7 August: 12.

Shakespeare, T.W. (2006) *Disability Rights and Wrongs*. London: Routledge.

Tammet, D. (2007) *Born on a Blue Day*. London: Hodder.

CHAPTER 9

Audit Commission (1993) *What Seems to be the Matter?: Communication Between Hospitals and Patients*. London: HMSO.

Banks, M.H., Beresford, S.A., Morrell, D.C., Waller, J.J. and Watkins, C.J. (1975) 'Factors influencing demand for primary medical care in women aged 20–44', *International Journal of Epidemiology*, 4: 189–95.

Bloor, M. and Horobin, G. (1975) 'Conflict and conflict-resolution in doctor/patient interactions', in C. Cox and A. Mead (eds), *A Sociology of Medical Practice*. London: Collier Macmillan. pp. 271–84.

Buckman, R. (1992) *How to Break Bad News: A Guide for Health Care Professionals*. Baltimore: Johns Hopkins University Press.

Bury, M. (1997) *Health and Illness in a Changing Society*. London: Routledge.

Cartwright, A. and Anderson, R. (1981) *General Practice Revisited: A Second Study of Patients and their Doctors*. London: Tavistock.

Department of Health (2005) 'Keep Warm Keep Well: Winter guide 2005/2006'. Published 30 August, Gateway reference 2005. Product code: 270225. (Available at: http://www.dh.gov.uk/assetRoot/04/11/83/79/04118379.pdf)

Department of Health (2006) 'Antibiotics: Don't Wear Me Out'! Published September 1999 (re-issued March 2006) Product code:16564. (Available at: http://www.dh.gov.uk/assetRoot/04/13/14/01/04131401.pdf)

Editor's Choice (1998) 'Through the Lens of Bristol', *British Medical Journal* (27 June), 316. (Also available at: http://bmj.bmjjournals.com/cgi/citmgr?gca=bmj;316/7149/0)

Freidson, E. (1970) *Profession of Medicine: A Study of the Sociology of Applied Knowledge*. Chicago: University of Chicago Press.

Graham, H. and Oakley, A. (1986) 'Competing ideologies of reproduction: medical and maternal perspective on pregnancy', in C. Currer and M. Stacey (eds), *Concepts of Health, Illness and Disease: A Comparative Perspective*. Leamington Spa: Berg. pp. 97–115.

Hannay, D.R. (1979) *The Symptom Iceberg: A Study of Community Health*. London: Routledge and Kegan Paul.

Jeffery, R. (1979) 'Normal rubbish: deviant patients in casualty departments', *Sociology of Health and Illness*, 1: 90–107.

Mulcahy, L. (2003) *Disputing Doctors: The Socio-Legal Dynamics of Complaints about Medical Care*. Maidenhead: Open University Press.

Oakley, A. (1980) *Women Confined: Towards a Sociology of Childbirth*. Oxford: Martin Robertson.

Parsons, T. (1951) *The Social System*. New York: Free Press.

Pensack, R. and Williams, D. (1994) *Raising Lazarus*. New York: Putnam.

Rhodes, L.A., McPhillips-Tangum, C.A., Markham, C. and Klenk, R. (1999) 'The power of the visible: the meaning of diagnostic tests in chronic back pain', *Social Science and Medicine*, 48: 1189–203.

Roberts, H. (1992) 'Professionals and parents' perceptions of A&E use in a children's hospital', *Sociological Review*, 40 (1): 109–31.

Sacks, O. (1978) *A Leg to Stand On*. New York: Viking.

Stimson, G.V. (1974) 'Obeying doctor's orders: a view from the other side', *Social Science and Medicine*, 8: 97–104.

Strong, P. (1979) *The Ceremonial Order of the Clinic: Parents, Doctors and Medical Bureaucracies*. London: Routledge and Kegan Paul.

Titmuss, R. (1968) *Commitment to Welfare*. London: Allen and Unwin.

Tuckett, D., Boulton, M., Olson, C. and Williams, C. (1985) *Meetings Between Experts*. London: Tavistock.

Tudor-Hart, J. (1971) 'The Inverse care law', *Lancet* (27 February), 405–12.

Waitzkin, H. (1991) *The Politics of Medical Encounters: How Patients and Doctors Deal with Social Problems*. New Haven: Yale University Press.

CHAPTER 10

Abel-Smith, B. (1994) *How to Contain Health Care Costs: An International Dilemma*. London: Stamp Memorial Lecture, University of London.

Abraham, J. (1997) 'The science and politics of medicines regulations', in M.A. Elston (ed.), *The Sociology of Medical Science and Technology*. Oxford: Blackwells. pp. 153–82.

Berridge, V. (1999) *Health and Society in Britain Since 1939* (New Studies in Economic History). Cambridge: The Economic History Society and Cambridge University Press.

Bury, M. (2008) 'New dimensions of health care organisation', in D.Wainwright (ed.), *A Sociology of Health*. London: SAGE. pp. 151–72.

Cartwright, F. (1977) *A Social History of Medicine*. London: Longman.

Field, M.G. (1973) 'The concept of the "health system" at the macrosociological level', *Social Science and Medicine*, 7: 763–85.

Field, M.G. (1995) 'The health crisis in the former Soviet Union: a report from the "post war" zone', *Social Science and Medicine*, 41 (11): 1469–78.

Ham, C. (2004) *Health Policy in Britain: The Politics and Organisation of the National Health Service* (5th edn). Basingstoke: Palgrave Macmillan.

Klein, R. (1989) *The Politics of the National Health Service*. London: Longman.

Maxwell, R. (1984) 'Quality assessment in health', *British Medical Journal*, 288 (6428): 1470–2.

Morgan, M. (2003) 'Hospitals and patient care', in G. Scambler (ed.), *Sociology as Applied to Medicine* (5th edn). London: Saunders. pp. 49–65.

OECD (2003) 'Health at a glance: OECD indicators'. Available at: http://www.oecd.org/

Pilgrim, D. and Rogers, A. (1993) *A Sociology of Mental Health and Illness*. Buckingham: Open University Press.

Prior, L. (1993) *The Social Organization of Mental Illness*. London: SAGE.

Wilcocks, A. (1967) *The Creation of the NHS: A Study of Pressure Groups and a Major Social Policy Decision*. London: Routledge.

CHAPTER 11

Atkinson, P. (1984) 'Training for certainty', *Social Science and Medicine*, 9 (9): 949–56.

Bosk, C. (1979) *Forgive and Remember: Managing Medical Failure*. Chicago: The University of Chicago Press.

Crawford, D.H. (2000) *The Invisible Enemy: A Natural History of Viruses*. Oxford: Oxford University Press.

Dick-Read, G. (1959) *Childbirth without Fear: The Principles and Practice of Natural Childbirth*. London: Heinemann Medical.

Eichelberger, L. (2007) 'SARS and New York's Chinatown: the politics of risk and blame during an epidemic of fear', *Social Science and Medicine*, 65 (6): 1284–95.

Fox, R.C. (1957) 'Training for uncertainty', in R.K. Merton, G.G. Reader and D. Hilfiker (eds), *The Student Physician: Introductory Studies in the Sociology of Medical Education*. Cambridge: Harvard University Press. pp. 207–41.

Hilfiker, D. (1984) 'Facing our mistakes', *The New England Journal of Medicine*, 310 (2): 118–22.

Kübler-Ross, E. (1969) *On Death and Dying*. New York: Macmillan.

Lamaze, F. (1958) *Painless Childbirth: Psycho-Prophylactic Method*. London: Burke.

Leboyer, F. (1974) *Pour une Naissance Sans Violence*. Paris: Le Seuil.

Porter, R. (1997) *The Greatest Benefit to Mankind: A Medical History of Humanity from Antiquity to the Present*. London: HarperCollins.

Rees Jones, I. (2003) 'Health professions', in G. Scambler (ed.), *Sociology as Applied to Medicine* (5th edn). London: Saunders. pp. 235–47.

Smith, Dame Janet (2005) 'Fifth Report of the Shipman Inquiry'. Available at: http://www.the-shipman-inquiry.org.uk/home.asp

Spock, B. (1946) *The Common Sense Book of Baby and Child Care*. New York: Dell, Sloan and Pearce.

Stacey, M. (1992) *Regulating British Medicine: the General Medical Council*. Chichester: Wiley.

CHAPTER 12

Annandale, E. (1998) *The Sociology of Health and Medicine: A Critical Introduction*. Cambridge: Polity.

Gerrish, K., Husband, C. and MacKenzie, J. (1996) *Nursing for a Multi-Ethnic Society*. Buckingham: Open University Press.

Mulcahy, L. (2003) *Disputing Doctors: The Socio-Legal Dynamics of Complaints about Doctors*. Buckingham: Open University Press.

Svab, I. and Katic, M. (1991) 'Let the patients speak', *Family Practice*, 8: 182–3.

INDEX

Page numbers in *italics* indicate definitions of useful terms

abortion 44–5
    impaired foetuses 142,
        143, 144
Acheson Report 75–6
achondroplasia (dwarfism) 138, 143
age
    and definitions of health 59
    and disability 134–5
    and inequality 83
AIDS see HIV/AIDS
alcohol/drinking
    individual choice 77, 79
    risk perceptions 97, 98, 105
    Russia 81
    sales restrictions 24, 26
    women 83
alcoholism, as a disease 54,
        55, 178
Allied Health Professionals
        46–7
alternative therapies 2,
        179, 181, 186
alternative therapists 6, 46
American Sign Language
        131, 139
anorexia nervosa 54
ante-natal care 154
ante-natal screening 141–2, 191
anti-psychiatry 187
antibiotics 13, 14, 31, 43, 61
    resistance 28, 31
Asperger syndrome *131*, 140–2
Aspies *131*, 141–2
autism *132*, 138, 140–2, 144
autonomy *51*
    doctors 9, 163, 177, 178
    medicine 52, 153
    nurses 186
    patients 150
autopathography *108*, 115
Avian Flu Virus 54, 178, 188

Baby MB 185–6
'barebacking' 99
Bevan, Aneurin 29, 163
Beveridge Report 164–5
biographical disruption *108*,
        114–15, 136
biomedical disease model 52–3
    deficits 61–2
    limitations 53–8
black minorities 11
    black bodies 123
    pain and analgesia 12–13
    racialized interventions 153
    young men stigmatized 113
Black Report 71–2, 74,
        75, 76–9
Blair, Tony 75
blame 99–100, 113–14
bodies 15, 119–30
    disappearing 126, 180
    embodied illness 121–2
    impaired 126–7
    as machines 124–6, 127
    mechanical model 180
    separation from minds 51,
        52, 122–4
    in society 120–1
    suffering 126
Boer War 24
Booth, Charles 33
Bovine Spongiform Encephalitis
        (BSE, Mad Cow Disease) 94
brain death 44, 125
breast cancer 33, 132
    BRCA gene 103
    Herceptin 168
Bristol Royal Infirmary scandal
        5, 166, 185
British Medical Association
        (BMA) 3–4, 23, 29, 177
BUPA 170

cancer 31, 33, 42, 179
    autopathographies 115, 116
    as failure 114
    mechanistic view 109–10
    stigma 113
    survival rates 32–3, 167
    see also specific cancers
capitalism 69, 73, 169
cardiac bypass 6, 43, 127 *see
        also* sham surgery
'care in the community' 33,
        169–70
Cartesian dualism *51*, 52, 122–4
Catholics 98
cervical cancer 33, 114
Chadwick, Edwin 33, 69
Cheyne, George 104
child labour 85
childbirth 133
    dangerous 32
    medicalization 7, 158
    reforming physicians 187
childrearing 187
Chinese medicine 46, 134
cholesterol levels 56, 103, 156–7
Christianity 123–4
chronic back pain 155
Chronic Fatigue Syndrome (CFS,
        Myalgic Encepahilitis, ME)
        40, 53, 155
chronic illness
    community care 170
    patient involvement 42
    patient responses 136–7
    relationship with disability and
        impairment 132–3, 135–7
    rise of 6, 22, 27, 68
    and subjective health 59, 62
cigarette smoking
    and class-based health
        inequalities 77, 79, 86–7

cigarette smoking *cont.*
  commercial interests 93
  and deprivation 96
  individual vs. population
    interests 91
  limited decline 96
  risk responses 102
  women 83
CJD (Creutzfeldt-Jacob
  disease) 94
clinical governance *161*, 166–8
Clostridium difficile 188
cochlear implants 139–40, 144
colostomies 120
commercial interests 2, 34,
  93, 170–3
Committee on the Safety of
  Medicine 172–3
Conservative governments 74–5,
  84, 90, 169–70, 171, 173
consultants 194
  division with GPs 23, 29
consumerism 35, 152, 158,
  179, 183
contraception 97, 98
coronary artery disease 27,
  153, 191
cousin marriage 100–1
cyborgs *119*
cystic fibrosis 135–6, 142

deaf community 133,
  139–40, 142
death
  association with medicine 43
  doctors' role 26, 43–5, 50
  reforming physicians 187
  shifting definitions 44, 125
death rates *see* mortality rates
Descartes, René 51, 122
d'Espine, Marc 54
developmental disorders 133–4
diabetes 27, 59, 60, 96, 136, 169,
  178, 184
diagnosis *37*
  breaking bad news 156
  GP 14
  legitimate and illegitimate
    illness 38–41
  by non-physicians 46
  and risk 102
  outstripping therapeutic
    abilities 25, 191
  technological 14, 38–9
  and uncertainty 183–4
diagnostic creep 177
Diana, Princess of Wales 13

Dick-Read, Grantley 187
diet 60, 77, 93, 104
disability 15, *119*, 131–44
  cultural model *132*, 139–42
  distinction from impairment
    126–7, 132
  and the life course 133–5
  and medical training 129–30
  relationship with chronic
    illness and impairment
    132–3, 135–7
  social model *132*, 132,
    137–8, 142
  special or universal needs
    142–3
disability rights 132, 134, 138
disease *37*
  describing 118
  discussing 63–4
  'lifestyle' 55, 104
  privileged over patients 5,
    39, 52
  social causes 67–88
  sub-cellular analysis 14, 126
  see also biomedical disease
    model; diagnosis; illness;
    treatment
doctor–patient relationship 15,
  147–60
  appropriate consultation
    149–50
  changing context 178–9
  co-operation and challenge
    157–8
  communication 155–7, 194–7
  conflict model 151–2, 178
  functional consensus model
    151, 152
  inequality 151, 153–5
  inverse care law 11–12, 152–3
  language 196
  listening 196
  negotiation model 152
  paternalistic model 6, 178
  relevance of wider context
    11, 198
  trust 4–5, 15, 178
  uncertainty 157, 197
  use of names 195–6
doctors
  challenging conventional
    wisdom 187
  definitional problems 45
  delegation dilemma 193–4
  diagnosis and legitimacy
    38–41
  difficulties 183–4

doctors *cont.*
  disappearing 179–80
  discontent 9
  dominance in NHS
    168, 178
  errors 191
  as gate-keepers 11, 39–41,
    166
  impostors 50
  individual vs. collective
    responsibility 11, 90
  as individuals 7
  overlap with other profes-
    sionals 46–7
  as patients 126, 156
  as political campaigners
    11–12
  public image 4, 14, 48
  remit 10, 15, 37–50
  role in death 26, 43–5, 50
  specialization 47–8
  trainee powerlessness 194
  treatment expectations 41–3
  'whistle-blowers' 185
  see also consultants; GPs
Down's (Down) syndrome
  13, 134, 142
drug use/users 76, 177
  and HIV 13, 34, 112, 113
dualist thinking 51, 52, 122–4
dwarfism *see* achondroplasia

Einstein, Albert 141, 142
Elias, Norbert 122–3
embodied *119*
embodied illness 121–2
emphysema 91, 136
Engels, Friedrich 69
Enlightenment 114, 122
epidemiology 69, 102
epilepsy 10, 111
ethnic minorities 197 *see also*
  black minorities; migrants
ethnicity
  and inequality 10, 11, 12, 74,
    81–3, 153
  and lay understandings of
    health 58–9, 60–1
euthanasia 44, 125
evidence-based practice 42, 150,
  182–3
exercise 93, 94–5, 102, 104
expert patients 158, 181, 182

face transplants 125
Farr, William 54, 69
First World War 22, 26–7

folk beliefs 61
French Revolution 70

Gaitskill, Hugh 29
gay men
    HIV narratives 116
    HIV risk 34
    HIV and stigma 112, 113
    horizontally transmitted
        culture 100
    risky sex 98–9
gender
    and inequality 10, 12, 17,
        74, 83
    and lay understandings of
        health 58–9, 60
General Medical Council
    (GMC) 3, 8–9, 22, 23, 47,
    177, 185, 198
general practitioners see GPs
genetic markers 61–2, 142
genetic testing 14, 39
germ theory *21*, 25, 61
global health inequalities *see*
    international health
    inequalities
golden age 9, 36, 177
GPs 14
    1900s rural 25–6, 34
    division with consultants
        23, 29
    fund-holding 166
    inappropriate consultations
        149
    independence in NHS
        165, 168
    use of folk models 61
Graham, Hilary 96
Grandin, Temple 141, 142
Great Depression 24, 27
Gulf War Syndrome 40, 53, 155

Haddon, Mark 141
Hart, Julian Tudor 11–12
Harvey, William 122
health
    biomedical model 57–8
    critical approaches 10–12
    lay understandings 15, 58–9,
        62, 63
    dimensions 59, 96–7
    effect of context 60–1
    post-war centrality 26–7
    World Health Organization
        definition 58
health inequalities
    and age 83

health inequalities *cont.*
    and ethnicity 11, 81–3
    future prospects 84
    and gender 11, 83
    historical context 33–4
    international 33, 84–5, 188–9
    physician campaigners 11–12
    and social class 11, 12, 33,
        71–81, 84
    left- and right-wing
        perceptions 87–8
    mechanisms 76–81
    policy approaches 71–6,
        83–4
health insurance system 163
Healthcare Commission 167
heart attacks 31, 94–5, 103, 114
    autopathography 115
heart disease 79, 102
Herceptin 168
herd immunity 95
historical context 21–36
    1900: 23–6
    1914–1918: 26–7
    1918–1939: 27
    1939–1945: 27–8
    1945–2000: 28–30
    costs and benefits of
        innovation 30–3
    health inequalities 33–4
    medical transformations 34–5
HIV/AIDS 14, 132
    autopathographies 115, 116
    bodily vigilance 121–2
    'Don't Die of Ignorance' 96
    identification 33–4, 54
    majority world 188–9
    prejudice 13, 99
    risky sex and gay men 98–9
    spread 178, 188
    stigma 112–13, 137
horizontal transmission of
    culture *89*, 98, 100
Hormone Replacement
    Therapy 55
hospice movement 187
hospitals/ hospital medicine
    appropriate consultation 149
    delegation of care 194
    diagnosis 38–9
    disappearance of the
        body 126
    historical context 22, 23, 24,
        25–6, 28, 29, 168–9, 177
    professional distinctions 46
    role in NHS 168–70
    treatment co-ordination 41

Huntingdon's Chorea 102
hypertension (high blood
        pressure) 56, 114, 184

iatrogenesis *1*, 6, 184
illness 15, *37*, 108–18
    as deviance 111–12
    embodied 121–2
    as failure 113–14
    legitimate vs. illegitimate
        40–1
    non-scientific explanations
        10, 113–14
    order and control issues
        108–9
    sick role 110–11
    and stigma 112–13
illness narratives 114–15, 136
    reformative potential 116
immunization programmes 11,
        13, 30–1, 43, 58,
        90–1, 132
impairment *119*, 126–7
    distinction from disability
        127, 132
    relationship with chronic
        illness and disability
        132–3, 135–7
individual behaviours 15, 33,
        77, 90, 91–7
individualism 74, 90
industrial accidents and
        diseases 68, 93–4
Industrial Revolution 23–4,
        69, 73
industrialization
        23–4, 68–9
inequality 10
    doctor–patient 151, 153–5
    in medicine 12–13, 17
    see also health inequalities;
        inverse care law
infant feeding 95
infant mortality 32, 69
infectious diseases
    misplaced optimism 34
    new threats 34
    retreat 6, 22, 27, 29–30,
        43, 68
infertility 104
International Classification of
        Diseases (ICD) 54–5
international health inequalities
        33, 84–5, 188–9
internet 7, 158, 173, 182
internetitis *147*, 182
inverse care law 11–12, 152–3

Judeo-Christian tradition 114

knowledge explosion *21*, 35
Kübler-Ross, Elizabeth 187

Labour governments 29, 71–2,
    74, 75, 84, 90, 167, 171
Laing, R. D. 187
Lamaze, Fernand 187
Leboyer, Frederique 187
leprosy 111, 113
lethal injection 45
Lettsom, John Coakley 11
life expectancy 6, 71, 76, 134–5
life tables *67*, 69
'lifestyle' choices 15, 33, 90, 91–7
'lifestyle' diseases 104
'lifestyle medicine' 55
Lister, Joseph 25
London School of Medicine for
    Women 23
longevity 13–14, 24, 26, 27,
    42, 68
lunatic asylums 12, 169
Lunatics Asylums Act
    (1845) 169
lung cancer 27, 96, 102

madness 12, 121, 169
    medicalization 7
majority world *176*, 189
malpractice 5, 185
Malthus, Thomas 70
Mandela, Nelson 113
Marmot, Michael 79
Marxist analysis 73–4
McKeown, Thomas 30
medical dominance 46–7, *147*,
    153, 168, 178
medical education/training 26,
    35, 46, 179–80
    and disability 128–9
    inequalities 12
    reforms 181
medical evidence 38
medical knowledge 46, 158, 162
    accessibility 7, 9, 58, 127, 182
    vs. lay health beliefs 58
    reverence for 9
    and uncertainty 184
medical monopoly 47–8
medical pluralism *37*, 46
Medical Registration Act (1858)
    22, 23, 47
medical sociology *1*
medical technology 14, 24,
    38–9, 43, 124, 167, 183

medical textbooks 26, 183
medical uncertainty 157,
    183–4, 197
medicalization *1*, 7, 177
medicine
    challenges to 15, 176–91
    change and continuity 193
    changing expectations and
        priorities 6–9, 22, 42–3
    changing practice 177–9
    critical approaches 10–12
    'geneticization' 180
    golden age 9, 36, 177
    hierarchies 17
    historical context 21–36
    inequality 12–13, 17
    non-human threats 187–9
    paradoxical 13–14
    place in society 48–9
    power, influence and
        reputation 2–4,
        52, 177–8
    prospects 189
    reductionist approach 109–10
    reform from within 186–7
    regulation 184–6, 190–1
        legal involvement 185–6
        self-regulation 7–9, 153,
            186, 193
        standing 9–10, 178
        trust in 4–6, 45
Medicines Act (1968) 172
melanoma 97
microbial threats 187–9
midwives 6, 46, 186
migrants
    class and health inequalities
        81–3
    horizontally and vertically
        transmitted culture 98
    ideas about health 60–1
MMR vaccination 31, 90–1, 93,
    105, 167
motor neurone disease 133
mortality rates
    cancer 32–3
    and gender 71, 83
    as measure of NHS effective-
        ness 164
    mothers and babies 27, 32
    nineteenth century 70
    and poverty 69
    reasons for improvement
        13–14, 30
    Russia 80–1
    and social class 71, 72,
        75, 76, 84

mortality rates *cont.*
    twentieth century decline 13,
        24, 26, 27, 29–30, 32
    twenty-first century 71
MRSA 188
multi-national companies 2,
    34, 73
multiple sclerosis 53,
    132, 135–6
Muslims
    and alcohol 98, 100
    cousin marriage 100–1

'nanny state' 74, 90
National Childbirth Trust 187
National Insurance Act
    (1911) 23
Nelson, Gareth 141
'neuro-diverse' communty *132*,
    138, 140–2
NHS (National Health Service)
    12, 15, 60, 75, 161–75, 177
    'blame' culture 183
    care context 173–4
    clinical governance 166–8
    commercial and industrial
        interests 2, 170–3, 175
    diagnosis and access 39–40
    doctors' and patients'
        interests 175
    establishment 27, 28–9, 33,
        71, 134, 178
    evaluating 164–5
    inverse care law 152
    medical dominance 168,
        178, 192
    patient choice 167, 197
    political importance 84, 174
    purchaser-provider split
        165–6
    reforming 165–6, 192–3
    rising expectations 6, 31, 104,
        164
    role of hospitals 168–70
    safeguarding 198
    structure and funding 162,
        163–4
    universal vs. special
        needs 143
NHS and Community Care Act
    (1990) 169–70
NHS Direct 7, 148, 182
NHS24 148, 182
NICE (National Institute for
    Health and Clinical
    Excellence) 90, 166–7
nurses/nursing 5, 46, 168, 186

obesity 60, 114, 170, 191
Odent, Michel 187
organ trading 125

Parkinson's disease 116, 120
Parson, Talcott 151, 152
Pasteur, Louis 25
paternalistic 1, 6, 178
patient-centred (person-
    centred) care 197, 198
patient choice 42, 167,
    159–60, 179
patients
    contemporary lives 35
    disease privileged over 5,
        39, 52
    non-compliance 150–1, 160
    social problems 198
    see also bodies; doctor–
        patient relationship;
        expert patients; service
        users' involvement;
        service users' perspective
Patients' Charter 158, 179
patients' interest groups 5, 62,
    181–2
penicillin 28
personhood 125
pharmaceutical industry 31, 34,
    55, 103, 107, 162,
    171–3, 175
pharmacological disasters 31,
    171
placebo effect 128–9
pneuma 122
policy
    approaches to health inequal-
        ity 71–6, 83–4
    individual vs. group
        interests 90
Porter, Roy 22, 189
poverty
    constraints on 'healthy living'
        91–3
    effects on health 12, 24, 33,
        68–70, 75, 198
    relative 79
Powell, Enoch 162
'pre-patients' 7, 56–7, 102, 173
prejudice 10, 12–13, 33–4,
    99–100, 127
premature babies 64, 133
prescriptions 29, 150
preventative medicine 58, 91,
    101–2
primary care trusts 166, 167,
    186, 193, 198

Prince-Hughes, Dawn 141
Private Finance Initiative
    (PFI) 171
private health care 13, 170–1
Professions Allied with
    Medicine (PAM) 46–7
prophylaxis 103
prostate cancer 56, 159–60
psychology/psychologists 2, 47
psychiatry/psychiatrists 28, 47,
    158, 169
    anti-psychiatry 187
public health 2
    education and advice 57,
        91–7, 148
    global reformation 85
    historical context 24, 28, 29,
        30, 69, 70

racism 1, 10, 82, 113, 123
Rainman 141
rationing 135, 166, 167–8
and responsibility 106–7
Reeve, Christopher 134
regulation
    drugs industry 171–3
    medicine 184–6, 190–1
        legal involvement 185–6
        self-regulation 7–9, 153,
            186, 193
risk 15, 89
    communication problems
        156–7
    cousin marriage 100–1
    cultural norms 100, 104–5
    and the pharmaceutical
        industry 107
    and preventative medicine
        101–2
    'at risk' groups 56, 102–4,
        173, 177
risk aversion 104, 105, 182–3
risk taking 98
    youthful 98, 106
risky sex, and gay men 98–9
Royal Society of Medicine 177
Russia/USSR
    mortality rates 80–1
    healthcare system 162–3

Sacks, Oliver 126, 141
SARS 188
Saunders, Cicely 187
schizophrenia 127, 153
screening 11, 32–3, 56, 58, 102–3
    ante-natal 141–2, 191
    language of 107

Second World War 27–8, 61, 71
seizures 10, 111, 127, 137
self-care 148–9
service users' involvement 5,
    41–2, 158
service users' perspectives 6,
    9–10, 62, 159, 181
sexism 2, 10, 83, 123
Shakespeare, T. W. 138
sham surgery 128–9
Shipman, Harold 5, 185
sick role 108, 110–11
signs (diagnostic) 25, 37, 38,
    52–3
Simvastatin 103, 173, 175
slave labour 85
Smith, Chris 113
Smith, Janet 185
social/socio-economic
    class 10, 67
    and benefits of health advice
        91, 97
    ill health and industrial
        revolution 68–71
    and inequality 11, 12, 33,
        71–81, 84, 153
    inverse care law 11–12, 152–3
    and lay understandings of
        health 58–9, 60
    Marxist analysis 73–4
    migrants 82
    occupation-based system
        72–3, 81–2
    and smoking 77, 79, 86–7
socialized healthcare 162–3
    pluralist 163–4
sociology 2, 10–11
specialization 23, 35, 47–8
Spock, Benjamin 187
standardized mortality ratio
    (SMR) 67, 68
state benefits 9, 40–1, 91, 198
statin drugs 103, 175
Stewart, William 188
stigma 10, 108, 112–13,
    127, 133
    cancer 113
    HIV/AIDS 112–13
    and knowledge 117
    seizures 10, 137
stroke 6, 27, 31, 33
sulpha drugs 27
sunbathing 97
SureStart 84
symptom iceberg 57, 148–9
symptoms 37, 38, 52–3
    minor 57, 148

symptoms *cont.*
  pathology without 56–7
  subjectivity vs. objectivity 39
  suffered in silence 110
  without lesions 40–1,
    53–5, 155
Szasz, Thomas 187

Tammet, Daniel 141, 142
Tay Sachs disease 135
thalassaemia 101
thalidomide 31, 171
Thatcher, Margaret 74, 75
therapeutic network *147*, 148

thrill seeking 98
Titmuss, Richard 152
transplant medicine 6, 32, 34,
  44, 124–5, 127
treatment 38
  expectations of doctors 41–3
  by non-physicians 46
  and risk 102
tuberculosis 27, 68–9, 113, 188

urbanization 23–4, 69, 188

vertical transmission of culture
  89, 98

Vesalius, Andreas 122
Viagra (sildenafil citrate) 55–6, 173
Villermé, Louis René 69

Welfare State 12, 27, 40–1
women
  informal care burden 148
  and medicine 12, 17, 23
  medical qualification 23
  'sexual dysfunction' 55
  women's bodies 123
World Health Organization 54, 58
'worried well' 56, 103, 181
Wyatt, Charlotte 185–6